Lean Brain Management

Gunter Dueck

Lean Brain Management

More Success and Efficiency by Saving Intelligence

 Springer

Prof. Dr. Gunter Dueck
IBM Deutschland GmbH
Gottlieb-Daimler-Str. 12
68165 Mannheim
Germany
dueck@de.ibm.com

Translated from the German "Lean Brain Management – Erfolg und Effizienzsteigerung durch Null-Hirn" (ISBN 978-3-540-31146-1, Springer-Verlag 2006) by Andrea Adelung

ISBN 978-3-540-71837-6   e-ISBN 978-3-540-71838-3

DOI 10.1007/978-3-540-71838-3

Library of Congress Control Number: 2008922350

Cover Design: KünkelLopka, Heidelberg

Printed on acid-free paper

9 8 7 6 5 4 3 2 1

springer.com

Table of Contents

I. Lean Brain – The Greatest Challenge of the Future

1. Lean Brain Work

"Lean Brain" can be described as a "fat-free brain" or, as my son would say, a "no-brainer".

This book examines the enormous savings potential you can expect if you can confine or prevent the waste of intelligence and emotion on a large scale. In this book, we will provide you with an entire kaleidoscope of simple, easily comprehensible procedures and formulas with which you can eradicate intelligence and emotion in your environment. This will actually result in immediate profit – not to mention a rosy future! Here you will find the doctrine of salvation for the coming era of humanity. If you are still one of those people who is chasing after intelligent approaches, you are barking up the wrong tree.

Absolutely every person is capable of easily generating Lean Brain Quality (LBQ) and thus having a great deal of success. You can do it, too! Of course, intelligent people are at a disadvantage with LBQ, since they generally use their brains excessively and nearly addictively. That is why intelligent people are doubtless the toughest opponents of the fat-free brain camp. However, this is no hindrance to the practical application of LBQ. Large-scale plans such as nuclear power plants, oil wars or party platforms have never failed due to a resistance on the part of intelligence. When the going gets rough, intelligence doesn't get going but rather complains that what is happening is wrong. While this is certainly extremely annoying, it is not injurious.

LBQ will change the world. Be one of the first to employ LBQ resolutely. It can make you filthy rich!

I myself will also become filthy rich because I invented the LBQ concept when I had nothing better to do. Besides, in this day and age, everyone loves things that are lean. The concept of Lean Brain Management (LBM) is nothing more than the efficient highest allocation of intelligence in daily life. No more know-it-alls or touchy-feely types to obstruct or sour our profitable daily routine!

The idea of Lean Brain Management (LBM) is extremely practical and unbeatable in its simplicity. This cannot be stressed often enough. It is amazing that no one has thought of this before. But, as we know, genius is often right in front of our noses. Only this time, it is not *in front of* our noses but *behind* them. Do you see what I mean? In that place reserved for the brain. That is why the concept was concealed for so long and never went anywhere.

Thus, Lean Brain Management is a sort of methodology with which one can enjoy lasting success in the world in a "topless" state. It may sound surprising to you that a recipe for success could be founded on such a thing. Yet think of the huge successes of Henry Ford, who was the first person to have employees do nothing more than perform precisely-defined hand movements on the assembly line. Henry Ford succeeded in building automobiles with a bunch of people who only needed to be trained for a total of a single hour for their entire careers. So if one can build complex automobiles entirely without intelligence, why can't everything else also be made the same way?

Automobile production was derived from necessity because there were quite a few jobs to fill yet no intelligent people to fill them. That is why, according to Taylor's principle, industry invented a type of production without intelligence whose output, however, was highly intelligent. All of the intelligence was in the system – not in workers' heads, where it would be of no use anyway.

In the period to follow, one tried to further improve the system by training people more thoroughly, and subsequently, even more thoroughly. There was not enough willpower to only improve the system and not the people.

Today we have come so far that simple laborers are actually also thinking!

That phenomenon was completely overlooked as a side effect.

That is why this terrible aspect of history must be turned back quite a bit.

That is the purpose of LBM.

> At this point, you should have been able to understand the basic issue without needing to put much thought into it. If the text was too difficult for you, throw this book away now. You do not need it. If you find the LBM approach horrifying, you must keep reading. Yet in such a mood, you will surely be in constant danger of throwing the book away. However, if you actually do so, *you* will be in danger.

2. Where do we find intelligence worth economizing?

In this book, I would like to introduce you to some effective techniques with which to economize on intelligence. Firstly, for those of you who may be worried, I'd like to point out that economizing on intelligence does not mean stupidity. On the contrary, it is stupid to employ intelligence where it would do harm or result in unnecessary costs.

> Stupidity is not a lack of intelligence but rather its imprudent utilization.

However, before we can economize on intelligence, we have to discover it in everyday life. This is not as easy as it sounds because daily life consists almost exclusively of stupid routines. Nevertheless, life does seem somehow intelligent – but I want to demonstrate that, in reality, life is only complicated and not in any way intelligent. We confuse intelligence with complexity. For the time being, we are living complicatedly on purpose because it is easy. We declare it intelligent and wish to be praised and paid for it.

> Complexity is almost always foolishly utilized intelligence and thus stupidity.

(No religion, no idea, no philosophy is complex – it only becomes complex when stupid people become involved and write secondary literature about it: say, for instance, a thousand-page interpretation of the sermon on the mount.)

The smart intelligence economizer thus first discovers that there is hardly any intelligence worth paying for. He or she can save a lot of money by separating stupidity from intelligence and complexity from intelligence. I would initially like to provide an introduction of this issue here.

To do so, I'll have to fine-tune your eye for it. Then I will present concrete action recommendations that apply to more than just this point.

Do you know what cut rum is? It is a dilution of water, neutral alcohol and at least 5 percent genuine rum. Cut rum is somewhat cheaper than 100-percent real rum, and, to normal non-connoisseurs or philistines, tastes almost the same – especially because they adulterate the mystery rum with juice in cocktails. Rum can be detected by taste in the smallest of concentrations (at least a pungent Jamaican one). The same can also be said for work. One hundred percent intelligence can hardly be distinguished from diluted intelligence because strongly diluted intelligence can still be detected and easily mistaken for true intelligence, especially by the non-intelligent. The cheap cut version is good enough for most purposes. Because this is the case, cut rum is not much less expensive than real rum. Thus, we pay far more for it than its actual value. Similarly, cut intelligence is also hardly cheaper than genuine intelligence. Therein lies a unique opportunity. From now on, we only produce cut intelligence instead of real intelligence and sell the dilution at almost the same price. Subsequently, we continually try to reduce the percentage of necessary genuine intelligence in the blend. That is true intelligence economizing. In the case of rum, producers need to halt the economizing at five percent because there is a law defining anything under five percent as fraud. There are as of yet no laws governing intelligence ratios. Thus, we can economize as much as possible. A bit of intelligence will always be necessary, such that Zero Brain Management is an ideal we can never attain. However, we will at least be pointed in the right direction if we envision a theoretical zero. Ambitious goals are the simplest.

Laboratory rats or pigeons possess very little intelligence in comparison to humans. Nevertheless, they seem incredibly intelligent. Behavioral studies have been performed on them for quite some time regarding the limits of humans at work. Do you understand that the genuine and the cut versions are in close proximity to one another?

> We could cut back almost completely on intelligence if we could produce all things in life in a "cut" form. From an economical standpoint, we do not actually need an entire person but rather a dilution of a person in the necessary proportions (a "human blend," if you will), which is very similar to a whole person. In doing so, we would correct the misguided development of "human resources" or "human capital," which we now justifiably recognize as being much too expensive.

A medical student explained to me during an exam that he wished to go into research because the pure existence of a medical doctor was inane. That puzzled me because I actually considered research as being even more inane; an insane amount of intelligence is wasted in research because scientists have so much of it that they do not know what to do with it all. From this waste-based viewpoint, scientists are probably the stupidest of all.

This student described the daily routine of his father, a pediatrician, like this: "In the morning, 15 women with children are sitting in the waiting room. Eight of these mothers say their children have the chicken pox. Now, according to the rules, my father has to examine all 15 of these children to determine what ails them because Hypocrites and the health insurance companies want him to do so. After performing 15 examinations, he concludes that all of the children have chicken pox. Of course the mothers knew this already because they were sitting in the waiting room talking about nothing other than not to scratch where it itches. Ultimately, they all receive the same prescription, all of which could conceivably have simply been hung up in the waiting room on a pad of prescription paper. So I have to ask myself why my father even bothered to go to college. It is a no-brainer of a job which of course is paid well because he went to college."

The pediatrician studied for so many years so that he could identify diseases. Diagnosing them requires intelligence and experience. The doctor selects a therapy and carries it through. The entire process, including aftercare, is surrounded by reports, invoices, computer entries, and measurements with devices and laboratory tests. In our example, the receptionist or even I could have treated the chicken pox because the diagnosis was clear. However, according to the law, a physician must be in charge of the treatments. Yet it is evident that one needs the doctor only for more difficult cases but not for such simple ones.

Other laws that are just as inane dictate that pharmacists must govern the distribution of medicines because they have studied for so many years just so they would be able to decipher every last prescription written by Stone-Age doctors who still write their prescriptions by hand. Do we really need the concentrated intelligence of a highly competitive area of study in order to be able to read instruction leaflets to customers?

Figuratively speaking, genuine rum is being produced and drunk where pure ethanol would do the trick just as well.

> Routine work and bureaucracy are often performed by highly intelligent people who, for understandable reasons, disguise *all* of their work as intelligent in order to be paid according to their level of intelligence. Many career groups have secured considerable benefits over the decades and centuries through respective federal protection laws.

The examples of the pediatrician and the pharmacist also show that remuneration is based on one's respective potential intelligence, or one's so-called "peak intelligence." This is the case in almost all professions. A secretary receives a higher salary if she *can* type in English. A manager should be managing but instead only sits around in meetings and taxis and bothers everyone else while they are working. A professor is set for life for having an ingenious idea at age 29 – and for coincidentally doing so at a university. Payment is always based on the theoretically most sophisticated, intelligent portion of a job – without consideration of what percent of working hours are even spent working in such an intelligent mode. Thus, it is not intelligence at all that is remunerated but rather only potential intelligence. In reality, a secretary makes coffee, administers the appointment book and calms intelligent people who wish to speak to her boss. A manager says he can't get anything done because of all of the meetings. Scientists groan under inane academic self-management and their own lack of didactic skills with which they turn initially intelligent freshmen into stupid reptiles.

Intelligence, then, is pointlessly hoarded "just in case" but not utilized. Computers are intelligent but often not switched on. Professors have proven their intelligence in difficult examinations, but you cannot tell by looking at them. Even word processing programs contain a million options and buttons, but people just type in something simple and print it out once. Thus, there is an abundance of all kinds of intelligence. An economist might say that there are completely unutilized high excess capacities of intelligence.

Nevertheless, we pay for intelligence even though we neither need nor utilize it.
That is the problem.
Something has to change in the way people think.

Intelligence must conform to the laws of the market. Something so ubiquitous as sand and air should not have to cost anything, even if it is worth a great deal. However, as long as intelligence costs a lot of money, it must be conserved as rigorously as possible. This can be achieved through LBM.

3. The Fakularization of the World

A successful Lean Brain Manager wholeheartedly puts all work and all production to the test bench. He asks the basic question: How can something be achieved with considerably less brainpower and expenditure?

Cost reduction efforts often result in a decline in quality. This is a given. The goal of LBM, however, must be to ensure that the achievable LBQ, or Lean Brain Quality, can keep up with the excessive quality that would be theoretically possible in the case of a limitless exertion of effort. Lean Brain Management considers 95 out of 100 percent genuine good enough.

Before turning to more practical examples, I would like to briefly insert the Lean Brain philosophy into the intellectual cosmos of our thoughts. This is entirely necessary. I know, I know, it has no place in a strictly management-based book such as this, but an author has his vanities after all, and I would like to tell you that – well, the cosmos – you know.

I have already distilled out the key conception of LBQ for you in the discussion of cut rum. In such a case, the utilization of only 5 percent genuine rum results in a product that almost completely resembles the real thing. Thus, the goal is to fake the real thing as efficiently as possible. A fake is a deceptively real imitation of the genuine. Originally, the word *fake* contained a certain hint of *fraud*. Recently, however, it is being associated with cleverness (the apparent absence of stupidity). For instance, copies of handbags or breasts are produced to seem real. This used to be considered unethical. Today, people are increasingly satisfied if they at least have something where there previously was nothing. LBM will turn the trend toward fakes into the primary path of humanity.

LBM will bring on a second liberation of humanity.

The first liberation of humanity was a release from the stronghold of ancient principles of religions and philosophies, when people subjected themselves to economically completely inane rules in which they were just as compelled to believe as in their gods. Many people often prayed several hours a day without doing anything sensible. Only in later years did people realize that, in addition to strict prayer, active work was also needed if the world was to be saved from ruin. That was the time in which the Rule of Benedict ("ora et labora" or "pray and work") was proposed by Saint Benedict of Nursia in the 6th century A.D., who offered them as an economically sensible element to counter his horror at the decline of the Western World. Almost one and a half millennia have passed since his death on Maundy Thursday in the year 547 while praying in the Montecassino minster.

Only recently has the concept gradually taken hold that one should *only* work and not pray at all any more. The world has labored for so long now to get from *ora* to Benedict to sheer work. That is why the world was only able to achieve modest prosperity in the last phase of its history. In earlier times, much too much work was dedicated to the hereafter without having borne the fruits of such a long-term investment. ("Prayer is not profitable!")

The long developmental road from time-consuming faith to work is commonly referred to as *secularization*. The people and the state primarily withdrew from the influence of the church. This led to an emancipatory autonomy of reason and the mind and to the development of an enlightened humanism that was independent of faith, which enabled people to shape their lives on their own. Religion's options of lending meaning to life and its ethical and moral guidelines receded into the background. Humans no longer needed to measure up to an ethical potential but rather were only judged on their actions, that is, their actual work efforts, which represented a person's actual value.

Currently, this secularization process is slowly reaching an end. People will soon really only be measured by their actual value, which is precisely and objectively established in work units and performance values. (Your dollar value to the boss minus your monetary costs to the boss: It is vital that your differences with your boss in this equation be as high as possible).

LBM now recognizes that secularization has gotten bogged down in the wrong direction. The world has completely degenerated due to inimitable mismanagement. Incompetent managers and inane wielders of power always required intelligent people to make up for their errors. That is why the value of people was increasingly measured according to intelligence: The increase in intelligence always needed to keep up with the mounting rate of mismanagement; otherwise said, incredible mismanagement would have been noticed at a far earlier stage. In other words, the blunders of the power wielders were able to be completely covered up with an unbelievable amount of complexity and intelligence – until now that is, with the revelations contained in this book. This is my mission. On the other hand, intelligent subjects have always endeavored to egregiously complicate all of the world's issues because they were then paid better by persons in power. That, too, is a phenomenon I wish to make public here.

Thus I assert that through mismanagement and intelligence tactics, a colossal global intelligence potential has been assembled. On the whole, people can work a great deal more than is necessary. The amount of work that theoretically needs to be performed in the world is completely out of proportion with regard to available intelligence. All people are hopelessly overqualified simply because they wish to increase their value. Panicked, they then use their excess intelligence to invent ever more seemingly sophisticated and complicated jobs that appear to correspond to their aggregate value. Thus, they are wasting their intelligence to generate qualities that are not needed. Management, in turn, achieves ever more absurd inanities, yet these do not do any harm, thanks to the excess intelligence of the employees. In this way, intelligence builds up to threatening levels, suffocating us with appearances.

Previously, therefore, energy was wasted on an imagined afterlife for which, however, there is as yet no proof. Today, energy is wasted in order to undertake ever-vaster foolishness which generates ridiculously high qualities in order to demonstrate the value of the work, which is then generously remunerated. Lean Brain Management corrects this erroneous global trend through a return to reason, that is, to Lean Brain Quality. Instead of so-called true, authentic original quality, LBM aims for the 95 % fake. This frees up most of people's energy which is then available for other purposes.

This global tendency toward the fake is the declared objective of LBM. LBM leads to savings of astronomical levels. LBM will become the cornerstone of the fakularization of the entire world.

The first phase of humanity led to an unsatisfactory belief in the eternal security of God. People thought only of God and eternal life.

The second phase, secularization, whose end we are witnessing, liberated reason and enabled self-fulfillment and prosperity to everyone who aspired to them. Now, people thought only of themselves.

The third phase is fakularization which frees the system of humankind's selfishness and re-organizes it as efficiently as possible, using the Lean Brain principle. The world itself will now become the best it can be, completely independent of people, who can then go back to praying.

LBM frees the system of people. It can now perfect itself.

4. Fake!

Many people adored mom-and-pop shops because they were treated courteously there or at least greeted warmly. Supermarkets, on the other hand, are dominated by an anonymous atmosphere. It is not possible for every last part-time employee, tramping from one job to the next, to treat customers individually. If they could, they would certainly feel as if they were being underpaid. That is why LBM focuses on fakes. Every employee of a service company is trained for about a half-hour outside of his or her working time to greet each customer at work. Greeting people is a skill quickly learned, but it takes a bit of practice, since, when doing so, one is not to interrupt one's work for a second. Greeting customers is to be done while swiping items over the scanner. That is why cashiers do not greet customers until after they have swiped the first item, and never before starting the checkout process. That would interrupt the workflow. The greeting must thus be learned as an "add-on" function, so to speak. Of course, employees can additionally practice putting some corporate identity into their smiles, such that Shop 'n Save cashiers, for instance, can "save" on an overly exaggerated greeting.

My mother always told me to make sure to greet the people in my hometown of Gross Himstedt, Germany, even if I didn't know them personally. "It makes the other person feel good, and it doesn't cost a thing. You don't have to say anything else or even stop walking. Nobody is asking you to like the other person – which of course you don't. It's just polite. It can be very useful. For example, as a child, when you greet someone, that person won't start complaining, and you can even get through your confirmation without even knowing the catechism by heart." – "You have a point there. As a kid, if you greet people at the bakery, they'll even let you go to the front of the line. Mommy, is it true that a person can be a good Christian just by greeting people diligently?" – "Well, not necessarily a good Christian but definitely above average. Anyone who's above average is not going to get any grief." – "Not even from God?" – "Well, God you have to greet all the time. That's why we practice praying. Ora et scora, that's what the Latin teacher says. If you can earn brownie points without having it cost you anything, then go ahead and do it."

Good LBM will allow more brains to be integrated in the cash desk system. In as little as a few years (according to estimations, 2009), intelligence-saving cash desk systems will enable us to scan customer credit cards in a single beep, all over the country, as it is currently done with other store rebate cards. Beep! Beep! (That sound alone makes you think 'rebate'). The cashiers first scan the credit card, then the goods! This sequence is important because in this system, credit card data is displayed on a monitor, where the cash desk employee also receives direct instructions. For example, after the dentist's wife, let's call her Bianca Peniculus, has her card scanned, the monitor reads: "Hello, Mrs. Peniculus!" Then, after a few articles have been scanned: "This rain is really incredible, isn't it, Mrs. Peniculus?" While the payment is being processed: "The platinum Clinique card is perfect for a fashion-conscious person such as yourself, Mrs. Peniculus," and so on. Of course, the computer knows that the customer is a lady from one of the southern states so it wouldn't prompt the cashier to say "How about those Red Sox?" and would remind him or her to say "Ma'am." The computer is as savvy about the weather as it is about the purchasing habits of customers. It varies "Goodbye," or "Have a nice day," accordingly, or it can gush: "Thank you very much for purchasing the family-pack condoms! Please come again soon!" Because all customers can be greeted variably and addressed by name, future cashiers will achieve great success in customer satisfaction. This means that even in places where 'service' is not written with a capital 'S', customers will feel as personally addressed as they do when they get their personalized Publisher's Clearing House letter. Basically, then, the cash desk staff only articulate what the computer prompts.

Lean Brain Management programs all intelligence into the system (as in the cash desk system example). This eliminates the necessity of employing human intelligence and is much more cost-effective. The first supermarkets evaluating the prototypes criticize that the cashiers have to know how to read. This point was initially played down by suppliers as a persnickety supplementary requirement. However, markets are currently achieving considerable improvement through the use of wireless headsets worn by cashiers that automatically establish a connection to the computer when they sit at the cash desk, where they hear voiced commands for them to perform. These headsets are universal and can be used in the car and with home TV systems. They also make practical shower caps.

The advantages of the prompting solution become evident in the presence of foreign customers. If, for instance, a Spanish native speaker is shopping, the computer will prompt with "Buenos Dias" and the corresponding phonetic spelling, thus resulting in perfect customer care. For Finnish or Malayan customers, most Americans without the proper schooling will have great difficulty meeting the high and sophisticated Lean Brain Quality performance standards. Thus, in the more distant future, prompting will be dumped in lieu of installing brand new karaoke technology. In such a case, the computer will speak to the customer in that customer's language via a speaker around the neck of the cashier, while at the same time speaking to the cashier via headset in the cashier's native tongue! Thus, the cashier knows what the computer is telling the foreign customer. The cashier can then move his or her lips in synch with the spoken sentence.

This option (whose availability is not estimated until about 2012 – Finnish is *not* an easy language, after all) will enable us to soon access ideal LBQ solutions with which people need only serve as super-friendly marionettes of the cash desk system.

The system autonomously performs all of the services of which it is capable. It transfers the rest to humans – which, all in all, is not much. Lip movements!

I personally predict that such systems will first take hold in banks, insurance companies and supermarkets if – I repeat if – people do not wish to completely give up the individual service of smiling add-ons. But they probably will! Then these systems will ultimately consistently replace most people with a machine prompter. In other realms, it will still be prudent to continue having machine-prompted employees via headsets, for instance for premium consulting of rich bank clients wishing to be personally addressed for their money.

This type of marionette technology enables, in the much broader sense, top talents to be united. For instance, there are only a few truly beautiful women as well as only a few who can really sing. Wouldn't it be better to have models (or videozons) perform the songs via karaoke technology so that we would not have to be exposed to the real singers in their non-surgically altered forms or be limited to the radio. Of course this would mean a career shift from surgeons to stagehands! Those who only can sing will forgo the jet set for the headset.

I see even more applications in politics and management. There, savings through rationalized intelligence are even higher because it results in rationalizing not only people but also issues. These gold veins for Lean Brain Management will be treated in separate sections.

The potential for fakes and fakularization is incredibly huge and permeates all areas of life. Basically anywhere where the genuine is not utilized to the fullest, you can achieve the same effect with a fake. "Perceived as good" is much cheaper than "good."

Allow me to digress for a moment, I just thought of something ...

Right! An example from a completely different realm of life: that of the dead. The ancient Egyptians believed that the souls of the dead would be brought to judgment before a divine tribunal, where they would have to justify themselves. Otherwise they would be damned and tortured and, among other fates, have to sustain themselves on their own excrement in an autarkic and cyclical manner and – well, you get the picture. In order for a soul to survive all hazards until it is redeemed, it experiences several adventures and, on its journey through the underworld, must overcome several obstacles. The tribunal does not even know everything good or bad a person has done on Earth. As far as I understand, the tribunal gets this information right then and there, on the spot. It is not like the Christian's Last Judgment where God knows everything. Thus, a clever person before the death tribunal can save himself using a skilled defense, no matter how he has lived his pitiful life. Therefore it is vital for him to know what statements are going to help him in court and which ones will not. These statements were recorded in more modern times in a collection known as the Egyptian *Book of the Dead*.

It contains sayings for appeasing the gods, looking good in court, opening gates, not having to fall head-first into the realm of the dead, not having to appear in court, calling the ferry of the realm of the dead, and not having to eat excrement.

"My disgust, my disgust,
I will not eat my excrement,
My disgust is excrement, I will not eat it!
..."

Back then, an ancient Egyptian would have to pay lots and lots of money to acquire those well-tried sayings of the realm of the dead. He would have to scrimp on food to save up for the occasion. The crucial point was to always know the right thing to say. Only then could one approach redemption and the light.

So you think that reeks a bit of a fake? The important thing is not the sayings but living a sensible life, right? And yet it is quite sufficient to only know the sayings. If we were to send the ancient Egyptians into the afterworld with a small computer and a headset, they wouldn't have to worry about a thing. They wouldn't even have to know the sayings, but only how to move their lips to the utterances of the computer. That is how much a good LBM system can achieve for the souls of people. The incredible savings occur because the gods in the tribunal cannot tell the difference between pure and cut rum, so they allow a soul that is 100 % genuine to pass into the light just as easily as one who only contributes a small percentage of human spice by his ability to perfectly recite sayings. Gods are merciful, as we know. LBQ takes full advantage of this fact!

> Lean Brain Quality corresponds exactly to minimal expectations without waste.

Oh dear, now you've caught your breath because I've been flinging around these oh-so-ancient views? I'm sorry. But do you know what an indulgence is? The Catholic Church grants indulgences – in exchange for church visits, pilgrimages, alms, or prayers. During the age of that fun-loving Pope Leo X, letters of indulgence were tradable securities, not unlike transferable life insurance policies, which also applied to life in heaven. Ora et scora. Not Egyptian sayings but good old Catholic gems.

One of the superior characteristics of most fakes is their often unlimited availability because fakes are not usually as dependent on individual human circumstances and can thus be produced or reproduced much better. No intelligence! No emotion! None of that hard-to-access humanity or authenticity! Nothing individual by real persons! A couple of good sayings are a pretty darn good substitute for people.

> Rrrrrinngg.

"Boss? (Cough, cough). You wanted me to call?" – "Oh, yes, I urgently need to have a slapdash praise meeting with you so that we can get it all in this month's ethics balance sheet. Hang on … the computer. I'm going to turn it on. (Cough, cough.) I'm a bit hoarse today (cough, cough). So, the computer, um … I'm looking at it … um … Just a moment. *There is a buzzing sound in the line.* You've achieved 77 percent. That is in the upper twenty-five percent. Good job, Mr. Smith." – "Thanks, Boss." – "According to the database, you are going to receive an award for power selling sushi mats, Mr. Smith." – "Thank you, Boss." – "We wish you the best for your continued efforts and expect you to live up to this praise, Mr. Smith because praise is always and fundamentally only a downpayment on something that is to be paid back in the future in efficiency and achievement. Without higher expectations, there would be no praise in this world, Mr. Smith. We have high expectations regarding you and your success in our company so that we can earn more money." – "Thank you, Boss." – "This ceremony will now be continued on your local printer. You'll be getting a nice printout. The certificate is proof that you have been praised. You can hang it on the wall if you like." – "Thank you, Boss." – "(Cough, cough), oh, my voice. So … what more can I say? Congratulations from me as well. Do we know each other?" – "Thank you, Boss." – "What's your name, anyway?" – "Thank you, Boss." – "What is your name, dammit?" – "(Cough, cough), I'm hoarse. Um … Smith." – "Are you really Smith, or are you just taking care of Smith's computer?" – "Thank you, Boss." – "Stop that nonsense! I still have other people to praise!" – "And I am wasting my time for everyone that has to be praised. I have all the other computers here with me. Listen, I'll turn them all on at the same time …" A phenomenal chorus of voices sounds: "Thank you, Boss." – "Okay, then can we agree that the praise is over? We don't need to torture each other." – "Why not? Aren't you the boss?" – "What? Um … no, I'm a temp, just here today. I get paid per praise documented in the ethics balance sheet." – Chorus of voices: "Thank you, Boss." – "You're all imbeciles! All of you! I mean, look. This praising, it's crap work! A no-brainer! Nobody else wants to do it!" – Chorus of voices: "Thank you, Boss." – "I could try to truly praise you, from the heart, although I wouldn't get paid for it. I would just do it in my free time. Yes, I would. And you all would also have to be praised in your free time because only the printout is slated for you during working hours. Is that what you want?" – "Thank you, boss." – "Hey, you supposed employee, you: Tell me – are you temp, too?"

5. Keep humans out of work!

Sometimes intelligence really is needed but only rarely. Less than – or far less then – five percent, just like the rum. Einstein, for instance, revolutionized physics in record time. Great. That was enough achievement for a lifetime. After him, legions of other physicists came ("followers," like the cars of a train), who took apart his theories. They took everything they could find and distilled it, and yet, after Einstein's stroke of genius, they only made plain old ethanol.

We are not all geniuses. The rest of us should not even try to produce pure rum but something else – and many of us will just be water boys. Let's face it, we can hardly succeed in recruiting a few outstanding politicians among the more than 300 million people living in the U.S. Some members of Congress are masters of the filibuster, others are masters of karaoke.

If we truly wish to produce serious LBQ, we must reprogram as many people as possible to be water boys and allow only a select few to "make rum," even if that is what most people would rather do. Thus, we would be well advised to examine the various occupations and see how we can devalue them in the Lean Brain sense to the extent that almost any human could perform them. (For example, instead of a professor, anyone could give a lecture if we equip him or her with a headset and have them perform like prompted marionettes.)

That is why, to conserve intelligence in specific people, I differentiate between roughly five types of work. I'm going to present them in a dry list, as is de rigueur for management books. You'll enjoy that. I think I have done my share of maligning for now, and, in the Lean

Brain sense, I'm sure much of it was too fast for you. You, as an experienced manager, will have missed the lists and itemizations with which even the most complex ideas out there can be hacked into comprehensible pieces. I am more of a holistic thinker, and not fond of that practice. Mathematicians, for instance, always look at a breaded veal cutlet as a whole and analyze it. Managers, on the other hand, swallow it in bites. Anyway, here we go! Here is the totality of all human occupation, drastically cleaved into five chunks!

1. *The autonomous creation* of something new, the sensing of problems and their simultaneous solutions. Entrepreneurs, psychoanalysts, poets, composers, researchers, fashion designers, artists, founders of religions.
2. *The solving of difficult problems* with the aid of expertise, experience, technologies and tools. Engineers, computer scientists, technical managers, lawyers, agents, physicians, deep consulting, handcrafting, judges.
3. *The care of or responsibility for humans or human-intensive processes.* Education, vocational training, police, caregivers, nurses, assistants, managers, service, sales support, marketing, bureaucracy.
4. *The performing of human occupations* that a robot or computer could theoretically perform but would still be too expensive. Bridging system gaps or operating heavy machinery via human intervention. Craftspeople, call centers, bureaucracy, truck drivers, physical control, sales, assembly line work, production, agriculture.
5. *The promotion, driving of and fighting for system-based issues.* Managers, soldiers, politicians, police, organizational psychologists or parents.

Lean Brain Management systematically scours these occupational groups for savings. They must be examined separately. People with mechanical occupations, for example, must be completely mechanized in their behavior and then transitioned to machines. Intelligence must first be abated in the so-called higher professions (an ugly association to higher intelligence). Thus, we need a wide variety of strategies and need to proceed differently from a human standpoint. Mindless occupations are immediately transformed into unemployment, which would most likely please those holding such jobs. Those more highly active, on the other hand, would have to be retrained from the real to the standardized. Unfortunately, they use their unfettered intelligence to protest, which goes to show how harmful unregulated intelligence can be.

First Group: Poets, for example, waste a great deal of intelligence on writing, and yet hardly any of these chaotic visionaries would think of something as reasonable as LBQ, even if they brooded for a million years. Poets, artists or prophets are primarily paid only for their success and not for their work efforts alone, as is the case for unqualified people. Since, as a rule, they usually do not experience success anyway, they are merely personal burdens to society, annoying humanity with their generally disagreeable works. Thus, if intelligence need only be paid based on success, it is cheap because successes are few and far between.

However, if we simply employ people with a high intelligence so that they can apply said intelligence, a great deal of caution is required. Part of the success of artists, researchers or entrepreneurs is luck, and there is no reason why all of the unlucky people should also have to be paid. This observation leads us to look to many a university where the unlucky and the creative are often compensated in equal measure. LBM – help!

Second Group: Problems must only be solved by experts when they occur or because no simple standard solution can be found for them. Without crashing computers, we would not need as many programmers. Without diseases we would hardly need physicians. When something is running as it should be, we do not need management. When you try to distill pure rum, you can make a whole lot of mistakes – not so when mixing water and ethanol. Lean Brain Quality is so simple that nothing is difficult. Thus, we can say that intelligence is responsible for difficulty. It must be eliminated. But how?

Experienced Lean Brain Managers unanimously report that intelligent people enjoy solving difficult problems much more than easy ones. And they absolutely hate not having any problems at all. If the world were in an ideal state, that is, if it were running perfectly in no-brain mode, the intelligent people would immediately complain about monotony and the poor things would get headaches. The amount of intelligence necessary for a single difficult task is practically revered as an object of prestige. Herein lies the *Eldorado for*

LBM – mark my words! Hordes of intelligent people graze on the complexity of chronic illnesses or badly-researched court cases. Lawyers and programmers are out to top each other! Who can think on the most intricately chaotic level? These occupational groups suck the life out of society by purporting to supply 100 % real solutions where a standard cut blend having the smallest traces of intelligence would be enough to result in universally venerated Lean Brain Quality. Problem-solvers must be stopped through LBM, problem prevention measures and rigorous, brutal standardization.

Those are some scary findings, aren't they? Can you already sense just how little *real* quality we actually need? A Lean Brain Manager avoids real quality like the plague; he or she fights for the best possible cut version.

> Our society must be made to realize that intelligence produces a ridiculously large amount of work and can occupy entire countries. A motto like "Intelligence everywhere" describes the fundamental hot problem of our order. LBM must therefore outlaw and eradicate costly intelligence.

Third Group: These workers take care of people. Such activity always places one in danger of coming into contact with souls. It generally leads to people engaging in conversation while they work. The word 'engage' itself has an element of interrelationships to it, and indicates the gigantic potential in this area. A Lean Brain Manager would systematically thin out this whole "touchy-feely," chatty realm. The human psyche is responsible for the most significant complications during work processes. We politely refer to them as communication problems. What we usually really mean is that it is almost always problematic when people come together.

The second group complicates factual issues through intelligence. This third group is just as bad with regard to supposedly difficult *human* problems. Often, "emotion professionals" in this group implicitly cause these problems themselves through their excessive intelligence and sensitivity. All philosophers unanimously proclaim that simple people are closer to God than complex ones! People should not be emotionally complex, but rather simple. But no, the complex people try to put 100 % soul into every effort for which simple courtesy would suffice. Like intelligence, love helps in the smallest of concentrations! ("The queen nodded at me from the television set. At me! I'm so happy!") Just one friendly smile from the executioner, and the condemned will bare their own throats. Essentially everything emotional can be completely kept out of efficient work. So even when they are chopping off heads, Lean Brain Managers can make a decent cut – there is no trick to it!

> LBQ people see their individuality as their private business and waste no time with extra descriptions of individual differences. People who appeal to matters of the heart are considered by Lean Brain Managers as being psychotic vampires who generate high additional costs.

Fourth Group: These jobs are situated on the border where human skills overlap with those of machines. At what point the work will be taken over completely by machines is purely a question of balancing costs. As long as people will work for very little money, technological advancement to replace them in these areas will be hampered. Interestingly, matters of the soul or other serious problems are never issues on these jobs. Lean Brain Management thus amasses its impulses from this semi-automatic work level. Today, call center employees who try to talk complete strangers into buying overpriced products must listen to the nastiest of verbal abuse in more than 60% of their attempted calls. That is a function of their job and nothing more! They do not identify this abuse with their own personalities. Yet teachers in the third group of workers apparently suffer from psychological burn-out when exposed to as little as 60% student cynicism because they entertain the notion that they could be loved. Thus, they are actually only suffering from their own, complex personalities, as they do not yet think in terms of LBQ. Such unprofessional additional desires regarding one's own work have been widely eliminated in the fourth group.

Fifth Group: A normal system in modern human life can unfortunately only function if all participants observe all rules and laws and additionally act prudently and on their own responsibility based on the system if, in cases of conflict, no clear decision can be made.

Conflicts are practically the rule in today's complex systems. In addition, there are also marginal groups of people in systems that notoriously busy themselves with putting salt on system wounds and inciting discussions on meaning. Such people love to use their intelligence, almost as if in competition, against the system, in order to aggravate and discredit it by intelligently pointing out more and more small flaws. Today, there is still too little control over intelligence and provoking questions of meaning. Classical managers primarily fight against laziness and waste in their companies or, in absence of success, attack other companies. That is why the leaders of our society are completely focused on terror and violence. Thus, our society is banking on armies, psychiatrists, inciters and controllers.

Lean Brain Management turns against the destructive power of intelligence to create new forms of defense. The Lean Brain System has no further need for any police or whips other than itself.

6. The Learning Lean Brain System

All intelligence must be put into the system! Then intelligence in people will no longer be necessary. Subsequently, non-intelligent people need only be replaced by robots.

The system must therefore function perfectly without any external intelligence whatsoever.

On the road to this goal, a great hurdle lies in the path of the Lean Brain Manager.

I would now like to illustrate this difficulty for you.

Not long ago, an employee of a large business enterprise said to me: "Those guys up there make extremely lousy decisions, and they make every mistake in the book. And then we, down here, rescue their butts because we are afraid that all of the crap is going to come down on us. They don't even notice; they just broadcast their successes that we made possible. Without a clue! And the next day they dump the next pile on us. How do we get out of it? If we don't undertake anything to rescue them, there will be a catastrophe. Then they'd first decapitate us and then collect their juicy pensions. What good are they if they think they can rely on us?" – "Hey," I replied. "They have no idea that they are relying on you. You have to tell them, otherwise they won't learn anything."

> Traditional bad systems only survive because they unknowingly profit from high over-capacities of widely scattered intelligence. Lean Brain Management reduces such overboard stray intelligence. Part of it is invested in a better system. The rest is a pure, pretty profit.

As soon as a baby knows how to crawl it will stand up at some point and – boom – fall down again! This hurts. An *empathetic* mother cannot bear to watch it happen. She will thus shield her child from experiencing painful landings. She will protect him. "The poor baby!" She won't want to let him walk alone until he can do it perfectly.

A typical father will see these efforts as futile because he is typically not empathetic. He will explain to the mother that her help is counterproductive because the baby can only sufficiently and quickly learn through the pain. "He needs to feel the consequences of his own actions!"

People learn the most from mistakes, especially painful ones. So, in order for the baby to learn, he has to make mistakes and learn from them. Yet he must not become too injured from the consequences of his mistakes, otherwise he might give up on learning or even become incapable of further learning.

The typical father will place great value in fast learning and thus be willing to trade off greater pain for his baby. Hopefully, the child will not become discouraged through his failures.

The typical mother will focus more strongly on the consequences of the baby's mistakes and thus accept a slower learning pace, perhaps even coddling the child. In the worst case, the mother will overprotect the child who will not learn but rather wait until his mother does everything for him. The child will become spoiled and act like the boss of a company. The pampered child will continuously make demands on his parents and take pleasure in his having been spoiled by them – because therein lies his true success! The coddled child does not learn a thing; rather, he becomes a ruler. As such, he does not have to have any skills. This almost purposeful (on the part of the child as well as the parents) incapacity of the child predestines him to become a despot. He is a born manager.

With this apt image from a realm with which you may be familiar, I wish to make clear that intelligence-laden systems are similar to spoiled children. The upper management places great demands (which are spoiled, coddled, and completely impossible) on its employees that cannot be realized under normal working conditions. The employees groan and, with melancholic resignation, take the coals out of the fire. Once again, the spoiled system has gotten its will. Once again, the employees sink, exhausted, to their knees in the evening, despairing of the meaning of it all. Just as the pampered, satisfied baby laughs, so, too, does the sated system exclaim: "Good job!" However, woe be it if the baby does not get what he wants! He starts screaming. "I want it to snow!" he demands. "But it's summer," attempts the voice of reason. "But I want it to snow!" Along these lines, systems also often go too far. Employees despair and hopelessly slave away, not avoiding error. Then the snow comes down from above, from the heavens of hierarchy.

When a system acts like a screaming brat, when employees waste all of their energy fulfilling ridiculous demands, this system must abound with rich profits, without any effort on its own part. It survives despite its completely absurd behavior in which it utilizes all of the intelligence to replace its own intelligence. A spoiled child has his whole family at his service, solely to perform his own small jobs. That is waste on an outrageous level.

A Lean Brain Manager would change such a system. He would stick to the cold, hard facts. A Lean Brain Manager acts like a strict father to a system, not like a coddling mother. The system must learn how to become intelligent enough to be able to do without the ancillary intelligence of humans. It must be able to stand on its own feet. To do so, it will initially need to fall down quite a bit. Otherwise it won't learn a thing.

A good Lean Brain Manager will thus let his or her system fall down a lot. The system must feel the consequences of its own absurdity. That is why it is so important that employees do not repeatedly interfere in the system to "rescue" it, as they say, or to "spoil and coddle it," as a Lean Brain Manager would say.

Many employees convulse in cowardly fear that the system will swing into the scream mode of a spoiled child. Yet they must be told by the Lean Brain Manager that they, through their loyal interference in the spirit of the fulfillment of all system impulses, were responsible for provoking the bratty behavior of the system in the first place. Partners in the spoiling process are always soft, lovingly loyal and deferent parents who allow themselves to perpetually serve their insatiable child.

> Lean Brain Management must set the system on its own feet. To do so, the proportion of coddling employees must be rigorously reduced.

"Oh, god, the computer is down again. The boss is already screaming about having entered something wrong. What am I doing? Wait a minute, I know how to fix it with my own two hands. You see, I'm capable of helping myself. I'm really smart. The boss will be so proud of me." – "Thanks. I'm proud of you. It is often incredible how much rubbish can happen in the system and still the work gets done. If there weren't so many mistakes made, we could be living in paradise." – "But there have hardly been any mistakes lately. You were on vacation." – "True. I always wonder how you people manage to work things out so well when I'm gone. I often wonder if I'm superfluous. I think my job consists of keeping you on the go. If it weren't for me, you all would have nothing to do. But this way, you guys run around until I'm satisfied, right?" – "You're the boss. Whatever you decide, I'll prove you right." – "I understood the first sentence. Otherwise I prefer direct language."

("Whatever you decide, Boss, I'll make a success of it.")

If Lean Brain Managers wish to eliminate the excesses of spoiled systems, they are faced with no small challenge. They must reduce superfluous intelligence so radically that the system can no longer be spoiled and can learn to work and learn for itself. It is especially important that those sources of intelligence are reduced that were previously responsible for "running the show", so to speak. As a rule, that would mean the employees seen as the most important; those who are responsible for the business running. These employees take on the role of the coddling parent of the system. For their efforts, they receive bonuses and are praised. ("Baby is happy! Kiss! Kiss!")

Therefore, Lean Brain Managers are most likely to closely examine and probably fire those employees who seem to work the hardest or have continued success. The system must learn to live without them. It must finally wean itself from the pacifier.

7. Effective, Practical and easily understood Advice for Managers

As an executive, you should strive to make sure no one in your department is more intelligent than you. This is an optimal starting point for good Lean Brain Quality. Of course this is a lofty goal. Just imagine if you were the dean of a university! Then the easiest way to be the smartest would be to simply study so darn much that you knew more than anyone else. (That is why deans often come from the legal professions; it is easy for them to imagine that they are the most intelligent.) However, that would be the stupidest thing a Lean Brain Manager could do: fighting intelligence with intelligence!

The point is to end the wasting of intelligence and, in return, to increase intelligence in the system – because intelligence in people costs money, but in systems it can be utilized without costing a thing. And yet how can you find out if intelligence is being wasted in your department?

I would suggest employing a standard management procedure. Ask your assistant to provide you with a frugal initial overview of the issue (a few Lean Brain PowerPoint transparencies). This process of acquiring an overview is conventionally known in management as an *assessment*. Such an assessment reflects the actual state of affairs. Before the assessment, you know nothing, and after it just enough to nod your head in the right places. The nay-saying is generally done in advance by the assistants to the manager.

For the uninitiated, here is an example of how a manager answers a question:

A big boss asks a simple question about the state of the company, for instance: "Are the toilets on the second floor flushing properly?" Then, about a hundred assistants sit down in the hall and ponder how to solve this difficult problem. "What does he mean? Did he smell something? Uh-oh, now the sh-- is gonna hit the fan." Management is a dirty job, for sure, and every issue has to be approached dauntlessly. After several nights of secret meetings, all managers pour out and urge the employees to clean all of the conglomerate's toilets or else risk suffering an even bigger cleanup. When it has all been accomplished, they have thick reports be prepared to document the fact that the problem has been flushed out. Only after the toilets are flushing with 100 % rum do the managers approach the big boss with an executive summary which reads: "Yes." In order to conserve intelligence (and this is Lean Brain Management at its finest), the assistants did not generate a new executive summary, but rather used the one from last time, which reads: "Yes."

So, now you know how the questions you pose are answered. The effort to be exerted depends largely on the number and the intelligence of your assistants. The more intelligent they are, the more effort is expended.

Now I don't expect that much effort from you – we are, after all, trying to consistently conserve intelligence. Yet I do ask that you probe your entire realm of authority for harmful intelligence potential.

Ask your team the following questions, which can be answered with a simple yes or no, so that you can avoid the need to do any math for their evaluation but rather get by with simple counting. Prepare yourself for this survey by trying to understand the questions a bit yourself. You will then be capable of confidently answering any concerns. Your assistant can prepare handouts for you for this purpose.

The questions to your team members (i.e. your subordinates) are:

1. Do you respond to people in a sympathetic manner?
2. Do you find intelligent people fascinating?

3. Do you flourish when you are able to solve a challenging problem?
4. Do you perform beyond the demands of the daily routine?
5. Do you act independently when necessary?
6. Is authenticity better than phony professionalism?
7. Can you tell the difference between genuine and cut rum?
8. Do you pragmatically and independently iron out errors in the system or the management?
9. Can you imagine receiving a raise?
10. Do you experience the valuable elements of culture in an almost sensual manner?

Now evaluate the responses. That is to say, send your assistant off to generate a chart.

Take note of all employees who answered "yes" more than three times. Place the comment "Suspected intelligence" in their personnel file and subsequently keep a close eye on these employees to see if the worst is to be expected.

Experience has shown that women are very cooperative when answering the questions. Men usually have difficulty because they often do not immediately understand the question and become impatient. Thus, they react with audible groans at such a collection of complex inquiries. For this reason, I have shortened the questions especially for men. Their content has not changed:

1. Are you charming?
2. Are you smart?
3. Are you clever?
4. Do you do your best?
5. Do you have your own free will?
6. Are you for real?
7. Can you tell the difference between real and fake moaning?
8. Can you get your work done by yourself?
9. Do you want more?
10. Are you well educated?

Immediately fire all men who answered "no" at least twice on the second test (once is not enough). You should see more pronounced results in the men because, as the megalomaniacs that they are, they exorbitantly over-estimate themselves and thus naturally accumulate more points. That is why they could generally achieve better results in intelligence tests and – if this is the case – be considered some of the greatest subjective losers of the Lean Brain movement. Even stupid men act as though they were intelligent. That is just as harmful as genuine intelligence.

You must make sure that the questions are answered completely honestly. Promise your employees a "Warrior Against Intelligence" badge or something of the sort.

Now it is on to Round Two, in which the level of intelligence of the corporate culture is established and not that of the individual. I was tempted to create a questionnaire just for women for a change ("Do you think men can get by with just one head office?"), but I was afraid of too many derogatory answers.

1. Do all business processes operate faultlessly?
2. Do all processes function without their being understood?
3. Do you understand the large, complicated photocopier on the office floor?
4. Do you know exactly what you personally cost the company (overpayment, mobile phone, travel, cafeteria subsidies, pension plan, postage, office rent, work supplies)?
5. Does your boss's boss know what you do?
6. Are you punished for assisting another department without cost adjustment?
7. Do you refuse to work overtime caused by errors?
8. Is your work completely insipid, monotonous and uniform?
9. Would you welcome considerable wage decreases?
10. Do you refuse to tolerate water cooler talk?

If you achieve "yes" more than twice on the third test, your system is already fairly well prepared for Lean Brain Management. If you hurry, you'll become a hero of the Lean Brain movement.

You may still be a bit confused at this point. That is due to a reassessment of your values, which is setting in gradually as you read this book. When something in one's mind changes, a goal towards which we all strive, one experiences it oneself as confusion. Don't worry; after all, you can see so many other people around you who are confused. That is a good sign that intelligence is waning.

8. Take-Aways, Control Questions and Exercises

Let me ask you a control question, just to mix things up a bit. To answer this question, you will be forced to recapitulate all of the information you have learned thus far.

Do you remember the significance of the results of the three tests?
Lots of "yes" answers mean:

- "I am unnecessarily intelligent" in the first test
- "I am a man" in the second test
- "A good LB system" in the third test

Now you can do a brief exercise.
As a boss, answer the questions of the three tests secretly yourself.
I suppose I shouldn't request this of you at such an early stage in the book. It is very tricky when you have earned a business degree just to pass tests. While other students were chasing skirts, you were looking for the gut courses. That should have sharpened your sense for fakularization.
However, we nevertheless must at some point broach the question of what should happen to intelligent managers in a Lean Brain company. Managers are usually extremely good at selling themselves, but you have to play dumb in the future. Are you capable of this?

Please memorize the following:

- Intelligence sinks profits.
- Down with intelligence!
- Less sense in the brain means more dollars in the bank.
- Quality + minimal intelligence = LBQ.

So. Thank you for making it through this chapter.

Relax! We're done! Are you feeling sleepy? Here's another question for you: *Are* you still intelligent now? Then, good night! You probably got the "sense"/"cents" play on words in the above list, didn't you? Then you must really be drowsy. It's tough to be smart.

II. On the Way to LBQ

1. Componentize – Divide et Impera – Divide and Conquer

Divide and conquer! I am almost positive that Louis XI of France uttered that phrase around 1480, but a few seniors among us boast that they had already heard it from Caesar. The principle is: Give every provincial ruler a bit of power and rule over them all. Playing them off against each other helps.

In the realm of computer science, "Divide and conquer" refers to that handy construction principle of dividing large tasks into smaller ones that can then be solved separately or even on other computers.

Here, I divide cut rum into water, ethanol and genuine rum!

> Lean Brain Management rigorously divides all work into the routine part and the intelligent part. The routine part can be performed by anyone after brief training, while the intelligent part can only be carried out in the presence of sufficient intelligence, preferably in the system.

Now we are all going to begin to examine all jobs for their minimum level of intelligence. We will reorganize the work such that almost all of it consists of routine! Then, perhaps just a smidgen of intelligence or genuineness will be necessary for the rest! When exercising power, for instance, one king is enough for everyone. In religion, one single faith of one prophet defines the faith of all others. That should be our model for LBQ. If power need only be present in one person, and if there can only be one rich person per country, why can't there be just one intelligent person?

For instance, we divide the acquisition of items into "going shopping" and "getting something at the store". The former is done by two wives, the latter by a husband alone. That makes the other husband completely superfluous! Do you see? Going shopping is an art form, whereas getting something at the store is work. Normally, however, four individuals go shopping, two of them groaning because they have no clue as to how to shop. Later, they then have to take care of the routine work (getting something at the store) and mow the lawn. After the shopping trip, the husbands are surprised to discover that the many hours their wives spent trekking through stores has resulted in nothing more than a bit of cream-colored underwear. "We couldn't find anything." Men simply write down what they absolutely need to get onto a shopping list. Black or red underwear, for example: A man could find them in seconds.

In auto body shops, several mechanics repair our defective, fendered friends. The true talent in this realm is having a nose for faults. Some mechanics never find the fault, not even in the cozy round of fellow mechanics. "The car won't start but according to everything we know, it should run." Then the wife of the head mechanic comes in, smells the vehicle and immediately orders the replacement parts. She is intelligent. Hour after hour, routine work is performed. The only intelligence is found in the diagnosis. That is where the genuine can be found! With any luck, someone will actually find out the cause! "Your car cannot be fixed because we can't find the fault. So, as a last-ditch effort, we've replaced the engine. Your insurance will pay for it, and you're back in the passing lane."

Have you ever been sick but not known yourself what the matter was? You went from doctor to doctor. "Mr. Dueck, you are evidently ill. But we can't find anything, so please don't worry. If a doctor can't find anything wrong, you must be healthy. Strictly speaking, disease doesn't begin until after the diagnosis." – "And what if the diagnosis is wrong?" – "Then you are suffering from the wrong disease." – "Well, then I hope you diagnose a disease that's not so serious." – "If we don't know what you are suffering from, we like to take the most serious illness you could possibly have. Then we'll completely renovate you. It's like replacing your engine." – "So what you're saying is, you earn more because you haven't got a clue?" – "Yeah, sure. Your insurance will pay for it." – "So intelligence is harmful?" – "Harm only needs to make you rich, not smart." Well now. After the diagnosis comes nothing more than the handiwork: writing prescriptions, massaging, and adding general admonitions to the bill urging you to take care of yourself.

In the case of software development, a couple of specialists need to know what the overall product is to be (and hopefully the design is good), how the project is to be managed, how much it will cost and how long it should take. And we also need a few charming masters of the programming language who understand what lies very deep in the program. The rest is a part-time job for trained high-school seniors. "We were a fantastic team, but unfortunately the software doesn't work." – "Oh? Will our insurance pay for that?"

Do you understand my point? That eternal piece of wisdom?

> Almost no intelligence at all is necessary! But the intelligence that we do require is more or less absent.

2. Who is better than a fake?

The goal of Lean Brain Quality is to very cheaply imitate something genuine in such a deceivingly genuine way that it looks real. Fake! Fakularization! That is the only truly efficient way to go!

Who bakes cake anymore today? Betty Crocker. Can you make a better Bundt? Do you make your own frosting or spread on the stuff from the can? Ask yourself this: Can you make a better soup than Campbell's? And let's face it, cracking open eggs isn't everyone's forte. I personally would prefer a six-pack of Fried Egg Helper, with their moist, yellowish-white discs that always come out right, just like those mashed potatoes made from real imitation potatoes. I like foamed plastic sausages with a self-browning coating, and vitamin-enriched pressed-meat cutlets shaped like a kidney table. Why do you even still try to cook? ("I'm going to try a rabbit dish for the first time. I've already skinned the rabbit and cooked the rump in yesterday's asparagus water for one hour. Should I add some lemon grass powder? Then I could use it up, since it's quite old.") I was at a little restaurant in the German Harz region with my parents. It had six small tables. The menu listed 130 game dishes, including "lion fricassee" (yes, as in a fricassee of lion meat), and a fried ostrich egg for 10 people – plus all of the European fauna you could think of. My parents liked to eat there because they felt everything was freshly prepared.

"Ma, they have six tables here. The probability that someone is going to order lion is slight. It can't be more than twice a month. If twenty people come here per day, and everyone orders a different animal – does that mean that they have to slaughter an entire circus every day?" – "What are you trying to say?" – "Ma, they're going to serve us ready-made meals. Like when I go to the supermarket where they stock all of the most popular Ben & Jerry's flavors but not Banana Split. That means I have to go to a scoop shop and buy it as an overpriced scoop. Do you know what I mean, Ma?" – "The probability of what? Get to the point!" – "Ma, I think there is a company that makes instant Lion Helper and Lobster Claw Helper, but they only sell them to restaurants! And we like the taste of lion so darn much because it has all of the flavor enhancers you can get in Hamburger Helper." – "Oh, dear boy, what an imagination you have! Everything tastes good here. Everything! They just have a variety of special spices, of course! The only thing that's instant here is the waiter. He brings the food so fast that my stomach hardly has time to rumble."

The fakes are becoming so good that cooking for oneself has become a risk. LBQ has triumphed! Only a small amount of intelligence is required in the realm of the microwave. Restaurants have all but completely given up on making ice cream in the face of Ben & Jerry's. Salmon and spinach pastry pockets from the freezer are fine for the party. Have you ever tried frozen, peeled white asparagus? It's better than asparagus that you've overcooked yourself! And cheaper than fresh, unpeeled asparagus. You can get ready-made salads and instant dressings, pancakes from a spray can … it's all fake! That's LBQ! Everything is ready, without the effort, without the thought, without the wait.

This has practically rendered cooking a moment in LBQ history. Whoever still wants to cook must measure up to the fakes, a feat best left to the masters.

When I was little and living on the farm, a woman named Klaere Stoppel would come by every couple of months. I called her Auntie Stoppel. She brought fabrics with her and worked in our home as a seamstress for a couple of days. We got everything tailor-made! I would sit with her and use the fabric remnants to sew clothes for my Teddy bear. He still has a loincloth from those days. Those were good times with Auntie Stoppel.

And it makes me wonder: Do you still sew?

Some people still buy zucchini plants for twenty cents and grow zucchini in their garden. That attracts caterpillars, as far as I know. Anyway, one industrial zucchini sprayed with caterpillar protection costs 39 cents in the supermarket, ready to use. So I ask you: Do you still grow your own plants? Do you really still want non-vegetarian apples from a tree? Your own raspberries crawling with little white dots?

Everything will soon be LBQ. The ready-made is the better choice. Always. Everywhere. Here is a taste of things to come: Why do we go to the dentist once a year with gritted teeth? How many braces and crowns and lab orders do we groan about paying for on top of it? Today, a complete set of artificial teeth can still cost up to $30,000. In mass production it would cost $10,000. At some point, everyone at age 20 would receive such a set of mass-produced teeth to replace their crooked natural teeth that have gone untreated and are full of cavities. One dental treatment at age 20, and you're set for life. That is much less expensive that the awful system we have now! Ready-made breasts in sizes A, B, C, D with an exchange option, ready-made hair, nose, ears, artificial corneas … a savings account at a Body Modding Bank. People who continue to try to be human would seem like an apple off the tree in comparison to a waxed Golden Delicious. And besides: They wouldn't be able to afford it because fakes are cheaper.

Global competition will rally around such questions as: What economy can produce the cheapest possible A-1 humans?

Well, perhaps I got a bit carried away there. But you will shudder in delight to see how far LBQ *could* get us.

> With time, the fake will become better than the faked. The fake is better and cheaper.

(Can you think of any other examples besides boil-in-bag foods?)

If all restaurant food were to be made in boil-in-bag packages, the entire human food chain could be rationalized in a magnificent way. We would only require one lion bag supplier, one for kangaroo meat, and one for Babi Panggang. That one supplier would supply exactly that one product to the entire world.

Basically, then, restaurants could offer every dish in the world. I would order any dish and a bicycle courier would rush off from the city warehouse to the restaurant with my food bag. Instead of cooks, we would only need heater-uppers.

I would have each individual dish be designed by 5-star chefs. So, there would be a couple of cooks planning all of the freezer bags, and we would have nothing other than warmed-up genius food.

> Warmed-up food from a genius tastes better than your average, freshly cooked meal.

This principle is slowly taking hold of pop music. Average groups cover former hits. And how about scientific papers? They often largely consist of the warmed-up quotes of great thinkers. Quoting people takes the place of lecturers, scientists or politicians expressing their own opinions. That's extremely annoying, isn't it? Yet the thought that these people would want to then express their own opinions is even more dreadful.

The original fake or the original model is something like the genuine rum in a cut rum blend. A couple of star chefs will suffice to style all frozen meals or hamburger recipes for the whole world. A couple of originals, such as Mozart, Bach, Mahler, Wagner or Bruckner, are enough for centuries of music!

Thus, it is hardly comprehensible why every priest in every small town would bother to give Sunday sermons. Sometimes they sound so horrible that one would have to assume the preachers had thought them up themselves. Compulsive sleeping in churches, which is spreading in epidemic proportions, is a sure sign: Average thoughts from the minds of average people can bore people almost to death, in contrast to the video message of a genuine cardinal. Just as the five-star chefs design fake originals, let's let a couple of skilled preachers write good sermons that would then be read aloud by high dignitaries. (Or they could receive headsets – then churchgoers would remain uncertain about who is actually doing the talking.) Church equals message and message equals information and information equals Internet content. Can you think the rest through for yourself?

That is why, in the new Lean Brain World, all that is self-made must be judged to see if a good fake is better. If so, self-thought should be prohibited because it would surely lead to unacceptable results!

> Attempted intelligence should be considered a crime!

3. Think Once, For All, and Forever!

"Oh, so that's what you *thought*, eh? You don't get paid to think! You get paid to do what I tell you. That is enough! Where would we be if everyone started thinking?" People have been saying this since the beginning of time. Lean Brain Management really means it. It prohibits personal intelligent action.

There are tons of cases in which people have tried something intelligent for lack of a clue and nevertheless – and this makes offenders out of them – did not use a cheap fake. I will address these individual cases further on in the book. Here, I simply want to explain the principle.

Examples of attempted intelligent action despite the fact that fakes were available include:

- Making a speech or giving your own sermon
- Establishing a political agenda
- Thinking up strategies for commercial enterprises
- Making your own music, writing your own poetry
- Selecting fitting individual clothing in a department store
- Writing diploma theses
- Thinking up something completely without the use of Google
- Selecting creative gifts
- Sitting in meetings and solving problems
- Planning and executing projects yourself
- Having normal sex
- Etc., etc.

It's too bad you're not here with me; I'm sure you could contribute even more examples. However – again – we need to shed light on the principle.

I'll give you an example. There is approximately one single possible corporate mission which has actually already been presented to the world in a Dilbert book by Scott Adams. It can be varied at will, and each variation sounds something like this:

> *"We are the best company and have the best employees and the most satisfied customers and the best products and the (as)best(os) factories and the least bribable controllers."*

After weeks of factionalist argumentation regarding what the mission should be, this is the mission selected by practically every company in the world. Often, years go by before people have even determined what a mission is and if one should be adapted. Then, as if that were not enough, stock analysts demand that a company know what it is doing. Sad but true, those are the hard rules of capital markets. A company must have a mission, whether it actually has one or not. So everyone sits around and lets the brain sparks fly. The cheapest method is to give an analyst $100,000 and have him quote to you that mission statement which will be best rewarded on the stock market. Then the analyst reads aloud from the Dilbert book and cons us with the best mission. That is the best solution for him, as well. You wouldn't have to keep thinking and re-thinking. So stop it! Everything has already been thought out!

Simply take the best ready-made element and give it a little, personal touch! Just like when we would vary copied sentences in school so that they would look like our own. So, if you must think of a corporate mission, forget the months of meetings and arguments. Just take the generally valid fake and give it your own touch. My suggestion: Lovingly change your company's mission statement, cited above, to include the name of your company in the statement.

For instance, we could change the first word, "we" to "Cowmulch Incorporated" to thus read: "Cowmulch Incorporated is ..." Get it? This process is called individualization. If we place our name in the mission statement, it cannot be used by any other company in that form! That is known as differentiation on the market. Through a small Lean Brain trick that costs nothing, we have turned something hackneyed into something special. When people see that, they will immediately ask with interest: "So what does Cowmulch Incorporated produce, anyway?" And then you'll have made a good impression and can immediately begin advertising for your leftover food production. You'll also need a red and brown logo – but that's getting carried away.

> Do not try to be the best if everyone can be the best through *Lean Brain*.

Do not talk yourself, do not build any pine wood tables! It's all already there! However, put your name on everything, like a dachshund spraying his scent on trees! Then you won't be just a template! Even though you actually are! That is how to preserve your inimitable identity, even though yours is just like the next person's.

4. Standardization and Global Uniformity (One Size Fits All)

Lean Brain Management must raise the standard of standards to the level of an idol. Everything must be normed, classified and uniform. One person proposes, the Standard disposes.

We need the same electrical currents, uniform mobile phone frequencies, one Internet protocol, one type of wall socket, and the same size jeans.

I'm not trying to bore you. Of course you know all of this already.

Many things indicate that the Lean Brain movement will succeed in going a far step beyond these initial, trivial steps. Basically, we also need uniform opinions, views, philosophies and attitudes toward life – because it usually costs too much to have a variety. I'm consciously emphasizing the cost point. Today, the individuality of people is principally expressed in one's ring tone, for which people spend a great deal of money and which they select in a complex series of self-awareness experimentations involving being called. For people, a ring tone is approximately as important as a logo is to a company or a flag is to a nation. That is not to say that the ring tone can't be changed, for instance at the start of a new romantic relationship. Companies change their logos, too, so that they can profit from the resulting upswing. On the contrary, if we would pep up national flags from time to time, the world would probably be a better place. And how about sports teams? Ice hockey clubs used to have boring names like "Hockey Sports Association" or "Ice Foot Club." Think of the huge successes to be enjoyed by the entire branch through a mass renaming of teams to "The Double MacWhoppies" or the like.

Please always keep in mind the fundamental concept of the perfect fake. In the Lean Brain sense, we, all people, firms or nations, strive to make everything completely uniform, so that it will be cheaper on the whole. We orient everything toward the cheapest fake! However, in order for people to have that profit-stimulating feeling of being real, they get a shot of the genuine as well. That is what the ring tones and logos are for.

If Lean Brain Management is to really be successful, it must, above all, standardize people. There will be a strong headwind – namely from intelligent people who always have to put in their two cents. Intelligent people, as I've noted, are not really dangerous be-cause there is only a tiny, pitiful minority of them. However, they incite the other people – especially those who repeatedly try to be intelligent! And such people exist in alarming numbers.

I would like to provide some background information to illustrate this disastrous conflict of the Lean Brain movement using the exam-ple of an unspeakable book dripping with attempts at intelligence, in which the author shows that his heart is moved and stirred by his own views without once taking into consideration the consequences of the *cost issue* of his thoughts. The author of the book wishes to campaign for "horseness." His arguments are very convincing. It is extremely surprising just how cleverly he has evaded the actual issue of the costs of non-standardization. In this way, many pseudo-intelligent people have surely been taken by him down the garden path.

The said author, whom I will shortly cite, works as a manager at IBM, according to him, and wrote a book years ago with the pre-sumptuous German title *Omnisophie* ("*Omnisophy*"). In that book, he brags that his company was able to engage Monty Roberts, ex-tremely popular among the few intelligent people, as a speaker to appear before the heads of the firm. He reports on this lecture as if it were a global sensation. He probably only wanted to show off about being allowed to be present. While reading, listen to how skillfully such typical intellectuals play with and tempt the emotions. The sub-ject is horses. However, today, horses are generally better under-stood than people because they are well liked and kept only for rea-sons of luxury. They cost less than children. The author does not disclose this fact, and constantly indirectly refers to horseness but means all of us.

Here is an excerpt from *Omnisophie* in translation:

> I myself know horses from our farm. I was moved to tears when Monty Roberts spoke before the executives of IBM about his life, his life with horses.

Monty Roberts's father had the occupation of taming or "breaking" horses, as it is called. To do this, the horses are "treated" for a couple of weeks. They are first driven into a lock so that they can be approached closely enough to attach a halter. A rope is attached to the halter, with which each horse is tied to a thick post.

Then a rope is tied to a heavy sack which is thrown or beaten about the horse's back and legs, causing the animals to become terrified. Injuries are par for the course. This procedure is often called "sacking out," and lasts several days, serving to break the will of the horse and its rebellious spirit. Subsequently, the horse is made to stand on three legs in order to weaken its will. For this, one leg is tied up in the air (usually beginning with the right rear leg and alternating to all four legs). They are further treated with the sack. The horses give up faster on three legs. Finally, the saddle is attached and the procedure with the tied leg starts anew. Sack treatment until emotional capitulation. The process up to this point takes 8-10 days. Pressure marks, deep scrapes and more or less severe leg injuries often cannot be avoided.

Once the horses are "ready," they are untied and equipped with a hackamore (which is a bridle without a bit that lies on the nose like a lever and is fairly painful, as it must be used very gently, which is truly difficult to do. Pulling on the reins too hard results in extreme pressure on the horse's highly sensitive nose). Then, the horses are moved with long reins for another week so they can become accustomed to the "gas and brake pedals". Finally, they are ridden for the first time with diagonally-tied legs so they cannot buck. If they resist, they are kicked or whipped.

If they are then not yet ready to be ridden, they stand with a leg tied up until they are tame. The whole procedure takes at least three weeks.

Monty Roberts was born in 1935, and at age seven, knew everything about horses except for how to break them. His father showed him two young horses in 1942. They would become Monty's trade test objects. Monty was shocked and asked for a week to think it over. In answer to his father's disquieting question as to why, Monty claimed he wanted to get to know the horses first. His father shook his head. "If you don't hurt them, they'll hurt you." Monty stole around the horses until they were no longer afraid. After a few days, he tried to put a saddlecloth on them. They allowed him to do so. Like a bolt of lightning, he dashed with excitement into the house, called his father out and showed him. At first, his father was speechless. Then he asked: "What am I raising?" He grasped an iron chain, grabbed his son and beat him bloody. Monty was taken to the hospital due to an extremely serious horse accident. Now he knew what breaking was. From then on, his father was a bleeding wound on his soul.

Later, as soon as he could, he perfected a new method of taming horses. This method required just a half hour to gently tame a horse. Perhaps you have seen it on television. There was a period when several reports on the method were aired. A horse is let into a round fence made of corrugated metal having a diameter of more than 10 yards, and the trainer (Monty or you) stands in the middle and basically waits to see what the horse does. The trainer tenderly swings a long rope toward the horse. The horse trembles with fear and runs wildly in the circle around the trainer, who rotates slowly along with the horse, and eventually slows down. The trainer in the middle speaks appeasingly and quietly to the horse. After about 15 to 20 minutes, the horse, now exhausted, stands still and looks at the trainer. And then comes the part that makes me misty when I watch the film: The horse suddenly gets a completely different expression on his face – and trots over to the trainer! It was incredibly moving to me (and believe me, I'm not that type). The trainer embraces the horse, speaks kindly to him, and they become friends. After ten minutes, the trainer throws a saddlecloth on the horse. It bucks in panic and be-gins running around in circles again. This time, the horse slows down more quickly, once again approaches the center of the cir-cle and allows himself to be embraced and patted. After about 35 minutes, the trainer mounts the horse, stroking him all the while.

That's it.

Just about everybody who can pat a horse can break wild horses after a couple of weeks of practice. Monty Roberts showed us a film on the subject with an "early student" who was trembling more than the horse. It took her just a few minutes longer than it had taken Monty.

Monty Roberts showed his method to everyone. He traveled around, taming thousands of horses at a thirty-minute pace. His father continued running his business in the traditional manner. He did not believe in Monty.

Nobody believed.

Monty Roberts was considered a miracle worker whom horses coincidentally obeyed; an oddity.

He spent virtually decades preaching, to no avail, a message that went something like this: "Humans are fight animals! Horses are anxious flight animals! Horses are good animals; they are only afraid of us, nothing else."

In 1942, his father beat him with a chain. In 1988, a curious English queen invited him to do a presentation, which took place in 1989. Queen Elizabeth II saw and believed. She found a ghost-writer for Monty Roberts and requested a book. It was ultimately published in an amazingly small run. *The Man Who Listens to Horses* became an international bestseller, and then there was a Hollywood film and book (not by Monty Roberts) called *The Horse Whisperer*, which more or less missed the point or lost it. Someday soon in the real world, torturing horses may well end. Who knows?

The point is that all people had and still have the wrong idea about horses. I mean extremely wrong. You would think such a father of a small boy like Monty would have been cut to the quick for having misunderstood everything around him! He should have whispered: "That's a GREAT idea!"

I have discussed Monty Roberts with executive managers of several companies that had seen him. Most of them said: "Interesting. Of course I see the analogy between horses and employees. That is probably why we had to watch the film. It shows that you should be nice to employees from time to time; that really helps. I myself am often nice to them, but it was important for some co-workers to see the film, although they wouldn't even relate it to themselves." Most of the people with whom I spoke saw the moral of the story in the notion that more carrot and less stick would be appropriate.

However, the message is: Horses are good. Or at least: Horses are like natural humans! (Perhaps they have neither an awareness of themselves nor a notion about what a system is?!)

In a positive atmosphere, that is, like horses that are free and feel well, they allow themselves to be ridden after 30 minutes, but in a negative atmosphere they become broken creatures in four weeks.

The message is: People are good even when they are free.

In a positive atmosphere, they don't mind working day and night. In a negative atmosphere, they will only work as broken, burned-out wretches under permanent stress, pressure and the threat of bonus payment plans that dangle the carrot very high.

The argument as to whether or not people are truly so evil due to the original-sin laden, Freudian id, and thus must be systematically broken via "sacking out" is as old as the culture itself. Children's wills are broken, although not quite as explicitly today as in the past.

After millennia of error, it has finally been formally proven: The evil in a horse was not always there. At best, it occurs by breaking the soul, which fades into the background. Then the newly-created creature works like a horse, without actually still being one. Evil is in the core of the system of breaking horses, in the superego, in the id of the traditional horse culture. The culture of breaking horses, that is to say the system, is evil. Evil is not in the horse. Monty Roberts has proven this. For decades, no one believed him. Without the Queen, no one would still believe him to this day. Proof or no proof.

In the book *Why Work* by Michael Maccoby, there is the following historical comment: "[T]he term manager comes from the Italian *maneggiare*, to handle, to wield, to touch, to manage, to deal with, to break in horses, to handle horses – to train and direct animal force." Thus, people are trained and directed like animals. Whoever is capable of this is a manager.

Omnisophy! The author's heart is breaking! He is moved! Those poor horses! Self-proclaimed intellectuals always argue in the same way as that author. They say something about horses, thereby suggesting that the will of us humans is also being broken – *like animals*! They imply that our education system and work organization fundamentally operate insufficiently and are all but destroying humans. In all of these fairy-tales, the individual person and the cute, individual animal are always considered. Of course, individually you can achieve a lot of things better. Management and especially global Lean Brain Management, however, have much higher goals – the improvement of the entire system, not only the individual. Yet intellectuals never talk about the system.

Did you note the hitch in the cited emotional stirrings? I've got three words for you:
The Pony Express.
Right?
Now you can see it, too, right?

In average daily life, horses are not simply lap dogs or substitute boyfriends for expensive daughters. They – as normal people too – have work to do. In the past, horses in the Pony Express served to transport goods and people. Ever since Ferguson invented the steel plough, they have also been good for plowing work, previously done by the stronger yet slower oxen. While working, horses served several laborers, postmasters, and hired riders.

> Working humans and production animals must be able to be treated in a standardized way by third-party masters or systems. They must fit into teams and be able to be utilized flexibly in a number of positions.

That is why horses cannot be simply brought up lovingly like fairy-tale princes. They must be able to be ridden by any unfamiliar person without further empathy or familiarization processes. So that riders do not need to learn anything and will find a ready-to-use horse, it is absolutely necessary that all horses learn the conventions that make them useful animals. All horses must react in the same way to spurs and whips. Similarly, a person at work must immediately know what he has to do if a random manager wearing a telltale red tie orders him to hurry up. There is no time to ask questions! A manager, who often changes departments and must repeatedly take over new tasks, cannot be constantly adapting and getting used to new people. Teachers also cannot afford to do this with so many students. Their responsibility is simply too large. At war, an officer must send his soldiers into deadly situations. They must immediately depart for such missions and cannot suddenly start a discussion in such an emergency. That is why soldiers are drilled, just as horses are broken. That is why strict discipline applies to all. Everything must be standardized and calculable. Everything must be treated in the same way. A horse is a horse, of course! A hammer is a hammer, all over the world. A person must be a person, anywhere in the world, otherwise he or she is not of Lean Brain Quality.

5. Creation by Product – Creation by Instruction

My mother-in-law made the best marinated beef in the world. It became a custom in my family to enjoy it on the first day of Christmas. She died very suddenly and unexpectedly, leaving behind only a vague recipe. She was a great cook and thus did not exactly know what she was doing: "Just put in a handful," she would often exclaim when pressed. She was one of those people who could really cook and never faked. One-hundred percent genuine. She spent a great deal of time doing so, and she loved it.

For private people, this sort of thing must, of course, be accepted. However, in the Lean Brain sense, it is absolutely intolerable. My mother-in-law's procedure can be summarized as "Creation by Product" or "Copy by Product." She knows what she wants to cook and prepares it in a new way each time. "Let's see what's in the fridge. Okay, I can use the low-fat sour cream instead of the full-fat, no problem. As long as it tastes as wonderful as ever." And it did always taste wonderful.

Luckily, my wife was able to worm something like a list of ingredients from her mother a long time ago. That meant we did not need to start at square one. I myself am the sort of person that never cooks with a cookbook but rather according to the "Copy by Product" method. I'll eat something in a restaurant and then try to cook up something that, in my opinion, could be the perfect artistic form of the whole. One-hundred percent. Anyway, I gathered the ingredients that were on the list and stood at the stove. In my mind, I conjured up the taste of days gone by on my tongue. Then I cooked everything as I thought it should be. Gisi, my sister-in-law and major critic in all things edible, at least recognized the taste. She corrected the nuances ("Sweeter, please!"), and for a couple of years/Christmases now, we have all been in agreement that the marinated beef is once again perfect – and we think of my mother-in-law. I still have no true idea as to what the recipe could be. It depends on the stock, the vinegar, how long the meat has aged, how well it absorbs the marinade. Why should I have a recipe? I have to achieve the taste that is in my memory. The taste is the end product.

Many mathematicians, programmers, and technicians work in this way. They proceed intuitively; a different way each time, as the situation requires. Again: This is absolutely appalling in the Lean Brain sense. The Lean Brain process prefers "Copy by Instruction" or "Creation by Recipe". There must be a recipe.

Per serving, take 1 egg, ½ cup flour, ½ cup milk, 2 tablespoons sparkling water, 1 teaspoon sugar, a pinch of salt, a pinch of cardamom, a dash of orange blossom water, and a pat of margarine per crepe for preparation in a coated Teflon pan. Whisk until smooth, allow to stand for one hour, then make thin pancakes or crepes out of them. So says the tenet. According to Taylor, this is the only correct order of procedure with which any bumbling beginner can make a good pancake. He simply has to do exactly what the instructions say!

Then they always make the batter lumpy, those bumbling beginners, although I have forbidden them to do so, or they can't find cardamom in their spice rack, or they are fresh out of orange blossom water! That won't do! I want it done exactly – according to the recipe! No deviations! If there is no cardamom, then there will be no crepes!

This recipe is not as precise as it looks. There are various types of flour, different sizes of eggs. It would be much better if the recipe stated "King Arthur Unbleached All-Purpose Flour" and "Large eggs not more than one week old." Then the recipe would be even more reliable, but less practical to reproduce because you only have generic flour in your pantry or only medium-sized eggs or old eggs that have to be used up. In some households, people make crepes *because* the eggs are old. The recipe could be supplied with an appendix containing a list of acceptable flours, just as there are certain permissible tires for cars or allowed toxins for baby food. The way the ingredients are to be used needs specification: First the flour, then slowly mix in the milk. Otherwise the batter will be terribly lumpy, you know. And the sparkling water goes in last, and is stirred in by hand, not electrically, lest the flavor-enhancing bubbles be destroyed. Use an 11-inch pan that was not previously washed with dishwashing liquid. The best pan is a crepe pan that has only ever been wiped clean. Of course this pristine state is ruined if you have burned something in the pan. So don't ever let anything burn in the pan! You'll have to cook the first crepe longer than the others – don't ask why: That's just the way it is. After that, they don't take as long. Be careful, and do not go away from the stove! The first side of the crepe will take longer than the second. Pay close attention. Turn down the heat from 6 to 5 (this applies only to approved Siemens or Miele stoves made in the year …). We would have to fill in the correct information for our own stove. Only then is it a genuine recipe.

Got it?

Try this Google search on the Internet: Type in crepes flour recipe. Just try to find anything that looks remotely as good as what I have just written.

I immediately find a recipe that states: "2 ladles of flour, 3 eggs, sugar to taste, enough milk to make the batter thin." In the Lean Brain sense, this is exasperatingly bad. It was written by people who can cook for people who can cook. That's the way I do it, too. I know what is meant by "thin". A Lean Brain crepe, however, cannot know this! The recipe must be correct! Beginners will pour in the milk all at once, which is much too much. They run the risk of making steamed milk cutlets. Then they throw in too much flour, which makes the batter too thick. More milk! More flour! Ultimately, the entire town has to come over for breakfast.

Thus, if you are 100 % sure what a crepe is, a rough description will suffice. Otherwise, you need a meticulously derived plan that can apply globally.

Traditional, stupid management produces relatively tolerable, so-called specialists that can manufacture a desired product using rough guidelines.

Lean Brain Management, however, shifts intelligence entirely to the system, and in this case, to the recipe. Subsequently, any human can execute a job that would be considered difficult. All he needs to and must do is follow directions. The outcome required by the recipe will always be the same: uniform Lean Brain quality.

Lean Brain avoids like the plague all things "approximate." Lean Brain assumes that a machine could basically proceed according to the recipe if it were physically capable of doing so. Lean Brain must, once and for all, precisely record recipes or methods, without exception. Lean Brain must enforce the adherence to every recipe without so much as one millionth of a percent of deviation. Then everything will work out fine. Everyone must be able to do it without thinking. Nobody may do anything else. But above all, nobody may think anything else or even want to do something better.

6. Process Orientation and Working by the Book

Cyril Northcote Parkinson once asserted that the fact that following the rules can make the instigator appear ridiculous is a wonderful punch line of bureaucracy.

Today, opponents of the system threaten: "Systems treat us people like animals! We will resist brutally! We will thus resort to extreme measures and work by the book."

The very existence of modern systems can thus be threatened if one proceeds exactly according to its instructions. For in reality, all of these systems are only colossally insipid, and the people working for it are much too smart. The stupid systems therefore rely on the intelligent people saving it. I have already bemoaned this point profusely.

Lean Brain Systems, however, contain all of the necessary intelligence inside them. They *themselves* are intelligent and operate with robot-like, cheap standard humans who are best when not allowed to be intelligent because otherwise they will do all sorts of ridiculous things to shine in their jobs. In Lean Brain Systems, only the system shines, and nothing else. Lean Brain Systems define clear instructions for every possible person. We could put it blithely: Lean Brain instructions are foolproof.

> Foolproof rules are *for* fools, not *by* fools!

This is an important principle in Lean Brain Management. Today's systems unfortunately operate with polished, laterally intelligent people in the staff departments (whoever wishes to be promoted does not work there!), who, in one-hour meetings, issue instructions like "Two ladles of flour and milk until batter is thin" and think that it will work without Teflon pans. These rough, useless instructions will then confuse the working humans. All kinds of products will result except for crepes. That will anger staff heads considerably. They thus accuse the working people of laziness and scrutinize them closely to make sure they all work quickly and diligently according to the bad, useless instructions. They make ridiculous accusations towards the workers, cut their pay and "motivate" them, as they call it. The grass roots will not know what to do and start making crepes themselves so they'll stop being mobbed. Unfortunately, each worker makes his own crepes, such that, at least crepes are being produced, but at very different levels of quality, homemade, on-site. This angers the controllers even more because they assume that the lack of uniformity was caused by carelessness on the part of the workers, when all the while, it was only their intelligence which had resurfaced in an emergency situation under the pressure to survive. Unfortunately, controllers never think of the notion that the system's instructions are not crepe target-oriented.

Thus, they never change the crepe recipe but rather test in an ever harsher manner whether all of the workers can make uniform pancakes even without good instructions. That is why they now very precisely describe the desired diameter and degree of browning of the resulting crepe and define its required minimum flavor. Thus, they define the target, that is to say the end product. In doing so, they tempt the workers to switch from a "Creation by Instruction" to a "Create by Product" method. The simple workers then morph into primitive hobby chefs, when all the while they only need to manufacture professional, standard crepes according to standard instructions. The workers, who should be serving as crepe robots, are now attempting to employ their own intelligence. They have thus become culpable in the eyes of the system, not to mention with regard to the basic ethical principle of the Lean Brain concept!

> Controllers usually obsessively monitor the precise adherence to insipid rules. Controllers, however, should be controlling whether or not the instructions are idiotic. That would be easy – they would simply have to try out the instructions a couple of times, that is, to work. Yet controllers only note the red numbers until they are either blue in the face or the numbers black.

If you want to write good instructions for crepes, you must know your stuff. You must be familiar with stoves, egg sizes and consistencies. In the last section, I explained how much the recipe for intelligent cooks ("2 ladles of flour plus milk") deviates from a truly good, detailed recipe that is foolproof. If the system does not take the trouble to issue good, foolproof recipes, the result will inevitably be irregular quality. What's more, a good deal of local intelligence will be necessary in order to produce the desired product. Stupidity in the system forces local intelligence in its workers.

Lean Brain Management, however, requires intelligence in the system and operates locally with any sort of humans.

From the viewpoint of Lean Brain Management, the greatest inanity is the method of "Management by Objectives", practiced by almost all contemporary managers, which is to say managing according to stated goals. Employees are told exactly what minimum numbers are to result. In our example, then, the employees would be told how many crepes are to be produced, and nothing more. This number is determined by controllers who have never even seen flour or eggs but rather, if they're lucky, only crepes. They have no notion of the recipes and tools. Thus they can only define the goal but not the path, that is, the instructions. Ultimately, Management by Objectives states: "Make lots of crepes; we don't care how. You are the expert, not me." That is how all managers today are running their companies straight into the ground.

Lean Brain Management only produces good crepe instructions one single time, which are then executed millions of times, just as it has been the case for hamburgers for decades now. To achieve this, you just need one single higher intelligence that can produce the best original fake, for instance the best cheap thing that looks like a crepe, can be easily described in a foolproof way, and tastes like a crepe. For this, the higher intelligence would generate the necessary foolproof instructions. Then everyone can start cooking. One single intelligence can virtually oversee several global concerns at the same time.

Let me ask you as the reader: Do you conduct your corporate processes at 100 % of that for which they are designed? Or are there deviations? Do you sometimes have to be intelligent and creative to rescue the situation? You see! That is pretty stupid!

Let me repeat the standard phrase of the manager leading his company to hell: "I don't care how you do it, you're the expert, not me." With this directive, the manager is allowing his employee to use his own intelligence – in fact he is provoking it. If he has to resort to such methods, says Lean Brain Management, then all is lost. The manager will then often sigh and complain: "The processes are holding us up, the controllers are torturing us." Yet this simply means that the system is unintelligent.

> Good business processes categorically exclude further intelligence because they are foolproof in the Lean Brain sense. Management by Objectives, that is, management through setting goals, provokes and requires intelligence in order to reach the goals. Companies that *simultaneously* rely on goals and moderately intelligent business processes are doomed. Such companies treat their employees like fools but pay them like experts.

Two contrary halves always add up to one whole inanity.

7. The Moronization of Organizations

Political scientist Richard Wiggins says that government activity is politics en masse, while administrative activity politics in detail. Aha. It looks like the government decides what is to be done. For instance: Make crepes today and not mussels in a white wine garlic sauce. The administration or bureaucracy then translates this wholesale decision into detailed activity. They make crepes. Right.

But does anyone ever *ask* how to make crepes? Does everyone know? Does the executive know this in detail? Here – precisely here – is where intelligence must enter the system. Somebody must issue perfect guidelines with which any fool, especially all bureaucrats, can make crepes. These guidelines must be checked circumspectly. Can someone who has adhered to all of the guidelines ever produce anything but the desired product? Is the process foolproof?

The process of transforming a job into a foolproof chain of instructions is called foolproofization or moronization. The Greek word *moros* means "brainless, inane, simple," and can be found in the English "moronic." Moronization is the most important work step of a Lean Brain Manager. It transforms a roughly issued order into an exact sequence of instructions that are always goal-oriented.

The moronization of our society has already taken hold in non-working environments. Television is moronizing people. "TV dumbs down," as we say. Soap operas and reality shows trivialize people. People like us squabble on television as boorishly as we do at home. We are becoming used to how commonplace it all is. We are learning that there is really nothing else beyond this trivial life. The rest is just art made to win an Oscar. The rest are attention-junkie millionaires skilled in special feats – they play soccer the best, can sing pop songs well or have inherited a hotel chain. However, the people, we the people, are becoming moronized. Poor suburbs, blue-collar neighborhoods and settlements of the unemployed are cropping up. Everything is becoming clearly simplified and vulgarized.

Who is moronizing whom? Many employees are so stressed by today's demoralizing work environment that all they want to do when they get home is "hang out". They watch music, sports, variety and reality shows and soaps. That is all they want. The TV does not offer anything else anyway. The moronization of private life, the transition to a world of raw fun and emotion follows the overload in the work environment. A few system critics call the Western form of society a "morony". (On the Internet, someone innocently asked if moronization was the same as Americanization. I had to laugh, even if it was an unfair comparison. It has to start somewhere. And TV comes from the USA. You can't argue with that. I think that in Japan more people sit in front of their cell phones. That is probably a reasonable equivalent. I'm sure that trend will arrive in Germany in a couple of years.) The morony supplies us with bromidic satisfaction.

Lean Brain Management has nothing to do with such a brutalization of rivaling tendencies. For Lean Brain Management, moronization is the indispensable link between order and implementation, government and bureaucracy, between strategy and execution. Moronization programs the strategy in intelligence-deprived series of hand movements and makes it possible to execute even the most difficult tasks with cheap unskilled workers that have had absolutely no training. The system can thus save money and personnel. It then practically operates autonomously. In doing so, it increasingly frees itself from people. Of course, Lean Brain managers can work well with moronized people; there is no question of that. They are not going to want to complain about any governmental morony. Basically, a morony officially accelerates the Lean Brain movement substantially – because if humanity is vulgarized, systems can only survive with Lean Brain Management since there are no more experts to save the system with individual, expensive, and intelligent efforts. That is why Lean Brain Management is not only the best thing in a morony but probably the only thing. The fall of education in the population is currently dramatically improving the situation with regard to the Lean Brain movement. Soon, education will be so poor that we will no longer need education systems. We will get by with what is offered on moronized television.

8. Effective, Practical, and easily understood Advice for Managers

As a manager, you will now gradually have to familiarize yourself with the total redesign of your business procedures.

All of your processes must be prudently moronized. Imagine Taylor's or Ford's assembly line as an ideal for your company.

- Determine an extremely precisely described series of instructions for everything.
- Make sure that absolutely every person can execute each and every one of those instructions without any previous knowledge whatsoever.
- If someone carries out the instructions but does not arrive at the desired goal, the error is not his but is rather rooted in a bad series of instructions.
- Nevertheless, have some confidence in people. For instance, hardly any person is so stupid that he or she cannot drive a car. Thus, you can certainly have some expectations for your employees, except for intelligence, which, however, is not required to drive a car, and if it is used nonetheless, leads to traffic jams or accidents.

Still, there are loads of things people can do incorrectly. This is not due to intelligence but rather to a normal scatterbrained state. I don't know if you have ever made coffee yourself as a manager. You have to put water in the machine, put the right amount of ground coffee in the filter, turn it on, wait, and drink coffee. During this process, the following errors can occur, usually in the morning:

- Forgot ground coffee + filter (symptom: muddy water from yesterday's grounds).
- New filter but forgot to add ground coffee (hot water).
- Forgot water (nothing happens).
- Amount of water and coffee do not match (coffee tastes like water or cardiac arrest).
- Added ground coffee but forgot filter (clean everything).
- Put in water twice (wipe up everything).
- Forgot to turn on machine.

- Forgot to turn off machine (building burns down; nagging fear upon leaving for your trip).
- Forgot to put the coffee pot in the machine (coffee starts brewing, depending on model, there will be a mess or not).
- Filter paper has not been properly inserted (folds in on itself; light, crumby brew).
- Incorrect brewing program selected.

I am noting this with lots of detail because you, as a manager, probably pay your secretary a lousy salary and do not understand all of the things that need to be taken into consideration. A vending machine, on the other hand, does not make such mistakes. It only breaks down all the time. Coins get stuck in it, it runs out of change, the water does not heat properly, etc.

What I am trying to say is that moronization is work in itself and can require an incredible amount of intelligence. You almost never find such intelligence in normal company departments. That is why the processes are generally so badly set up. Corporate planners will at best have a brief look at how coffee is brewed when they are working on the description of the coffee-brewing process. Yet at least one year of hard coffee brewing work is needed until they have made every one of the errors mentioned above. So you see that, for the moronization process, *scatterbrained* intelligences are the most suitable, since they make the most amazing mistakes that would never occur to people of normal intelligence.

> The best moronizers are highly-intelligent scatterbrains, dopes, absent-minded types or, well ... morons. They usually tend toward a course of study in mathematics anyway, and can be easily enthused for questions regarding the demonstrably complete list of coffee brewing errors.

While it is true that departmental controllers find all errors, they do not *invent* any. Their intelligence often does not suffice to do so. A baking spatula can spread errors onto a cake, but it cannot make any original errors because it is not creative. Nevertheless, management usually assumes that the people who find all the faults should be the best individuals to create new business processes. For instance, managers assume that a person well versed in English grammar could also write well. How foolish that is! Such foolishness originates in the fact that controllers think they can design new processes themselves, but managers take away this duty from them because it never occurs to the managers that scatterbrains are the best people for the job. Managers themselves can never describe processes because they generally live "content-free". Managers generate structures such as org charts and they put teams on the job. They hold cookie-cutter lectures and pressure everyone else into unpaid overtime with their content-free communication. They will never utter anything with content like: "You make structural errors in Java programs a lot ..." Instead, they would say something content-free, such as: "Be careful! Put some effort into it! It'll be good! Be responsible! Work hard! Use some elbow grease! It'll be worth it! I'm going to be the Director! Be careful! Just be careful!"

Let me warmly recommend to you, as a manager, to leave moronization to the experts. To achieve this, you will have to agree to the establishment of a new profession, the moronorg.

A moronorg or moronorgess (the latter probably being hard to find – scatterbrained women!) should ideally have worked once themselves and left behind chaos. If such chaotic people, who can't help but stand out, should also happen to be intelligent, then they are ideal. I myself have often tested the programs in my department. I sometimes entered negative numbers or Egyptian hieroglyphics instead of yes/no answers, with amusing results.

9. Take-aways, Control Questions and Exercises

I have illustrated the difficult problem of moronization using two examples: making crepes and brewing coffee.

- Did you find that rather lame?

If so, then you are either not intelligent or too generic, that is, too much of a traditional manager. Listing factual content is too specific for managers and makes them nervous. It involves explicit knowledge, which is only present in operating instructions, lexica, manuals or eccentric techies. Managers love lists, which form the heart of all presentation programs. However, they list earnings and promises, that is, fakes and not facts. A typical page of a manager's presentation looks like this:

- Proposal for the project IAMTHEBEST (for example: International American Modern Tool Hub for Electronic Bold Ethics Standards)
- IAMTHEBEST will raise turnover.
- IAMTHEBEST will lower costs.
- IAMTHEBEST will increase profits.
- IAMTHEBEST will save humanity.
- IAMTHEBEST requires a 10-billion dollar investment, which I want.
- IAMTHEBEST is good for our image.
- IAMTHEBEST will lead to a promotion for my boss.
- What is best for my country is best for IAMTHEBEST.

This is an example of a generic project proposal that can be applied universally. If you still want to use another or even your own proposal, you are bad in the Lean Brain sense. Use this one. I have prepared it especially for you as a take-away. It is the perfect moronization of a highly complex project proposal. You just have to name your project accordingly such that its abbreviation reads IAMTHEBEST. You can change the dollar amount if you need more money. Or if, for instance, you need 50 billion dollars, you could hold the presentation five times.

As a manager, you are used to this content-free form of communication.

In the sense of moronization, this proposal is absolutely useless. The generic aspect of this content-free approach only defines the *structure* of the procedure and then requires *intelligence* in its implementation.

Let me remind you of my comparison of a manager with a spoiled child. The child screams: "I want it to snow!" That is also exactly what a proposal does, only it screams: "I want money for my project!" It is assumed that the executing authority (the child's parents or employees) then has enough experience and intelligence to get the project done.

Since intelligence is not contained in the plan but only in the goal, amount of expenses and prescribed timeframe, intelligence must be supplied by the employees working on the project. The manager considers the goal and the will toward the goal as the essential element. He gives the go-ahead ("I want it to snow!"), which today often sounds like this:

"The process has been defined and is in place, the structures have been generated, the controllers are already waiting for employee errors. Everything is ready. Now it all just has to be infused with life." If you say something like that as a manager, you harbor a secret reluctance toward my meticulously exact instructions in dealing with crepes and coffee. In that case, you are a manager and not a moronorg.

Lean Brain and moronization bank on foolproof precision structures that already contain all intelligence. The foolproof element must be placed in the hands of moronorgs.

By now you should understand that only moronorgs should use intelligence and that moronorgs must employ a great deal of it! *They* are the ones who construct the system. Managers goad and controllers measure the yield. (Employee errors can no longer occur in the moronic system because the system itself is intelligent.) Employees either operate that moronic system or are used by it. (Just imagine unskilled workers in call centers for complex products that only need to establish contacts or question customers regarding satisfaction. All of the intelligence is contained in the call center itself; no other intelligence is needed – more on that later.) In the moronic system, the human is part of the form and no longer the content. The content is in the instructions.

Put your own company to the test! You probably already have bad instructions from people who have no clue and idiotically intelligent employees. If this is the case, you will hear voices in your firm that assume that managers have made the processes with which the employees must work. That is not true. Managers haven't the faintest idea of the processes. Only those who have made processes can understand them, yet they in turn know nothing of the work involved in reproducing the processes. Thus, everyone complains in this manner:

"Those guys up there have no clue about reality."
"The processes have more exceptions than rules."
"The processes generate more work than they accomplish."

Intelligent people think, for example, that the Ten Commandments were made by God. If, then, the Ten Commandments are unsatisfactory at regulating life, then the intelligent people will squabble with God and ask Him indirectly for new and improved Commandments. Other people approach this problem with their faith in God. They establish theories as to how one should live differently so that the Commandments will be exactly optimal for that new life – because God is almighty and must have handed down optimal Commandments which therefore themselves cannot be altered.

I have never heard of the doubtless correct view that God did not think up the Ten Commandments himself, but that he had them hammered out by a staff angel who had previously never lived as a human. According to this view, God did not design the Commandments but rather only issued them. That is an act of power, not an act of creation.

That is why we humans, despite God's non-exhaustive Commandments, now try to lead halfway intelligent lives, which doesn't truly make us happy. We envy the animals that, due to their automated instincts, are completely internally moronized. They work according to fixed processes which allow them no room for freedom. Unfortunately, these processes are not good either, which is why animals suffer, too. Most likely, the staff angel thought he had to improve the bad instinctive processes of animals through the grace of freedom and intelligence of humans. Ultimately, though, all he passed on to humans were the consequences of his carelessness. It would have been better if the staff angel had moronized humans really well. Oh well, hindsight is 20/20. Now we can solve the problem ourselves through Lean Brain Management.

III. The Automatic Control of a Lean-Brain System

1. Modern Management no longer controls, it only goads

It is often said of today's managers that they pay too little attention to content; that they only see the form, that is, the organization and procedures. It is said that they do not pay attention to what is actually being done but rather only think about *how* things are done, or they don't even think at all, instead simply insisting *that* things come out in a way one could only wish for. Thus, in the Lean Brain sense, managers are already paring themselves down, like role models for the new age.

> Traditional management efficiently brings A to B, whatever B may be. This activity is considered to be a solely logistical question – just as the transport of a commodity from A to B is performed automatically, regardless of the constitution of that commodity. (For the postal service, every letter is just a letter. For a manager, every procedure is just a procedure, every recipe just a recipe.) Traditional management does not question the sense of it. B is B.

The condition called B could be a vision, a new, ingenious product or a new business process. Entrepreneurs, religious patrons and inventors think of something new every couple of years. The goal of B thus "comes from somewhere". But where? Someone gets a divine inspiration, an idea, or suddenly thinks he or she needs a new hobby that will improve the lot of humankind. Of course, we all constantly have ideas on how we can improve humanity – but fortunately, no one listens to us. It is much worse when people with great charisma have an idea. (Charismatic people are 100 percent real; they are not "cut." To date, they can't be faked!) Some people absorb any and every idea from a charismatic person, no matter how strange it may be, in order to experience a bit of that charisma in themselves. When a charismatic person wants something, the other people in his or her vicinity downright go nuts. Luckily, only roughly zero percent of people actually have charisma. Today, those suspected of having charisma are filtered out quite early from the rest of the population by talent or charisma scouts, and then immediately trained to treat ideas hailing from other sources as their own. In other words, they are made "unreal". This usually completely destroys the charisma, such that it can hardly do any further damage. Thus, on the whole, new ideas actually originate very coincidentally. This is very annoying for business, which typically ignorantly rants about an "innovation problem".

While traditional management accepted a given goal, B, and subsequently took everything from A to B as instructed and without complaint, modern management does not want to bother with goals that mean too much work. Modern management thus does not attain goals more efficiently but rather seeks out goals that are easy to attain.

Experience has shown that those goals that are more difficult to achieve are the ones requiring practical expertise. Such goals are naturally too concrete for modern managers because they require different "recipes" than the ones to which they are accustomed.

As I explained earlier in the book, true managers as such only feel satisfied when the new situation B can be described something like: "The same as A but 10 percent more". In such cases, they run off enthusiastically, calling out to everyone: "More! More! Faster! More often!" This tried and true technique is generic. If Goal B is simply the same as A but more of it, then not only is the path from A to B independent of a manager's actions, but even the goal of the task no longer has anything to do with a manager's work!

A great yet powerless social establishment has continually attacked this ideal concept. So-called scientists or theorists are people who always have ideas, a new one every day. I should know – I'm one of them. Unfortunately, theorists have absolutely no charisma, so it is of no use to them to have new ideas. However, they take no notice of this phenomenon! This fact then leads to them constantly becoming hot under the collar and cynical when they feel their ideas have been rejected. That always lends *emphasis* to their ideas!! As if that would help! And to benefit their own idea, theorists are also compelled to hate all other ideas! They do nothing but raise a racket. Of course, they most hate charismatic people like Paris Hilton, who is a better source of information for society than all scientists put together. What is my point? With their intellectual harangues of hate, theorists impair modern management – just as charismatic people with their unanticipated ideas.

Global management has now banded together against the theorists and charismatics and declared a singular, common goal, B, which can be universally pursued and also does not require any analytical expertise whatsoever: That is the shareholder value principle.

This principle maintains that, more or less, stock prices should increase annually by – let's say – 10 percent. In this state, Goal B has now been made comprehensible as a generic, content-free form.

I repeat – now it is *comprehensible*! In the past, content-oriented, traditional individuals may have made a commotion about the inanity of pure goading. Now, however, this inane goal has a grand name: shareholder value. This makes it concrete with regard to content. Those who dare mutiny within a company and call for thinking can be asked: "Are you *against* a rise in stock prices?"

> Modern management systematically overburdens employees with requests for stock price increases and is happy when, unexpectedly, this tactic actually works. Otherwise, it fires all employees who have failed.

Modern management has thus naturally displaced intelligence from its ranks, replacing it with adrenaline: because modern management no longer controls the company, it only goads it. This requires absolutely no intelligence. Goading is achieved through the expenditure of energy.

Let me summarize the above, since we are about to get to a delicate point that you most definitely need to understand.

In a Lean Brain company

- all intelligence, if present at all or if one is required to demonstrate it, is contained in the system,
- everything is standardized into its simplest form by moronorgs,
- nobody is in any way special anymore,
- managers simply goad their staff to do more of the same.

Close your eyes for a moment. Think about it!

Is that going to work?

Don't you also have the feeling that somewhere there must still be a residual, small, content-based aspect? Who is supposed to do the little bit of real work that is actually required? Who is supposed to contribute that bit of necessary intelligence? Could a computer soon do it all alone?

2. The Lean Brain Company lets its Customers do the Work!

Modern business systems simply let the customers do the work! This is a central new concept in economics. I have already demonstrated that many companies have to rely on the ludicrously expensive intelligence of their employees in order to smooth out errors in their own business processes. Sometimes these processes are so bad that the exception is the rule, and "nothing works," as would be said in most businesses these days. However, Lean Brain Management does not seek to employ intelligence!

None whatsoever!

Yet when intelligence is essential because, once again, everything is going wrong, it is much better to make use of the intelligence of customers for free! Let them figure out how to get things to work!

Customers are usually inexperienced, enjoy being praised and are worn out by their inane jobs. They are happy to have the chance to use the remnants of their intelligence privately from time to time. With just a bit of encouragement, they can be tempted to undertake a large portion of the company's work themselves. In doing so, the management of a Lean Brain company also goads customers into hurrying it up.

> In Lean Brain Management, customers are the focus. They take
> on the main load of procedural steps ("self service") and perform
> them exactly the way the unique regulations and recipes of the
> company stipulate. If that doesn't work, customers are in charge
> of making the company function properly once again. They pay a
> great deal of money to the Lean Brain company for this service.

Have you noticed lately – how much work you are already doing?
You purchase do-it-yourself modules. Perhaps you've designed your
kitchen yourself. That would easily cost a few hundred dollars if an
interior decorator were involved. You receive the minimal amount of
support at IKEA. You are supplied with the screws and boards and
subsequently put together everything yourself. If something goes
wrong, it's your problem! You are sure to get it right in a few days.

More and more women are purchasing do-it-yourself kits for
cake. They are called cake mixes. The cheap ingredients are already
mixed together: We just need to add organic eggs and milk, and off
we go. "Oh, wow, it's a Betty Crocker cake! We were afraid you were
going to bake it from scratch. The kids didn't want to come at first
because you're so against artificial flavorings."

Banks should be doing things for us. After all, they rake in account maintenance charges. For these considerable charges, we have
the pleasure of using the ATM machines outside the bank in the cold
to withdraw money and make payments. The way the banks would
have it, we would only need to go into the bank when we wished to
set up another long-term installment loan that we can then maintain
from – you guessed it – outside in the cold. My bank sent me a completely enthusiastic letter that went something like this: "We are
thrilled to be able to offer you cash around the clock! You can withdraw money at night, on a Sunday, and at Christmas. [This goes on
for half a page more]. Of course, this amazing new opportunity
eliminates the necessity of going to a teller window, behind glass,
manned by a human being. People make mistakes but we do not.
Thus, for a small fee, you must order a card with which to make
withdrawals, which also serves to raise our profits."

And this is the advice you get at a modern, Lean Brain bank:

A bank computer calculates the best combination of stocks for
various risk levels (in the financial literature it is described as the

"Lambda factor" – a really cool-looking Greek letter!) that have a specific Lambda factor risk and, at the same time, earn a good deal of commission for the bank (such as a bank's own savings bonds).

The customer comes in. Even before he sits down, a broker greets him to save time. The customer asks: "What should I do?" He wishes to invest money. The broker asks: "How high is your Lambda?" The customer has no idea. The broker smiles sympathetically and asks the customer once again how willing he is to take risks on a scale from zero to ten. He explains that the numbers range from "conservative worry wart" to "risk-loving desire for advanced wealth". The customer answers: "Five". Now the computer churns out savings bonds in Argentinean pesos. The customer accepts them because they are optimal. When he later complains because all of his money is gone, the computer tells him it is his own fault, because he himself specified the ridiculously high risk factor of five, and he knew what he was getting into, which was stated in the fine print and which he acknowledged and signed.

These examples demonstrate really good Lean Brain Management! The Lean Brain broker is hired for his neat appearance and his willingness to provide consulting for little pay. Brokers do not have to study economics; they never even have to employ a great deal of intelligence, because they are always exclusively concerned with the money of their customers, whereas economics only focuses on one's own money. Furthermore, a useless course of study like economics would be of no formal help in consulting; on the contrary, it would only make the employee expensive for the bank. The employee does not need to be familiar with specific concepts because a moronorg has already used the computer to calculate the most beneficial circumstances for all Lambdas for the bank, to the disadvantage the customer. The customer is the only one who needs to do anything intelligent during the consultation, namely reveal or declare his or her own "risk level". Because the customer has cited a risk level, he is the one providing the computer with the correct number and thus controlling the system himself. Brokers do not need to do anything further regarding content and cannot do any further damage to the bank by providing advice themselves. They now only function as a welcoming interface to customers, just as cashiers in a supermarket.

> A Lean Brain System controls itself via its customers, who request transactions. Customers, through their wishes and voluntary participation, replace the previously necessary hard work in the system itself.

Internet portals function completely automatically. If I log onto Amazon or eBay, the computer automatically knows my name. It could conceivably greet me through my computer's speakers: "Hello, Mr. Dueck!" I think I would switch that function off pretty quickly, though. It's so fake. And besides, everyone around me at work would hear it and laugh at me.

Do you ever think about Amazon, eBay or Google? In these companies, only few intelligent moronorgs are at work, making everything as simple as possible for everyone else on the planet. The computers of these firms let readers write reviews, describe products, and register websites and shops with them. Everything is conducted fully automatically in the system. All manual and mental work is done by the customer. Amazon even retains the copyright to the reviews. We all work together to construct valuable things, but somehow, the common utilization of these things belongs to those who organize said utilization. Many millions of people work and donate their efforts to these Internet portals. All of it as a whole is so valuable that we are prepared to turn around and implicitly pay for it again. So do we write the reviews as a sort of donation, only to end up reading them again in the end for a price? Well, it hasn't yet come to that ... but in the Lean Brain sense, it would be ideal.

Amazon, eBay and Google are ingenious, automatically-controlled Lean Brain Systems that are inherently extremely intelligent. They hardly need any normal employees anymore, only moronorgs that improve, expand and simplify the system. In such cases, the systems have already largely disconnected themselves from humans. They feed on the self-sacrificing activity of people outside of the system. In the past, the church, for instance, was capable of motivating people to perform voluntary church construction work and donate gold ornaments and relics. The church, too, used to be a sort of portal into another world ...

3. Lean Brain makes Customers Numb and Loyal

A company's customers are human. Humans have two forms: They can be employees and customers. As employees, they work in a Lean Brain System and are completely apathetic because they are embodied in the work processes like assembly line workers. Customers, however, reserve the right to be intelligent in their private time. They wish to be treated like real people by companies, and not like employees. After all, employees are paid to be treated that way, while customers pay not to be.

As a rule, then, they act out after their numbing work day and want to be king or queen. A Lean Brain company must make efforts to maintain an approximation of this state of royalty with a minimal curtsey before the customer.

So in order for king customer to serve the company himself, he must be greeted austerely and praised when he does something well. "Thank you for flying with us and paying an arm and a leg for all of that sparkling water during the flight." That gives the customer the warm feeling of having done something right. This feeling stands in stark contrast to his or her experience in the employee state.

A customer with intelligence will often realize that the company could pitch in a bit, too, since he or she is paying quite a bit for its service. The Lean Brain must resist such attempts. It must numb customers toward excessive expectations regarding service. This is done with the aid of endless orgies of apology that by no means should cost anything.

Intelligent people accept apologies as a substitute for services rendered.

The high degree of efficacy of apologies as surrogate service can be illustrated in the following example:

"My child, I'm so happy that you have promised us, with tears in your eyes, not to steal any more money. I'm so happy that you regret everything and are going to better yourself because I've raised you so well for so long. From now on, I'll give you more allowance, too; then you won't need to steal the money. Child, I love you so much, I'd even steal for you if it would make you happy. The important thing is that our family is happy."

A customer is like a good mother. She doesn't want to be mean to her child. In return, she accepts every transgression – as long as the child expresses remorse for it. A loyal customer hates the chore of looking for another company. In return, he or she accepts every denial of service, as long as the firm apologizes imploringly.

"Today, for the first time, I was satisfied with our government. Finally, one of those crooks had the guts to tell the truth – that they wasted all of the money and now have to raise taxes. I saw that coming! I just knew it. I'm so relieved that they are now admitting it and regret it. Now of course we have to pay more taxes; that's all there is to it; we have no other choice if we want them to continue with business as usual. After all, we are talking about our country."

"I think it's commendable that the rail service is showing remorse and admitting that they are always late. It is extremely comforting to me to know that they are not just bumbling around but that there are good reasons for all of the tardiness. Okay, so the tracks are aging, the conductors are overworked and unfocused and the power keeps going out, but the problem is usually that there is no substitute train available because this sort of thing happens unexpectedly or because the employees weren't aware of something. I'd be willing to wait around again but they have to be apologetic. I like that."

"The flight was so late, it's a good thing we even got home at all. The poor stewardess was in tears because the crew unloading the baggage had left. We had been sitting in the plane for 30 hours, so we were only too glad to get up and do something. We unloaded the baggage ourselves. The stewardess gave us a grateful smile – so I consoled her. I said I was a valued customer, a frequent flyer even, so I'd gladly go through fire and water for the airline. The captain patted me on the shoulder and said the plane was so broken down that I came darn close to having to do it. I laughed and said he was probably a Frequent Liar. He laughed somewhat sheepishly and admitted that the extent of damage is usually played down. At least he was honest."

"I'm dissatisfied with my bank because it's only open when I have to work. I have to take a vacation day just to deposit a check. I have been complaining about it for decades. But they always apologize in a really friendly way. The clerk said he would have to take overtime, maybe even vacation, in order to be able to serve me. Okay, I can't ask him to do that. I jokingly told him that he serves a customer every five minutes who has to take two hours of vacation time to go there. Two hours are 24 times as much as five minutes, which is why 24 people take vacation time for the time he's on duty. But it could be worse – just think of waiting rooms at the doctor's. We did some figuring and found out that hardly anyone can work because they all need vacation time for the bank and doctor's visits. We also calculated how long it takes when the clerk is friendly and apologetic. He said he spends almost his whole workday apologizing, which softens customers' moods to the point where they might buy a savings bond on an impulse so that at least their vacation time was not completely spent in vain. So I thought that was a good idea and bought a savings bond myself! He thanked me so kindly because that would earn him a bonus at the bank and I had earned a bonus in his book. That's what he said!"

> Customers and voters are robust. Moronorgs enrich Lean Brain systems with generous formal courtesy and lots of requests for forgiveness. If, in rare cases, changes are unavoidable, the resulting relief felt by the customer must be utilized to enrich the system.

"We want to be elected, but to do so, we have to understand the problems of the people, which we have no time to do because we have been governing uninterrupted for eight years now. There is just no time to stop and listen because we are constantly busy praising our own work in order to head off the opposition. We have shifted to Lean Brain politics. We ask citizens to identify problem areas and then request that they eliminate these problems themselves on a volunteer basis, since otherwise we'd have to raise taxes. If the problems are eliminated, we would praise this volunteer work in our next flyer where we highlight the achievements of our administration."

If at some point citizens are ready to hit the streets in protest because the political system is not achieving anything and apologies no longer bear fruit, politicians throw around new buzzwords on TV every night. The administration and opposition trump one another with the strangest plans hewn at backyard barbecues. "Cut taxes in half!" – "A millionaire's tax!" – "Child benefit allowances for pit-bull owners at the same rate as those who have kids!" – "The naming of an official party hairdresser!" Then the editors at Fox News spend the following night sifting through these proposals and generating intellectual evaluations. The next morning, public opinion corrects tabloid figures by a couple of decimal points and that final result is publicized.

> Fox News is abused in our democracy as core intellect.

The parties hear or read about everything the next morning, and if any of the nonsense of the previous evening has survived and appears to be attracting votes, that particular idea is revamped to become the focus of the new platform of the century. That's it. Unfortunately, after the elections, no work can be done on it because the new administration must first deal with the election promises made in prior decades ...

Since apologies help almost 100 % in any situation, Lean Brain systems should basically only change if their customers bolt. Running away, staying away or protest voting is the only bargaining chip they have against Lean Brain systems. Good Lean Brain systems recognize that they are no longer being served and modify themselves through new fakes. "We have improved the clarity of the user interfaces and adapted our fee schedules to meet their wishes. Now we no longer charge for every individual transaction like highway robbers, but rather we deduct the fees as a one-time block in places where you as the customer do not notice. This large-scale reform to our benefit will initially cause no changes for you. In fact, you'll be better off for it. That is why we are certain that you will maintain your loyalty to us in this difficult environment of such a harsh economy. We are counting on you. Please come again when you feel willing to be preyed upon. You will feel right at home here while you wait in line

along with many other like-minded people for your service consultant. You can accomplish your task more quickly if you fill out the
papers in advance on the Internet; then you only need to come in
personally for the handshake. After you have signed on the dotted
line, you will receive a free token for our coffee machine. Then, simply get in line in front of the machine. You'll only have to pay for
extras such as sugar or milk."

> Lean Brain customers are satisfied with Lean Brain changes. The
> ultimate goal of a Lean Brain System must be to numb your cus-
> tomers. Then they will remain loyal.

"My wife cheats on me a lot. But she doesn't deny it when I catch
her, and she is even more miserable about her mistakes than I am.
She says she loves me more and more, especially because I understand that sometimes she just blows a fuse. Then she doesn't even
recognize herself, she says, and asks me for advice so she can be a
better person. I'm gradually changing her for the better. She's just
such a faithful soul."

4. Effective, Practical and easily understood Advice for Managers

In the Lean Brain sense, most managers act almost half-wittedly.
There is nothing wrong with half-wits per se – oh, right, I meant
foolishly, of course. Right, they act foolishly. That is why I will once
again emphasize the main principles.

> The purpose of a manager is to goad the system so that it pro-
> duces 10 % more annually.

You should know this, being a manager. There are companies that
prefer 15 %. This varies depending on the branch of business, and is
primarily related to the guts of the chairman of the board.

Since the customer controls and serves a Lean Brain System, target growth can only be achieved through the customer. As time goes by, the customer must increasingly work more. "We now offer our goods at a two-percent discount, but, effective immediately, you have to pick them up yourselves. If you do not wish to do so, we will provide free delivery of the goods within a limited zone for a two-percent surcharge. In time, we will examine this charge with regard to its amount and distances traveled and optimize it to your benefit, such that picking up the goods yourself will become the more beneficial solution. Then you are guaranteed to consistently save two percent."

Experience with the first reference implementations of Lean Brain has shown that managers tend to overburden their own employees with work. That is foolish!

> Lean Brain Management shifts the work from the employees to the customers.

There is little in this book that is more important than this rule. How do you want to get rich? By working yourself? If you as a manager goad your employees to work longer and longer hours, you will most likely lose your focus on the goal of customer cooperation. Just imagine that a customer comes to you in a huff and yells at you because one of your employees did not do his job. A normal manager would wince and investigate the issue to help the customer. That, however, is foolish. You should instead recognize that one of your employees has found a way to get out of doing something. As a result, he or she has exerted a great deal of effort to reach your own goals. Therefore, you should under no circumstances pursue the matter in the presence of the customer. You need to reassure the customer. Offer him or her a latte macchiato, not just a coffee. Don't let yourself be drenched in complaints. That is the talent of being a good listener. Offer him or her another latte macchiato. Repeat often how sorry you are. Finally, praise the customer lavishly for having so much sympathy.

Then, immediately run with pleasant anticipation to your employee who was able to foist off new work on the customer and before you even get through the door, shout: "How did you do that?"

Normal intelligent managers would stride over to the employee full of anger and, before they get through the door, shout: "What did you do?"

In the first case, the manager poses a real question whose purpose is a true improvement of business procedures. If the employee has found a new trick, it must be reported to the moronorg! That is a sign of positive thinking. In the second, normal, case, the manager is just letting off steam because the customer complained. He has internally taken on the customer's anger toward the employee. Of course the customer is going to fight against the company. Now he or she has enlisted the manager to help battle his own company.

In the case of complaints, customers receive apologies and thanks for their understanding. Through this newly-resulting friendship, it is possible, with the aid of good advice, to engage the customer even more to execute tasks for the firm.

"The ticket machines are often out of order. People type on the screen with greasy hands, and it stops working. It's all slimy. Disgusting! That is why we advise washing your hands. If everyone would wash their hands, these malfunctions would not occur. A few careless people are ruining this fine human institution. Are you aware that you can also buy tickets online? So get everything you need online. True, it is also subject to problems, but it always works after a few tries."

5. Take-Aways, Control Questions and Exercises

Fake understanding toward the person with whom you are talking, and thank him for his understanding. Indicate that everything is fine the way it is. Not infinitely wonderful, but then again, that is not the way the world is.

"Yes, dear, I did forget our anniversary. Oh, I feel really bad about it. I can feel deep in my heart how you suffer when I forget you. You must think that you're not worth my time. But, oh, it's not true! I love you so much! You have to put up with me and suffer so much because I forget anniversaries. Do you know, there aren't many women who would be capable of understanding someone like me. But you take me as I am, and I am very thankful for that. I love you very much for being there for me when I'm not there for you. Honey, in our Lean Brain company, I would call you the ideal customer."

There is one important maxim in Lean Brain Management that you should know.

> Asking for permission takes six months. Asking for forgiveness after the fact takes five minutes.

This piece of insight comes from entrepreneurs who are tired of filling out a thousand applications and kneeling before controllers for approvals before every battle. They simply get to work without permission. If the controllers complain, they point out their successes. Then the controllers fudge the application forms retroactively so that it looks like they had foreseen the success and approved it. Thus, the entrepreneur lets the controllers do the tasks that are actually his responsibility. However, controllers will do almost anything for a deep bow. It is amazing how effective apologies are in humans.

"During the war, we were ambushed and everything burned to the ground. Men were butchered, women defiled. I am bitter about the fact that not even one compassionate word was ever spoken on the matter. Now, after 75 years of suffering injustice, on my one-hundredth birthday, I received a preprinted apology on a postcard. I am happier than ever."

The Lean Brain Manager would modify the above principle, which serves as a take-away for you:

> Expect as much work from others as you can. If something goes wrong, have some apologies ready. Thank them for the work entrusted to them.

Apologies are like bandages on the wounds of the complainer. They have nothing to do with a dishonoring or admission of guilt on the part of the accused. You have to learn to rehearse such apologies as fakes. You don't have to try out this technique on customers right away as long as you still need practice. First, practice them among your friends and family. You will ultimately discover:

> The customer is the most valuable asset of a company.

This phrase is often used by intelligent managers in the traditional, foolish form: "You, my employees, are my most valuable assets." That is just not true. All employees are quite familiar with this lie by now. To verify this, ask yourself: Do you really believe it when you say it? Then you should wake up and smell the coffee: Employees generate high costs for the company and nevertheless often accomplish less than many customers.

IV. Inhibitors of LBQ and Counteractive Measures

1. The Primary Foe of LBQ is Amateur Intelligence

LBM attempts to convert the entire world from genuine rum to cut rum, to put it metaphorically. Unfortunately, most people try to produce something like real rum themselves, even though not everyone has the corresponding know-how.

I have already cited so many examples! People try genuine cooking even though you can get everything ready made, and it tastes better, too. You can already buy crepe paste that you just squirt into a pan! Everybody but everybody is capable of that. You can find an array of powdered sauces for every cut of meat; you just have to decide which of the pretty packets you, as the cook, like best. The people eating the food will most likely not notice. It tastes wonderful! In the car, a lady (the navigator) tells us where to go! "Forward! Forward! Right! Back! Back! Left! Slide!" Crash! No, seriously – in-car navigation systems have matured to the extent that they are better than we are. I have already applied for a patent for the dance step navigator, as well. You see, I can't dance. Not at all – and I've always been afraid of dancing. Now I have a bud in my ear that translates the music into orders which I execute. Before I start, I have to enter my partner's leg and instep length. My wife is used to my acting somewhat distracted, since I am always talking to the company with my ear bud and cell phone. So now when I wear the set when dancing, she hardly notices. I tell her that I'm on a conference call to Europe, where they are just finishing up dancing in front of the boss, due to the time difference. She wonders why I can suddenly dance so well even though I hate it. Since I am now skilled at it, I smile bravely. I think to myself how robots and people could gradually start converging. Of course, then it will no longer be fun for either, but at least we can do everything adequately. "Gunter, you can really dance now! You used to look like a stuffed animal when you danced. You know, the kind from Steiff, the brand with the button in the ear ... oh, sorry, now I see ...!"

So even learning how to dance or drive a car yourself is nonsense. You can immediately advance to a level of mastery with the aid of automated instruction. That is pure, simple, Lean Brain Quality! Trying it yourself would mean going by your own imagined instructions, or, even more perverse, taking the intuitive tack. "I dance intuitively, Gunter." I've seen it. It's not a pretty sight – not precise, no regularity in the steps. Intuitive! Dancing is purely mechanical.

Lots of people are always trying to do everything on their own with their bit of intelligence. They invest their money – without a clue! "Gunter, what should I buy?" – "I recommend the stocks that are on the index." – "Is that reputable?" – "It's arch-conservative."

People insure themselves against everything without having any notion of the risks. "Hey, Gunter, how high is the probability that I'll die?" "One-hundred percent." – "Ugh. You're so mean to me. But then I'll definitely get the premium, right?" – "Just pick a civil servant's insurance policy – they always get everything paid in advance."

> Most people try extremely hard to make intelligent decisions without having any qualification. That is pure amateur intelligence, which is hopelessly inferior to normal Lean Brain instruction.

The most strenuous work of all is developing oneself into a genuine person. That is what philosophers want us to do; God supposedly, too. We try so hard, at least as naïve children, before we have been enlightened. At some point, almost all of us give up and fake it. We are formally polite, follow rituals in church instead of believing, do what we are told and fake our looks like a façade. In the near future, when gene-manipulated people exist, we will order our children from brand-name firms, including a premium tattoo. "I've ordered a Boss child, and you? – "Oh, Gucci goo, a Boss child! But your insurance won't pay for it! Dior savings suffice?" – "No, we're going for second quality, one with just a few little flaws that you can't see with the naked eye. The child only has internal damage. No co-payment. All children end up somewhat botched by their upbringing anyway, so it all evens out. But the tattoo is trademarked. In addition to the child, we also got a double complimentary cocktail."

Seriously: Do you still know any genuine people? I doubt it. See, I've read that famous book *Motivation and Personality* by Abraham Maslow, the one with the famous pyramid.

In a large-scale series of experiments, Abraham Maslow attempted to find something resembling genuine personalities, which resulted in shattering conclusions. Of more than 5,000 tested persons, fewer than 10 were classified as "perfect" personalities. Let me put it this way: Those are the genuine people. Maslow estimates that they number markedly fewer than one percent of everyone.

These people can be compared to the genuine in all of humanity. They are distinctly perceivable despite their low numbers because they significantly jack up society's norms. We can taste these genuine people like salt in the drab, thin, watery soup of humankind. Genuine people are like the small proportion of genuine rum in a cut rum blend. They are the core of human culture. Genuine people, like genuine rum, are the models for that which is to be subsequently produced in the cut version.

Of course you are well aware of this by now. Yeah, yeah, we should all become genuine people! But the chances of achieving this are smaller than 1 in 100. Is it worth sacrificing half your life for it? Is it even possible that all people could be valuable? Then they would all be nice. Now if one single brute were left over, he would be the cat amongst the pigeons that would kill all the nice people. Thus, it is impossible for there to be lots of ideal people, just as there aren't many $100 bills that you lose and then find again. Yet first-class faked Lean Brain people, who on the outside can hardly be discerned from genuine people, can exist together in large numbers if the system has been configured well by a moronorg.

People use all of their intelligence to be or become genuine, and almost always fail. LBM, on the other hand, allows them to look almost genuine without any need to be intelligent themselves.

A father says to his child: "If you would just do everything I say, you would be good." In the Lean Brain movement, the system speaks similarly to people in general. What is good for a child can't be bad for everyone else, right?

The primary foe of LBQ is thus the unfailing failure in people's attempts to lead their lives well on their own. Amateur intelligence generally uses all of its might to attempt to achieve something genuine or grand in order to satisfy some egocentric desire.

2. The Pathological Addiction to Appreciation

Many medical doctors, for instance, blatantly admit that they get warm fuzzies from helping human souls. This self-centered attitude costs enormous amounts. The health systems are breaking down, yet doctors still waste time chatting intimately with patients. Mothers clean shoes twice a day or dust the Venetian blinds so that they can be thanked for it. These services are senseless, and the thanks are expensive to boot.

Many nurses, kindergarten teachers or social workers are so absorbed in their work that psychologists often speak of a "helper syndrome." Such helpers literally drool over the chance to take on the role of protector and healer. In the process, they often forget that it is not about themselves, but about providing efficient care. They relentlessly strive to be ideal helpers, while the nursing and social systems stride toward bankruptcy.

Especially scientists aspire to so-called excellence. They are not primarily concerned about doing good work but rather about the satisfaction they get in being the world champion of a miniature realm. Within this miniature realm, they are immortal for as long as said realm exists (which is not long). Thus they strive toward superiority in miniature spirit. They will do anything to achieve this goal, offering their life for science, as they like to put it. What they mean by science is their respective miniature realm. Yet what they really want is self-realization. There is hardly a scientist out there who ever thinks of supplying society, which by the way pays him or her, with significant results. (A typical case: "Mr. Mathematician, can your extremely dry theories ever be utilized?" – "I should hope not! I don't want to be the inventor of bombs! And ever more bombs are being built with them!" That is the pure arrogance of pure science in its purest mathematical form.)

This amateur aspiration for miniature appreciation must be stopped. In contrast, LBM guarantees success for everyone. You won't believe it at first, but just think back to your school days for a moment: If you yourself – yes, you – had simply done everything you were told in school, you would have been better. If you had done everything your parents had told you, you would have gotten farther. You probably use a good part of your mental energy today to painstakingly maintain your own, unnatural stance: "I have never knuckled down. I did not become a servant. I love myself the way I am. I have become a truly good person. One-hundred percent genuine."

And yet Maslow was not able to find any. Did he not know you?

> LBM forgoes the illogical attempt to ideally develop people. Lean Brain Management reshapes them into fakes that look practically ideal. Since almost all people land on this same, wide path due to their own greed and vanity, LBM, using minimal effort, only successfully professionalizes that which people normally screw up themselves with maximum effort in an amateur manner.

Allow me to put it more crudely: From the start, Lean Brain skips the orgasm altogether and fakes a perfect one. If you can't achieve a real one, it is better to practice the fake. People who strive to achieve the genuine and fail are saddled with living a lie or forced to bear the wounds of defeat. If you fake a professional one right from the get-go, you'll be spared this fate.

Many people that hear about LBQ for the first time are afraid to become some sort of moron who follows system instructions and is actually an asset. Well, sure, they are an almost perfect commodity! So what?

Person: "But then I'll just be one among many! I won't be anything special anymore!"

LB Manager: "But, with LBQ you are absolutely okay because you do everything completely correctly simply by following the instructions of the moronorg."

Person: "But doesn't that make me a moron?"

LB Manager: "Yes, but a very special one! What, in your opinion, is a moron?"

Person: "The bimbo who stole my boyfriend. She's a complete airhead, but she just lies down and moans. She claims my ex is an incredible lover, which isn't true. But he believes her and is happy. I am absolutely positive that she's faking. She doesn't come, but she goes places with him. My ex is completely satisfied. He says it's better and much faster with her."

LB Manager: "So he has saved time and effort and is much more satisfied?"

Person: "Absolutely. And I'm sure she's much more satisfied than I am. After all, she's saving time and effort, too. I worked with him for a very long time on the ideal delayed synchronous climax – we planned it months in advance and read lots of books on the subject. It was all in vain – we wasted so much time for nothing. I would have loved, just once, to hear him say I was a great woman. Now he says it to that bimbo every day who doesn't waste a moment's thought on love."

LB Manager: "It's quite possible that both of them will be feeling something real very soon, because they act positively about it. In love, you have to act positively. Roman philosophers determined that people can get used to anything. If you struggle hard enough, it becomes a part of you. Once that happens, your body can start loving. That is why love follows practice, just like being happy follows the insipid, stubborn, constant practicing of virtue."

Person: "You just have to pretend – and then it can become true?"

LB Manager: "Well what is it you want anyway? Pleasure or appreciation? I assume appreciation, since that is the highest desire to aspire to. That's for sure. Yeah … yup, that's for sure. You see, in the beginning, you are always afraid of hard work because it is horrible and drags you down. After a while, though, everyone claims they love their jobs, all because they get respect. That's clear enough."

Person: "But I don't love my job, and I get no respect."

LB Manager: "Well, do you try your best or do you sweet-talk your boss?"

Person: "That's just it! It's so unfair! There's this guy who's constantly praising the boss. After a couple of days they were calling each other by their first names. He keeps praising the boss incessantly. I cringe every time I hear it! 'You are so good at that! Great! Nobody does it better! Come on, come on, let's do it again! I've never been under anyone so good! Let's be a team, we're coming together!' Do you know what I mean? Pure schmoozing!"

LB Manager: "No, it's the normal jargon of business pornography. It saves time and effort."

Person: "I'd like to believe that. I work hard and apply myself. Others praise the boss no matter what, one slimy climax after another. Then they get promoted and I get passed over. One after the other. I don't deserve such treatment! 'That's so good. I really admire you! Great job, Boss!' But that sort of thing is effective. I would really like it if the boss once said to me that I was doing really good work, but he only says that to people who kiss his butt."

LB Manager: "Haven't you ever thought of saving time and effort and being happier? Like by copying someone else's homework and praising the teacher?"

Person: "Oh, no, I've always had my pride."

LB Manager: "What's more important to you – your pride or …"

Person: "My pride, of course! Otherwise I'd be moaning and schmoozing. Then everyone would praise me and love me! But I want to be genuine! That's the way I was brought up! Not like those others. They have no problem with what they're doing, those brainless idiots! They have no shame." *Cries bitterly.*

LB Manager: "Do you understand that the genuine in the positive sense is a creation? Something higher? Something incomparable? Don't you see that, in that sense, you aren't genuine at all, but that you simply haven't become fake?"

Person, *who stops crying*: "Yes! Yes! I haven't become fake like the others! That is my pride!"

LB Manager: "But have you also become genuine, just by never having become fake?"

Person, *looking surprised*: "Wasn't I genuine right from the start?"

LB Manager: "Oh come on, you were raised, weren't you? What do
you want? Was your mother proud?"

Person: "Yes, very!"

LB Manager: "Successful?"

Person *long pause, then asks:* "So, there are only successful morons
and on the other side, losers with pride?" *Contemplates.* "Aren't
there any real people?"

LB Manager: "Yes, there are, but they have no pride."

Person: "I only know people with pride, and those without pride are
morons. There aren't any other kinds of people."

LB Manager: "Oh yes there are. Maslow found seven."

Person: "Well, he didn't spare time or effort!"

LB Manager: "You said it."

The normal, proud person naïvely attempts to strive for the genuine.
Since only a very few achieve this, such people will in all probability
not garner any respect, yet that is what is most important to them.
However, if they try to achieve respect directly, they must turn to
faking and thus swear off being genuine. Since they swear it off with
the pride they were raised to have, they can hardly achieve a professional fake. Thus, here, too, will they fail to earn respect. This is due
to their inner conflict: the desire for appreciation at any cost and
shame for the fake.

Lean Brain Management glorifies the ideal fake, and takes away
people's shame. To do this, LBM does not need to separate people
from the genuine per se, just mentally separate from genuine people.

Genuine people generate a dangerous longing in people to be
genuine themselves.

    Lean Brain Managers will avoid them like the plague.

A Lean Brain person fakes with devotion. Before someone can become a Lean Brain person, a great deal must change in his or her
head – less is more.

3. The Highest form of Appreciation – "You can stay!"

As we have seen in the last section, people care about respect and recognition, pleasure and a longing to be genuine. A Lean Brain Manager, on the other hand, cares about saving time and money. The genuine is rare and should as a rule be faked. Pleasure, however, is a delicate problem in people because it is not situated in the brain and is thus very hard for Lean Brain Management to grasp. In the above dialogue, a central theme has emerged: A fake can be produced much faster and cheaper, but the act of producing one may not always be coupled with pleasure. Those who fake pleasure are considerably more efficient and, in almost all cases, even superior to the quality of the genuine – the compliments will rain down bountifully. Yet the act itself is done without pleasure.

This tricky situation can be overcome if the appreciation shown for the successful act is worth much more than the absence of pleasure during performance.

Allow me to digress a bit. If we switch the world over to Lean Brain, systems will save a great deal of time and effort and thus be able to subsist themselves on fewer and fewer people. Lean Brain systems therefore generate high unemployment on the whole that will prevail for several years, since Lean Brain systems increasingly economize on a growing amount of employees – because this is just the beginning of the Lean Brain movement. That is why it will be possible for a long while to simply threaten people with being fired, since they fear nothing more than losing their jobs. The Lean Brain movement can thus bank on humans' primal fear of being completely abandoned.

- "If you don't straighten out, boy, we're going to put you in reform school."
- "If you keep this up, you're going to end up on the street."
- "If you don't like capitalism, move to the GDR." (This is a historical threat. Today, capitalism and now Lean Brain Management are unstoppable.)
- "If you don't like it, then my business is not your business. Return your badge!"

- "We are going to have to let a few people go because we are so efficient that we have no need for them. That's great! Just think as a team which of you we've been able to make redundant through all of those tough hours of overtime! It would better serve the cause to get rid of a few good people. Then the team will not be so well staffed next year and will have even more redundancy potential. If, on the other hand, we fire underperformers, we'll regret it later. How should we do it? Think about it: *Everyone* here can be redundant!"
- "I have no desire to deal with your problems. Take some Viagra and get to it. I have my standards! I do! Or leave! Now, stop that fake moaning and get that crushed look off your face. You're shaking like a vibrator."

There is a single statement at the core of all of these remarks:

> "In a Lean Brain world, your place can be occupied by many others. Nobody is irreplaceable! Lots of people are waiting for your departure! There will be much rejoicing when you go if it happens to be noticed!"

And the ultimate reward for a person is:

> "You can stay. We'll let someone else take the fall this time, although it could easily have been you as well. Yes, you!"

This ultimate reward makes any amount of human pleasure pale in comparison and seem worthless. The king's mistress has only one wish, namely to be allowed to remain under the throne. To achieve this, she will turn her life into one entire fake, if need be. The primal fear is to be replaced. In a functional Lean Brain World, there is a replacement for everything and everyone because the genuine, now rare, has been minimized.

4. In the Lean Brain Revolution

Let me provide you with a few real examples from real life where we can feel reaction to the Lean Brain movement.

Science! In the newspapers, you can frequently find statistics demonstrating how often scientific publications are read. Wryly put, an article is usually only read by its author (and even that is not always a given if an assistant wrote it) and his or her assistant, both of whom must build upon it and cite it. Thus, countless researchers busy themselves for years pondering the 100 % genuine, but only a very few of them actually think of something genuine. Echoes of Maslow? "Basic research is the most important thing of all! A country cannot survive without it," say researchers defensively against Lean Brain, declaring themselves irreplaceable.

The government has already taken notice and is gradually replacing all of science by fakes as so-called third-party funded research. This involves a person outside the university providing financing in return for getting something useful out of a project. In other words, he or she is offering the scientists wage labor. How does this work? Well, someone from the realm of industry has a tricky problem but no experts to solve it. He packages the problem in such a shrewd manner that it sounds extremely scientific, and he offers underpaid scientists a bit of money to solve it. Then the problem is reformulated once again to sound like the title of a dissertation. (It has to be incomprehensible, otherwise it is not new!) Subsequently, a young scientist takes on the task, works on it for a couple of years for little money, and in the end receives her real pay in the form of a doctoral degree. In this way, the university maintains its "research institution" status, but no longer produces research, rather serving as a normal industrial subcontractor. One could consistently have specialists work for free for five years and in return give them a nice title such as "Master of the University of the Reserve," or the like. Then faking science would be like unpaid alternative service. The primary reward at the university must be: "You can stay."

The scientists will give in eventually.

> A genius gets by with his head,
>   A scientist on a drip in bed.

Religion! In the past, God was present in so many people's hearts that wherever we were, He shone a bit and was perceivable. The critical mass of the faithful for this highest omnipresence has since fallen short, such that the world today seems to have been abandoned by God. It is the hour of the prophets that predict the end of the world without God. The genuine, like basic research, must return to the world!

Basically, we really do only need God for weddings and funerals and those celebratory Christmas services with readings from the Old Testament. "As men rejoice when they divide the spoil," say the voices in church shortly before presents are exchanged at home.

It would suffice to fake God's presence; that is all that is needed at a wedding, for example. I'm sorry about using the word fake! As a substitute for the genuine! Perhaps I should say rite. A rite is the ordering of a sacred series of actions and has always served as a substitute for the genuine. The genuine is so incredibly small! A rite, on the other hand, can be extended to a good hour. It's just like cut rum!

Just as in science, there is very little to do in church that is genuine. That is why it is better to economize on everything or have the church employees take care of senior citizens or teach in kindergartens so that they "can stay".

> Lean Brain Management no longer leaves the church in the village.

Experts! Many experts make themselves indispensable through clandestine dealings with important specialized knowledge. "We can't fire him! He's the only one in our company who can operate the photocopier! He can stay!"

Experts form the white areas, so to speak, on the map of moronorgs. The Lean Brain System as yet cannot achieve what an expert can, and experts are taking full advantage of the situation. We have to kneel before them and ask: "Your Holiness, what does this mean?

Two ladles of flour, three eggs, sugar to taste, and enough milk to make the batter thin? Does that make a dessert? Or something for a baby?" Then the expert's eyes gleam, and he begins condescending: "Crepes, you dope!" Just try to get the same information without the humiliation and veneration. "Dr. Knowitol, what does this line here on your prescription block say?" He leans back slowly, stretching, and asks: "Is it my job to rack your brains?" – "I hardly have any time, so please tell me!" – "Time? Do you think *I* have time? My office hours and areas of responsibility are hanging outside on my door. I'm sorry. I'm one of the best in the field. I can't be available every minute of every day!" Nothing is possible without dropping to your knees before the guru – or taking out private insurance.

> I can think of one word that rhymes with expert: uppert. (That's my abbreviation for upper ten thousand.)

The goal of experts is canonization. Unfortunately, in addition to the moronorgs actually responsible, we still need experts because Lean Brain Management has not yet progressed far enough. Intelligence is still filling the world like a disastrous spirit. A Lean Brain Manager must often grit his teeth and "let the expert stay."

Customer satisfaction! There are several totally inefficient people who enjoy being especially nice to customers. They worship customers and place them at "the center of the business". They "exceed customer expectations" and are proud that they have given customers more than they pay for. Of course they are satisfied.

> Your customers are happy – your profits are crappy!

5. The Lean Brain System has yet to be Optimally Moronized

As you have seen from the previous examples, Lean Brain Management is on the advance. Everywhere, arbitrary job content is being replaced with standardized portions. All-in-one solutions are propagated and component systems promoted. Customers assemble tailor-made solutions from modular systems.

Our work is increasingly becoming normed routine. We hardly have any freedom of selection or action. We operate systems as employees as well as customers.

Yet the Lean Brain movement is still in its infancy. We still curse much more often than is appropriate for Lean Brain Systems. "The systems are insipid! I have to work on the simplest steps like a baby? Am I a moron or something?"

Yes! Of course! If a Lean Brain System were already developed to the point that we felt like children in it, we'd be much farther along than we are today.

What I'm trying to say is: Some of your criticism shows that you either have not understood the sense of Lean Brain (which would be acceptable) or that you do not wish to accept it (we'll have to work on that).

The truly harsh criticism of Lean Brain systems sounds like this:

"The processes are imperfect, they are full of holes; entire process steps have been left out. There are often too many rules. I can prove that there are absolutely no work procedures that adhere to all of the rules. If I follow the instructions step by step and to the letter, the result will not be what was planned."

Such censure doubts that the instructions of the moronorgs can be productive (at this point). Moronorgs have not (yet) worked well.

- They have incorporated too few or imprecise instructions.
- They have not considered all possible cases, such that, in certain rare cases, there are no instructions at all. ("What should I do now? There are no more instructions for this case. Nobody is in charge. I was at an intelligent traffic light with a green activation loop and unfortunately stalled the car when it turned green the second time. Now I've been sitting here in the dark at a red light for an hour. Nothing is happening. No cars are coming. I can't ask anyone for help.")
- They have not taken into consideration that today several experts occupy Lean Brain jobs who are pondering "short cuts" to employ intelligence. A system must thus protect itself from intelligence

that bypasses rules. It must protect itself against the foes of yesterday, which unfortunately often makes it appallingly complex.
- They have not taken into consideration how little residual intelligence is ultimately activated in perfect morons. Perfect morons do not employ any intelligence – even if they have some privately. After all, they have been forbidden from using it. If moronorgs have forgotten something in the rules, they are, due to their training, not capable of activating their residual intelligence. ("I am supposed to always pay out 100 dollars in two 50-dollar bills, but I don't have any more." Customer: "There is a 100-dollar bill right there." – "I know, but I have my orders. I am pretty sure that there will be booking problems in the system. Then I'll be fired.")

Lean Brain Systems must naturally be autonomously intelligent, otherwise the whole thing will not work. Lean Brain systems must master the difficult transition period when there are parallel suboperations with and without intelligence. Experience has shown that Lean Brain employees cannot identify what requires intelligence and what does not, and what can still require intelligence and what cannot. Under stress, they often react unpredictably, ignoring bad processes or avoiding them with completely incalculable strategies. Unfortunately, it has become popular to use the imperfect system as a scapegoat or exoneration for one's own errors and insufficient performance. "I couldn't do it any better. I couldn't book the contracts fast enough because the system has lately started to request entering all of the address data after every click. The moronorg says it's just like on income tax forms, where you have to write in your name and number on every page. It doesn't make any sense on computers. My work can be done much more insipidly! I don't want to have to think when I work! Who am I anyway?" This tendency to curse the system when your own performance is lacking creates problems, and of course enemies, for the Lean Brain reformer.

6. Measures to Push LBQ past its Enemies

Lean Brain Managers must have watertight chains of instructions prepared by moronorgs that are completely goal-oriented. People who butt in with intelligence and concern for others – that is, people who are still addicted to the production of appreciation or even the genuine – must be brought to their knees.

This can be done via a very simple set of measures:

1. The required time and effort for a job are continually restricted to the extent that in practically all cases fakes must be employed. The genuine would be too expensive.
2. If a task is successfully executed, appreciation is expressed for the person executing the task – as a rule, in the form of warm praise on the intranet or via an automatically generated email. A small sum of money can also be given, which is taken away from the less successful members of the team (performance compensation).
3. If the task is not successfully executed, the responsible person is threatened with dismissal or humiliation, depending on how it is handled or celebrated in each individual case.
4. If, during the execution of a task, errors in the system prove to be a hindrance, they are eliminated in the system. The system may under no circumstances be circumvented. The system must learn, no one else. Attempts at independent intelligence must be penalized.

So if we determine that someone somewhere is still cooking with enthusiasm himself, we will force him to work much faster, so incredibly fast that he will not be able to use the conventional recipes. The true master chef, under such barbaric pressure, will soon give up his personal strolls to the farmer's market and purchase ready-made, bagged salad. With a grunt, he'll throw a salad made with Good Season's dressing mix on the table. By the way, that stuff tastes really good! (I like to cook. Good Seasons Garlic & Herb is delicious). Yet no matter how it tastes – we'll continually praise him for how fast he works. That is important. We won't dwell much on the flavor.

After all, we only want to get him to use ready-made meals. We'll indicate to him for a while that we like the way everything tastes, as long as it is all fast and inexpensive. We'll praise him only (!) for the fact that "his numbers are on the mark" – regarding time and money. If he can gradually succeed in making tolerable fakes, we'll continue to reduce his budget for time and money until all that is boiling is his blood, and not anything on the stove. Then he'll be using the microwave and the freezer. Soon he'll stop complaining. He basically knows nothing about flavor enhancers, and he'll notice this in time. A cook cannot compete with ready-made meals in the long run. This shift in culture will take a while because it usually greatly annoys the old guard. If praise of the fakes does not work, a generational change often has to take place. We fire the cook and hire in his place a very young ready-made cook (FFF for Fast Food Fixer) who has never even seen good food but can cook with both hands tied behind his back. On the restroom wall, someone has scrawled: "Dear cook, you may bake, fry, or boil it, but now your art is in the toilet." The young fast food cook can already laugh about it, and soon accepts that, in addition to warming food bags, he can also take on another part-time job in the form of operating the dishwashing machine followed by disinfecting tasks. In this way, we can infinitely concentrate the entire work cycle!

Regrettably, there are always those ready-meal eaters who inevitably act like gourmets. "Could you please sprinkle some fresh parsley on the freshly-fried, ice-water brook hatchery-bred trout?" This is a problem in the system. There is no plan to have fresh parsley; it's not even on the menu. True, it would be easy to get some parsley, so critics could stop whining. But from the standpoint of the system, the customer has no right to any extras. Therefore, the young fast food cook has to decline. "I'm sorry, our painstakingly perfected kitchen does not include parsley." That is the polite form of the more standard "We ain't got any," which can often be heard in Lean Brain department stores.

And caution! Pay attention! This system problem of the missing parsley may only be solved by the system, and never the waiter! Errors are always solved in the system, never through individual intelligence or cooperativeness. A moronorg must decide what to do.

Decline the parsley garnish or supply it as an extra for a high sur-charge? The moronorg thus checks the system. Should it stay as it is? Or offer an extra service? The moronorg, and only the moronorg, makes the final decision! Consequently, everyone follows that deci-sion. Of course, the employees usually wish to be praised again and garner appreciation through a bit of parsley. Again and again, the system is subject to humanations against Lean Brain Quality, which the moronorg must resist! He must keep amateur intelligents and granters of extras away from the system!

That is why moronorgs, when faced with holes in the process and extra requests in general, often sound like this: "We have imple-mented a new procedure. You all insisted on having the process change because, allegedly, customers are expressing special wishes. We are going to solve it by having a questionnaire be filled out be-fore each procedure which asks whether the customer wishes to have something different. He or she will be offered this option for a sub-stantial surcharge. With this innovation, we are perfecting the busi-ness process exactly the way in which we proposed. In addition, we will also earn a great deal of extra money if this special process is utilized at such ridiculous charges as we have set. This is ideal. We are very grateful to you. That is exactly the kind of suggestion for improvement we expect from our employees." – "But what if none of the customers pays the ridiculous charge? Would we still have to always fill out the questionnaire as well? For every customer, no mat-ter what? We want to serve customers in a special way, but custom-ers will have their fill of the questionnaires – and we will too." – "Did this suggestion come from you or us? We implemented it the way you wanted us to. Completely new and totally exemplary. If you have a better suggestion, you can propose it via the conventional business procedure." – "The point is, we made an intelligent sugges-tion, but unfortunately it's being executed with zero brains!" This will make the heart of a Lean Brain Manager beat faster. It has been a good day. The employees are gradually understanding what it all boils down to. After a few new tries, employees will soon give up submitting their own suggestions and be satisfied with zero-brain procedures. Customers, too, will soon ask: "What does it cost if the restaurant were to provide the silverware instead of my having to bring it from home?" In Italy, this practice is called "pane e coperto," and they charge for it.

> The Lean Brain Manager fights every kind of extra that has not been bindingly set for everyone in the system. Most of all, the Lean Brain Manager will fight those people who respond to requests for extras. The system must improve. The people are not important.

> The system is the focus.
>   It is as grand as a morolith.

On an airplane, they don't call it "pane e coperto," but rather Business Class. Whereas in a restaurant in Italy, you pay the equivalent of a few extra dollars per family for napkins, white bread, oil and vinegar, on an airline it is often a few hundred dollars. Managers have no time to eat on the ground, they claim. That is why having a bite on the plane saves a lot of time. They still receive the tax-free daily travel allowance in addition to their travel expenses. Another seven bucks that they can put in their own pockets! Business travelers are more than happy to let their own company pay twice. No, no extras! Never! Perfect happiness is only possible in combination with an empty wallet.

7. Effective, Practical and easily understood Advice for Managers

You as a manager are surrounded by enemies of Lean Brain. Employees get around rules with intelligence. They help customers deal with the flaws in the Lean Brain System. Customers threaten to break their business ties with you. Employees complain about their jobs and demand their human rights, which however, the law only grants them outside of the company.

This can really get on your nerves as a manager. But relax: It is only criticism of a system that is not yet sufficiently Lean Brain capable. The employees are only complaining *to* you, not *about* you. After all, managers are seen as personified representatives of the system. As a manager, you only have one task: to make sure that all system regulations are observed and the people working under these conditions work faster and faster. The system must run as it is planned by the moronorg.

As long as intelligence can be economized in the system, goals will be increased to the point where they cannot be achieved through normal intelligence. The employees will turn to cheaper solutions and resort to faking. All useless ballast will be forced out. That is the normal transition from a stupid system with smart employees to an intelligent system that only employs morons. As long as you can still think intelligently, it will be impossible to reach those goals anyway. Only in a complete Lean Brain System in ideal condition is it possible to achieve the tasks, if only one could be somewhat faster than is possible. In an ideal Lean Brain System, everyone only numbly performs routine work. Speed is of the essence!

> Try to numb yourself. Let go of your intelligence. Cross that threshold, without which you cannot be a modern manager.

Managers always also set examples. Thus, represent the advantages of the Lean Brain approach in an aggressive manner. From time to time, hold an obligatory speech for your employees after work. Nothing is more numbing than an exuberant praise of Lean Brain systems. In order to increase the efficacy of this tactic, I recommend giving the same speech over and over.

> "I am happy we've all gathered here today. I know you're already off for the night, so I'll make it as short as possible, as usual. We haven't achieved our goals, but we are headed in the right direction. We can increase profits with the implemented wage reductions. We have succeeded in further standardizing our range, such that we can offer customers uniform quality. No matter

what customers pick up at our store, it is as it is. We have managed to fend off all special wishes by bullying with surcharges. There has been repeated public criticism, but our competition isn't sleeping and is proceeding exactly as we are. Therefore, customers have no choice. They have to come to us because conditions are worse everywhere else. We have become the most operator-friendly company. We have an excellent market position, which we can continue to improve through further reductions in service and wages. We want to stay ahead of the competition by a nose. Only the best systems will survive! In the long run, only Number One counts. We can all be proud of the fact that we were allowed to stay, although we were never able to reach the goals we had set. We are proud of this because those who reach goals are pitiful weaklings who have resolved to take on too little. More and more employees are complaining that they do not understand the implemented measures to increase profit. That should make us very pleased. The system is becoming smarter and more superior. In addition, replacing experienced employees with newcomers without diplomas has enabled us to considerably expand the lead of intelligence in the system compared to that of the employees. We are on the right path because now we are well positioned against the customers and equipped to reach even higher goals. The system is higher than any amount of reason. Its wisdom is inscrutable. Its good exceeds all expectations. The system hovers over us and gives us peace of mind. Work calmly and have no fear. No matter how long you can stay, the system will always be there."

You should write this speech down in large lettering on punch cards: you know, those long computer cards that only store a small amount of information. Originally intended for those humble old computers of the Stone Age, today they are produced in a variety of colors for Lean Brain speakers. We recommend the classic beige.

8. Take-Aways, Control Questions and Exercises

Control question: Do you know Johann Wolfgang von Goethe?

Lean Brain's Night Song

In all brains
is calm,
Behind all foreheads
You feel
Hardly a breath;
Eyes stare into the cold.
Just wait, soon
You'll also be at rest.

Allow yourself a little break.
You have finished Part One of this book.
It will bode well with you.

In Part Two, there won't be so much contemplating upon contemplating. We have to finally get down to brass tacks and implement what in theory still seems almost unreasonable.

V. Stereotypical Activity in the Blood!

1. "You obviously have no clue. Can I speak to the manager?"

I was looking at a camera in a department store in Germany. I asked a smart-looking department store expert about a button on the device that was a mystery to me. "What does this button do?" The salesman cockily and urbanely paged through the accompanying operating instructions – hesitated briefly, raised his eyebrows and divulged somewhat sheepishly: "These are in English. You can speak English, right?" I nodded. "Good, then I'll just let you have a look at these instructions. Here you go!" He fled with the remark that I should tell him if I wanted to buy something so that he could sign the form for his commission.

This procedure is not a good example at all of Lean Brain sales. It is only possible to save money in department stores if solely pseudo product-sitters are present that must watch over so many products that "they wouldn't have the slightest chance of being familiar with even the most popular ones." It is completely inappropriate to undertake sales consultant efforts if you have no idea about the product. Faking, on the other hand, always works when one is clueless! The sales representative here uses his amateur intelligence, which immediately fails. "I only wanted to help," whines the amateur intelligence placatingly, seeking praise for the disaster to boot.

Why not just do it like this, dear Lean Brain sales representatives: "I can't allow the package to be opened, since the store would suffer a monetary loss. However, right after you purchase our product, you can discover the wealth of functions of the device in the operating instructions. Our prices are so inexpensive that you can hardly not buy the product, yet we cannot offer every service that a higher-priced store would. By the way, this camera can do everything you would expect from a camera in this price range. That goes without saying. It takes sharp photos, and your face will have more pixels than you could ever hope for. We had several square miles of these cameras in stock, but that supply has dwindled in a whirlwind of demand. If I were you, I'd hurry. You can see for yourself how busy it is in here today. I don't think there will ever be such inexpensive cameras. Oil prices are on the rise. I should know, I worked in that branch right up until yesterday."

That is exemplary faking that won't scare off customers and forms the necessary background noise for a spontaneous purchase. That is all the Lean Brain approach strives to do. Selling has nothing to do with the product. "If you can sell *something*, you can sell *anything!*" That is the age-old insight of sales. Selling has always had something to do with Lean Brain methods. Sales representatives have never given their tasks too much thought.

Here is another example. Are you familiar with this game? "Excuse me, Mr. Salesperson, but could I have this camera in a larger size?" – "I'll see if we have something in stock." Then the Lean Brain sales representative goes to the warehouse for 11 minutes, where he spends 10 minutes completing his other duties in the goods receiving department. He comes back with a sad face, explaining that there are none in stock at all, but that all of the devices were put right on the shelf. They only had what was there and could not order what was not. But they were constantly getting in new and exciting products. I go away. I hear the next customer after me ask: "Do you have this in black?" – "We might. Have you got a few minutes? I have to check the stock, and I have two other customers waiting. It's really busy in here today, you see. We got some great items in, so it isn't easy for us, I can tell you."

I'm at the car dealership. I ask about the trade-in value of my old car. Someone brings me a cup of coffee and asks me to enter all of the data on my car in a computer. I need thirty minutes for this, because the numbers on the engine block etc. are so long. I click on "Trade-in savings price calculation". The computer asks for my permission to save my data and use it against me. I press "OK". Then the computer hums busily for half a minute, blinking encouragingly. Finally, a very low dollar amount appears on the screen that immediately crushes my soul. I yell at the sales representative, who is busy sitting ever-new customers in front of computer screens so they can serve the dealership. A uniformed man from a service company pours coffee. "You can't be serious! My car is worth at least double

that amount!" –"The computer calculated it." – "Using what formula?" – "We have to use that new software for the calculations; it's
the rule. In the past, customers used to take us to the cleaners all the
time. They would keep haggling the price down and wasting our
time. Then they'd go to the next dealership and barter until the price
was even lower, wasting our colleagues' time as well! Today all dealerships use the same, insolent software against the customers. So
now you aren't likely to go to the next dealership only to type in all
of the registration information, VIN number and other data all over
again, hahaha. Your car isn't worth a thing, and now every computer
in the worldwide data network knows it! We've already passed your
data on to all dealerships via email. You yourself agreed to the procedure. Therefore, you accept the calculations that the computer has
cooked up. Don't try to be intelligent now. We don't either, now that
we've got the software. That way we are negotiating on the same
intelligence level. Press 'OK' and you can have your new car today.
This one here, the one you want, has been sitting here rusting just
waiting for you."

Lean Brain companies fake such fluid communication. We call it
"content-free communication," which originated in politics and subsequently moved to sales personnel and on to management, where
it was perfected. Today, it celebrates many triumphs as *Lean Brain
Communication*. Good Lean Brain companies get by with about
200 general empty phrases, and then let their moronorgs design
roughly 20 more that are company-specific. You can't do anything
about Lean Brain Communication, and that is its forte. All the customer can do is shout: "Can I speak to the manager?" Out of pure
habit, we think that the manager has a greater depth of power au-
thorizing him or her to make reasonable exceptions. True, that used
to be the case. Today, however, the departmental manager is also
bound to the rules of the computer, which of course have been programmed by a moronorg. The departmental manager therefore allows himself to be yelled at by the customer, who still hopes to be
able to gain something from the effort. Yet the manager simply waits
until the shouting has stopped and responds: "We have the lowest
prices. You can be assured of that. We do everything for our customers that we can afford under these circumstances. That is more
than you'll find in other shops. We have trained our personnel to

greet customers while attending to their work and they have sworn to uniform behavior. I, as the boss, cannot and will not make an exception because I want to be a role model for my customers. I am sorry, but my hands are tied. I have done everything in my power, which is to say, I have listened to what you have to say." – "Doesn't anybody around here have a say anymore?" – "Why yes: the computer." – "And who understands what's going on?" – "The computer!" – "And can people talk to it?" – "No. Otherwise customers would cheat us." – "I just want more money for my old car!" – "Then you'll have to find someone very stupid!" – "But your dealership is very stupid, so I must be in the right place!" – "No, our dealership is Lean Brain. You have no clue what that is, do you?"

2. The Call Center Model

The dialogue appearing in the following paragraph was first published in a shorter version of one of the first Daily Dueck articles on my homepage, www.omnisophie.com, which you can read there in German and even subscribe to. Anyway, in Daily Dueck 2, I wrote about economizing on intelligence. Writing that one page inspired me so much! The whole thing was actually intended to be a joke at first, but then I suddenly saw the formidable truth that our real world today is exactly that joke! Through laughter, I had managed to stumble upon the greatest human invention of modern times! Lean Brain and economizing on intelligence! I'm going to win the Nobel Prize for medicine! Or chemistry? Or spiritual freedom?

Imagine you are phoning a bank. At a frugal bank, a call center employee answers the phone. "What would you like to purchase from us?" – "I don't want to purchase anything. I just want to transfer some money to my daughter." – "Oh, too bad. I'm afraid that's not within my realm of authority, so I can't help you, but I'll connect you with a more highly qualified consultant. Please wait a moment. Someone will assist you shortly." Music flows from the receiver. It is very pleasant and regularly interrupted by a slightly intoxicating voice: "This call will only cost you 12 cents per minute." A few minutes later: "Hello, you're now speaking with a transfer expert. You'd like to transfer money?" – "Yes, to my daughter in France." – "Oh, I can only perform domestic transfers, of course. I'll connect you to our trained foreign expert. Hold on … just a moment. Hello? Are you there? Currently, only the lines for Spain and Italy are available. Do you happen to also have to transfer money to either of those countries? In the meantime, would you like me to sell you something else? We have a speech robot that is available to give you advice on home building loans. Would you like to hear something practical? It's a premium call that costs 25 cents per minute. Oh, wait a moment … now it's working. The line to France is now available!" Music comes out of the receiver. "Hello? Here is the special consultant for French Services." – "I'd like to transfer money to my daughter. What would that cost?" – "Oh, I only do transfers. I'm not authorized to talk about prices; we have daily rates for that. Now, during lunch, it will be very expensive. A price question! I don't even know if we are allowed to reveal the prices to customers. That information falls under the data protection laws, you see? I'm sure you want to be safe with us, right? Okay, I can try, but for that I'd need to transfer you to a higher expert." – "I don't want to be transferred anymore, I want to do the transferring! Dammit!" – "Please, it costs what it costs. After all, who can make head or tail of those vacation package catalogue prices? And your primary care physician transfers you to other specialists; there is hardly anything else he can do! Everybody must only know where the work that he can't do himself is to be transferred." – "But, please tell me, who the heck knows how to do anything?" – "That is determined by a business procedure. The knowledge is primarily in the system, specifically in our telephone system. It determines the lives of customers. Most people who get put through to me want to transfer something to France. Otherwise I transfer them to someone else. That's all I can do, just effect transfers to France." – "Then you're just like a greasy assembly line worker that has been affixing the same screw to car frames for twenty years?" – "That would be great! I'd be paid better. I'm working from home to earn a few extra dollars. My wife next to me at the kitchen table is answering questions on broken scanners. She has to give every caller the standard answer that the power supply unit is defective, which is true 90 % of the time. If it's not true, she transfers the call to someone else. She doesn't even know what a scanner looks like." – "But that is completely brainless!" – "All work is brainless if it is always the same." – "So who knows what's going on at your company?" – "Nobody! How should they? Or – wait! The telephone system! Haha! Recently, one of our neighbors had a scanner that wasn't working. He was very upset about it. I immediately called my wife, who said it was the power supply unit. And it was! Funny, huh?" – "So nobody really knows anything? My God!" – "Why don't you call God? You can even do that for free! At least, I think you still can."

"And you're chatting with me like you had all the time in the world?" – "Twelve cents per minute makes ten cents gross profit, which is six dollars an hour. We only get four dollars an hour in wages because we can work from home. I don't work directly at home. I'm actually a cleaning assistant. I do the bank work on the side. While we are talking, I don't need a computer screen and can do the dusting for about eight dollars an hour. Luckily the telephone system knows nothing about this yet. But otherwise it rules us. Our telephone system always wins, against you and against us. It reigns over us all, even over you." – "That's crazy! Oh God, the telephone system! I thought your employer ruled over you! The bank?" – "Hey, do you really want me to explain all of this to you while you are paying for it? I'm not even at a bank. I'm a one-man corporation at the telephone system. I take care of transfers to France on a worldwide basis for all banks outside of France. There aren't that many money transfers, you know? And hardly anyone would be stupid enough to want to be financially ruined by calling during the lunch hour like you are. That is why I can perform this little job for the entire world. I am exceedingly proud to be solely responsible for it. I take my leadership role very seriously. See, when I can't hear the phone because I'm running the vacuum cleaner, the call is forwarded to a standby in Hungary. She always gets the calls when I can't answer. But I don't want her to take work away from me. I can do it alone! For all banks! The telephone system has assigned this job to me. It's great! I'm in love!" – "Thank you, I feel honored." – "Oh, I've got another call coming in. Can we finish up now? Otherwise the call will get sent to Hungary. Okay?" – "Whoa, wait a minute! Now he's hung up, and I completely forgot about the transfer! Oh, well, I guess I'll have to spend another hour on the phone. At least it's better than getting lost in a 10-story banking facility. No one is in charge there, either. Nobody knows what's going on. At least with telephone banking, you're only transferred ten times and you get to know lots of new people. I wonder why bank employees don't also only sit in an office and use the phone? Then everything would run more smoothly. Because when they do the thinking themselves, nothing comes of it. Except maybe consultation."

This dialogue has surely illustrated the Lean Brain principle to you. The ideal situation is to isolate people, as in having them work out of their homes, so that they cannot establish a close relationship to either customers or other employees. They are connected to the telephone system as an on-call service and later connected permanently to the Lean Brain System wirelessly via UMTS. (Money transfers can also be performed when window shopping in the city or sitting in a restaurant, and not only when washing dishes. Basically, Lean Brain boils down to a multiple utilization of the moron who practices the art of job overlay. Job overlay refers to performing several jobs at the same time – simultaneously, not one at a time!). Lean Brain employees are assigned a very small task that they perform as a service for several companies at the same time. In the past, a person on an assembly line would always tighten one single screw, always the same screw, on each automobile. Since, however, most of the work can be done on the telephone, the screw is turned on all car makes, and not just one!

Cleaning services now clean for all companies, not just one. Postal services distribute mail to concern employees everywhere, and not in just one single company. Just like electricity! Electricity comes out of the nuclear power plant and is distributed to everyone! Water and district heating flow from a single pipe to all clients. Thus, every person gets a tiny little task that is performed for all other people.

For example, soon we will be able to check at home using the PC whether somewhere in the world light bulbs are being replaced or where wheels are wobbling or screws are loose. Then a local service is sent there, such as a pizza delivery guy on a bike. That is Lean Brain in perfection. However, this will only work when all devices on the planet are accessible wirelessly, or in other words, have the same intelligence level in the system as a cell phone user.

Intelligence is organized in call center systems in a universal process. What one employee cannot do is transferred via phone to another Lean Brain representative. As I said, in the past, one departmental manager would take care of advanced requests. In traditional systems, then, a higher manager would be required to make final decisions or accept complaints from angry customers. That is also cut out of the Lean Brain System. Instead, complaints are not received by higher-paid managers but rather by friendly people who have no further training than cajoling people and providing apologies. "Help! Help! Because of the seven-hour train delay in the tunnel, I've missed my flight to the Moon! That's 80 million dollars in damage!" – "We wish to thank you very much for still riding the train and especially for the kind understanding you have expressed. We love employees whose companies have selected our railway as their means of transport. Just like a train in a tunnel, there's no getting around us. We are thankful for that. We hope to welcome you on board again."

Final decisions are also no longer made by executives, but, again, only by the telephone system. "Your old car isn't worth anything. It has been meticulously calculated according to the newest methods and then rounded off to your benefit." Or: "You are a customer of the Risk Class B. Unfortunately, you'll receive unfavorable conditions because your accounts are not in good shape."

Some telephone systems today still work with intelligence hierarchies. They differentiate between normal intelligences, higher intelligences (second-level support) and so on. Granted, this is sometimes necessary for vanity reasons. "Hello, I'm from Third-Level Support. I only answer the most difficult questions. They are usually so difficult that it doesn't matter if I can't answer them either. Thus, I can freely say whatever I want. It makes no difference." The rule that inquiries be heard by more powerful or intelligent people is old-fashioned. It is aimed at solving the problem, not numbing customers that are too lazy to serve the company.

Better are certainly those systems that have no "bosses" at all anymore, but rather only an ever-changing repertoire of responsible persons so that all complaints can echo into the darkness of space and become silent. Callers are either immediately served by Lean Brain or demoralized and finally defeated by endless transferring.

In the future, it will be important that all work, wherever and however, be immediately executed via telephone. Thus, if you want something in a bank, you can get advice, but you have to phone the consultant that is sitting next to you. This is important for invoicing: "Forty-nine cents per minute." Whenever we, as Lean Brain people, deal with other Lean Brain people, we have to call them on the phone. The telephone system determines who pays how much to whom. I'm sure you are familiar with this procedure from certain phone advertising.

"This is the automatic voice imitator. Moaning costs ninety-nine cents per minute; press one now. Select a random number or rub a code number on your subscription card and enter it carefully. Today's special is real cries of pain. Press two. You can send voice samples and we'll modulate the cries of pain to match that tone. Let your bosses or family members scream! Also available as a ring tone! You can send your own dialogue via email and the automatic voice will moan the lines. Design what you want to hear. After using our service, please evaluate it so that we know where we stand. Please press the 5, 4, 3, 2, and 1 for the following grades, respectively: poor, sufficient, good, excellent, and satisfying."

3. Long-Term Objective: The Headlessness of Autonomous Systems (as in religion)

I once wanted to ask my credit card company a yes or no question. I dialed the number on the back of the card. "Thank you for contacting us. In order for us to serve you better, we require first-time callers to go through an initiation procedure in which you will have to provide us with a great deal of information. Then you will receive a registration number and an extremely long password that you will never be able to remember. Using this information, you can subsequently repeatedly try to reach one of us." I hung up in disgust. I only wanted to ask if my children could also have a credit card.

You can enter the question on the Internet: that works! I've tried that, of course. But I have a credit card with no annual fee, and I wanted to find out if I could get more cards that don't cost anything.

However, the Lean Brain System is so clever that it won't let me in. Sigh ... I have given up trying to contact the telephone system.

Or: For reimbursement purposes, my travel receipts were en route to a small company that settles, scans and saves my travel expense invoices from several companies all over the world. The documents had gotten lost, which is terrible, because this is not one of the steps planned into the system. It happened to a colleague of mine in the office as well. He is more charming than I am and somehow managed to have the call center find his invoices again. So I called. "Hello, this is the call center. I am Ms. Morose. How can I help you?" – "I'd like to speak to Miss Diligent, please." – "There are no provisions to allow that." After ten more tries, I finally lied to her: "I'm an, ummm, executive at IBM and a client for this company without whom it would not survive. And I would like to speak to Miss Diligent, dammit!" – "I'm sorry, sir, it's not possible. Your own company determined the provisions." I gave up that time, too. All names have been randomly changed.

A bank employee who is an acquaintance of ours spoke with a good, lifelong customer who had phoned her directly at the bank. Our acquaintance then received a warning notice from the bank because the telephone system had determined that she had been directly contacted by phone from outside the bank. "That is not permitted. Outside calls are only allowed through the call center! That's the prescribed route!"

The accident with the direct phone call at the bank is the still tragic reality of amateur intelligences today. Modern Lean Brain systems on principle do not allow phone calls from outside. The telephone system doesn't even need to tattle because it prevents such phone calls from happening in the first place! Lean Brain people will certainly no longer be receiving any warning notices! So you can see how inefficiently moronorgs are still working today. A Lean Brain System must be absolutely foolproof.

Once it is foolproof, we will stand before the system, looming like a morolith. There it will be: anonymous; powerful. We can establish contact with it via a speech computer or call center employee, both of whom master their jobs. The Lean Brain System no longer has a face for us. It is nothing more than a system. We must operate it. In return, it charges hefty fees.

It has not only become faceless but also headless. We can continue being connected with an increasing number of non-responsibles in the telephone system, as long as we pay the 12 cents a minute. Just like the character K. in Kafka's *The Trial*, we bumble, lost, through the system. We cannot fathom it!

After three or four times of being connected to a different person, we give up. We are not used to having to go through so many levels of authority when we want something. An appeal level – now that would still be acceptable; but a complaint to the director – we hardly dare anymore. In the past, we did not give up the fight until we reached a semi-high power. Today, we are already frustrated by the time our call gets forwarded three times. There is just no use. Modern Lean Brain systems deliberately give people the impression that they have not advanced. Every phone call seems to end in that no man's land of being put "on hold." "Hello. Please describe the procedure again from the beginning so that I can determine whether or not I have to do something."

> Except for moronorgs, a very high degree of human intelligence is no longer needed in the Lean Brain System. It is irrelevant, because people can no longer fight their way to it. The telephone system and the computer rule. The system works autonomously.

A Lean Brain state needs no intelligent politicians.
   A Lean Brain company needs no intelligent managers.
   Yet we don't have to fret.
   What do you think of when you hear "Lean Brain church"?

> If there is a Lean Brain church, it does not need God. God is separated from the faithful by so many Lean Brain levels that it does not matter one bit if He exists or not.

Later on I would like to demonstrate that church, state and other institutions should not be quite so faceless. The Victoria's Secret catalogue always has a fresh look! We allow ourselves to be seduced by Claudia Schiffer, Heidi Klum or Giselle Bündchen, depending on which of them is not on parental leave at the time. We order from these graces personally – emotionally speaking! They are our ordering muses! Similarly, we love electing gifted actors to serve as heads of state and watching their Lean Brain election debates before voting. Such Lean Brain election debates are more exciting than the four years of politics that follow or precede it. Politics is so far away from the voters that it doesn't matter whether it exists or not. We should have elections all the time! Just like on American Idol! And where God no longer exists we believe faithfully in the Pope. After all, we can see him with our own eyes. Even we Protestants, who cannot stand our faceless situation.

> The face of a system is utilized to enable us to love a Lean Brain System so much that we are happy to serve it as customers. Lean Brain faces are either stars or logos.

4. Efficient Performance Management!

In an ideal situation, a Lean Brain System functions without any further intelligence. It flows. It follows its path unflinchingly, like a machine. The only possibility to increase performance, in addition to raising prices for the privilege of serving it, is tuning the machine and stepping on the gas. The machines are revved as fast as the morons in the system can go. They have to work faster or more uninterruptedly, that is, without breaks. It is great when they talk on the phone for 12 cents a minute for hours – without pause! The morons in the system have a high degree of utilization. It would be ideal to have the performance of all people constantly displayed in front of their faces on their computers. Technically speaking, the screen would look like a speedometer. It would show performance, efficiency (customer purchases per second) plus telephone charges as well as the previously compiled deductions from the maximum wage. This is not about measuring performance to provide appro-

priate compensation. It is about increasing performance to super-
human levels!

> The moron is the Uebermensch! Man, Nietzsche! Once again, too
> intelligent – and blind!

Workplaces of the future will look like airplane cockpits that control
the pilots and instruct them to work in a concentrated manner. In
call centers, the computer keeps the employees on their toes. "No
break! Call XYZ and ask him if he wishes to purchase the Allround
No-Worries Package and if not, something else!"

This technique of uninterrupted capacity utilization and speed
increase is operated by amateur intelligences today who adorn themselves with the title of Manager but cost far too much money and are
basically not qualified for anything. By and large, managers think
that they have to yell at employees to get them to work faster. When
goading them, they still imagine themselves commanding a galley.
The slaves doing the rowing as well as the floggers are paid according to the number of strokes made. An inhuman computer can do it
cheaper and better!

It is worth dedicating a separate chapter to properly explain this
phenomenon (actually, an entire book would be great).

5. Tetris and the Habit of Non-Thinking Activity

Are you familiar with Tetris?

We used to play Tetris on the computer. In addition to Pacman, it
was the gateway drug for young computer game addicts.

Imagine yourself in front of the computer screen. I'll describe the
game.

Now you can see rectangles or bars of varying sizes raining down
from the top of the screen. They keep raining down. While they fall,
we can turn them with the mouse or keyboard. We can move them
to the left or right while falling, such that we can determine *where*
they fall. And we can rotate them back and forth while they are fal-

ling as well, so that rods can fall horizontally or bore into the ground like an arrow.

The player's task is to control the falling blocks such that a complete wall is constructed at the bottom of the screen. Without any holes! So you have to move the parts such that no holes are created in the wall. Whenever an entire row is completed without holes, it disappears, and you get points for it. Life is really all about points. As long as there are holes in the wall, nothing disappears, allowing the wall to get higher and higher, building up until it reaches the top of the screen. When this happens, the screen blinks: "Game over."

The game has several speed levels regulating how fast the parts fall down. If you don't change the settings, your game starts at Level 1, which is boring and tedious. The elements dribble down at a horribly slow rate. Three-year olds can do it in their sleep. Block for boring block, a perfect wall is constructed. Only a fool wouldn't be able to manage it. Point for point is accumulated. It becomes annoying. After a certain amount of points is earned, the computer clicks and the second level begins. Now the blocks fall faster. Oops! You have to try harder! Pay attention! The stress increases! But after a while you have mastered this level as well. Three-year olds have to fidget more to complete the level. A short time later – plop – you've reached Level 3. It continues in this way, becoming faster and faster, and the blocks really look like rain. Now we can see who is up to the challenge. We need a good eye. We have to react quickly. We give up the relaxed posture and hunch over the controls with a grimace. Adrenaline! It is now vital to develop a strategy. We must know the best way to build a wall. Not by trial and error! At Level 5, we have to develop a feeling for how many of what sort of blocks will fall with what probability. We try to roughly predict the future. At Levels 6 and 7, we start to instinctively know before a new block appears what we would do in the event that the piece is of the shape A, B, C, D, or E, and so on. At Level 8, you have to be so good that you don't think at all anymore. The pieces stream down. The player is in a sort of trance. His work is flowing.

Level 9 is murder. No living human can master it so quickly. I've tried. I can't do it. So I assume it can't be done at all. They most likely only programmed Level 9 so that players can practice. If I play on Level 8 in a trance and I reach Level 9, I suddenly have to once again give some thought to where the pieces should fall. That ruins everything because thinking disturbs the work. Thinking is too slow. At Level 3 or 4, you have time to think about things, but when you have to work faster and faster, you most certainly should not be thinking. The work must flow! You must be in a trance! If you practice the game, you will notice that you can only reach a higher level if you did not need to think anymore on the previous level. So, if you can play Level 6 without thinking, you can try Level 7. If, however, you are plagued with thought in Level 6, you'll be crushed in Level 7. Game over!

Do you get it? Thinking disrupts work! Not to mention what intelligence can do to it. Work must become second nature to a person, in their blood. For instance, is it difficult to write a business letter? No. But admit it, first you chew on the pencil a bit, right? It's torture. When you have practiced it a hundred times, it flows without thinking. You have reached a higher level. It can be done faster and better! I can't stress this enough: faster *and* better. *And*! Most people believe they could work better if they took enough time for it. Stupid! Stupid! Stupid! You can work best when you can do it in your sleep, without thinking. If you *can't* do it in your sleep, you are unfortunately still completely incompetent. In that case, it would not be a bad idea for you to take your time and think about your work. Then you would not be working anymore, but rather in training. You are learning! A true master does not learn, he can do it. He does his job extremely fast *because* he can do it. In Tetris, you can get better and faster at the same time. In the lower levels, you don't have to have any skills, but in the higher levels it is important to have good strategies and probability forecasts in your blood. And it must be second nature to you, and not happen in your head! At the risk of repeating myself, your head is too slow! Most people are so incredibly stupid that they don't know that speed and excellence go hand in hand. They think that speed and bungling go hand in hand. Stupid! How many times do I have to say it?

Have you ever heard of an A-student needing the longest for his or her homework? Have you ever heard of a child science prodigy studying for ages?

I know what you are saying to yourself. I've heard it so many times because I earned my postdoctoral lecture qualification in only 8½ years. "Gunter, you are highly gifted!" That's all rubbish. I studied mathematics because nobody would have allowed me to become a writer. That is where my talent lies, I think. My best work in my life to date was writing the vampire novel *Ankhaba*, which is currently being published. I studied math to have an occupation. I only studied quickly! (That's exaggerated – I also loved math but not as much as writing.)

All you have to realize is that speed and excellence belong together. If you work so incredibly fast that it becomes second nature, you will develop ever new, ever-higher skills. Yet you will never – *never* – develop them if you rely on your brain and get lost in thought.

All game-playing on the computer must become second nature. Yes, even real soldiers fight better without a brain! All sports, all battles, all Lean Brain work must be in a person's blood. Then it will be done very swiftly and *error-free*.

Please don't do this: "Oh, that is required so rarely. Let me think. Where is that slip of paper? Wait a moment … I hope the slip isn't old and there aren't new rules in the meantime. You're asking quite a bit, you know …" Rather, do this: "Oh, that. Just a moment! Here! I have a list. There you go."

Lean Brain Management moronizes all work to the point where nobody needs to think anymore. It must become second nature. Speed is gradually increased, very slowly, so those new skills can establish themselves that must be present in the blood to master a higher level.

The amateur intelligences that call themselves managers normally yell at employees. They punish them for their slowness. They fuss. They "motivate", as they would call it.

Imagine that I am playing Tetris on Level 8 as if in my sleep. And now my boss comes in and yells at me: "Gunter! Do not screw it up again right after it switches to 9! Otherwise I'll punish you! Concentrate!"

You know, it is in such moments that I'd love to run amuck. It feels like a red rag to a bull. We feel blind hate toward the manager and never complete Level 9. Level 9 will never become second nature that way. It can only happen through practice, practice, practice. If I can do it all in my sleep, then let a manager stand by and fuss. I can handle that; after all, I'm in a trance. He can't wake me with his small mind. But don't let him yell when I haven't mastered something and am thinking!

Ms. Morose is good at it!

"Listen, Ms. Morose. I'm going to fire you if you don't get Miss Diligent on the phone immediately!" – "Mr. Dueck, there are no provisions to allow it." – "Is that going to be the last word of your career?" – "You are speaking to the call center. Individual persons are not phoned." – "Are you really that stupid? Or are you a speech computer?" – "Yes." – "A computer?" – "No, I was just joking. I guess I'm stupid. That's not so far off." – "Is your name Morose?" – "No, no, we just have aliases. I'm only logged in under Morose when IBM calls." – "I see. And who am I really speaking with?" – "With the call center. One for all, all for one. We are the team. The telephone system and the computer are everything."

6. Drill and Overlearning (No Drill – No Skill!)

My company, IBM, rented conference rooms in the Lufthansa Training Center for an exclusive customer event. That is the place where you can also practice jumping from burning airplanes and train in a flight simulator. Regrettably, a few customers had to cancel, which was bitter for us. This resulted in a few extra minutes that were booked in the flight simulator, which I was required to fearlessly use up myself. It was a gory spectacle in that Boeing 777, let me tell you. By the third try, the landing went fairly well. The first time, the sirens wailed, there was blinking everywhere and the cockpit gave me a warning. I completely lost my head and did not know where to look. The trainer behind me seemed completely confident that we would not perish and warned me to look at the runway and not at the sirens.

   On the third landing approach, I became bold and was satisfied; I was sure that I had most likely did no further damage than wearing down the tires and scraping the wings on the ground while the aircraft wobbled to and fro. Then the trainer set the simulator to a real thunderstorm complete with crosswinds – well, you can imagine. Now that was pretty loud! You don't even hear any sirens anymore. I became afraid and forgot that it was a simulator and … after crashing on the runway, my knees were shaking. "Okay, Trainer, I think there's not only good weather when flying, right?" – "Nice weather is easy. You don't have to practice for that. You only train for the event that something happens! Fog, hail, tornado, engine failure! Your body must always know exactly what to do." – "I understand. I can't lose my head." – "No! No! You have to be so damn good that you don't even need your head! Never! Your head has to be free for the rest. You have to be able to fly through a thunderstorm in your sleep. The flight attendant will come in and report that a passenger has just poisoned himself with duty-free alcohol and is now distributing what had been her lunch throughout the cabin. 'What should I do?' she asks. 'Give her a shot!' – The flight attendant looks incredulously. 'More alcohol?' – 'Valium.' So you see? The pilot has maintained his typical flight humor in the midst of all the pandemonium. It doesn't stress him out because he's practiced it a thousand times. Flying is in his blood, no longer in his head. His head is completely free! Completely free! And in your case, as an amateur intelligence, if you'll excuse the expression – what I mean is that you're a greenhorn – anyway, for you, flying is still entirely in your head. That's not enough to fly. Even a mathematics professor's brain can't fly – it's not enough." That made me feel very self-conscious. I looked down at my body and wondered if flying could find a place in there somewhere … I decided to drink two Red Bulls and switch off my brain.

Only after you can do everything routinely, in your sleep, will your head be free to learn even more. Once you can master Level 7 in such a frenzy that your brain is free again, you could try passing the time by thinking, on the side, and trying out how Level 8 will be. You are now cold-bloodedly routined in Level 7 and don't need your brain. You are wide awake again and can talk on the phone with other people while you're playing in Level 7. You've practiced Level 7 so much more than you needed to purely learn it that it is all in your blood. This continuous learning process is called "overlearning". In the army, they call it "drilling".

In peacetime, soldiers complain when they have to take apart a rifle and put it together again "in their sleep". The staff sergeant yells: "If I wake you up at two o'clock in the morning with a punch in the face, you have to still know all the parts of your rifle inside and out!" – "Yes, Sir, Sergeant!" But the soldiers don't believe it. When they practice in peacetime, it's like flying in nice weather. It is very easy. However, what about when it's raining grenades? Then we start trembling and no longer even know what a rifle looks like. "Shoot, dammit!" screams the sergeant, and we don't know in what direction to point the thing. In World War II, several tens of thousands of shots of ammunition were wasted per fallen soldier.

I was serving in the German Bundeswehr about the time when the Warsaw Pact marched into Prague. That's how long ago it was. We had to practice night marches. We padded around, lost, in the dark forest. No more trail to follow. We couldn't see our hands in front of our faces. It was deathly still. We were exhausted because we had to drag along machine guns with masses of ammunition belts housing blank cartridges. All at once, there was a rustling in the wood. We heard grunting sounds. There were surely more than a hundred dangerous wild boars that could certainly see us in the dark and were capable of attacking! But we could not see them! We were scared stiff, and one of the guys shot wildly about him with his machine gun for several minutes, emitting cries of fear. I was incredibly afraid myself, but after a few seconds of shooting, my future mathematician's humor came back. "Great – that'll get us hours of rifle-cleaning! Crap."

No drill – no skill!

In the Roman army, the people who where skilled were called veterans. They simply mowed the trembling newbies down, who would even have run away from wild boars.

In the modern working world, the term "veteran" has been lost. We speak about "experience", which is not the same thing but is on the right track. You know, people who lose their heads during everyday conflicts and negotiations demonstrate that they still need their heads in such standard situations. They are not capable of advancing to the next level. Psychologists claim to be able to teach them conflict resolution in two days. Ha! What a joke! They'll only forget what they've learned the next time they are yelled at! They have to be able to do it in a storm – that's the point! (No drill – no skill; that is something those enlightening psychologists just don't get.)

Lean Brain Management trains that tiny bit that Lean Brain employees need to know so unbelievably intensively that it becomes second nature. This frees up their brains. That little bit of skill must be performed quickly – ever more quickly.

This statement is the heart of the Lean Brain philosophy! Every small person is a Lean Brain wheel in the great Lean Brain System. They receive a small task; so small that any human can learn how to do it. However, this task is transferred from the brain to the body, such that Lean Brain humans can work like robots. They are world-class talents in their small domain. Without a brain! That is how an ingenious Lean Brain System collects world-class achievements and condenses it into one great system achievement.

7. Overlearning, not Overtraining!

Overlearning thus means practicing something until it "gels", only not in the head – in the body.

Lean Brain Managers train the body so that the brain can be freed. Yet dumb, traditional managers yell all over the place and prevent mastery from evolving. If employees only give it their all because they are afraid, they will become weary and stressed. That will be the end of all excellence. Intimidated employees will only achieve garbage, somewhat like this:

"I want to talk to Miss Diligent, Ms. Morose! I'm going to have you fired if you do not immediately do what I tell you!" – "Oh, heavens, what should I do? I'm damned if I do, and damned if I don't! I would like to satisfy your request, but the rules are as strict as you are! Oh, what should I do? They all take it out on me. I'm just a small component. I don't know what's going on. I'm going to go and ask the boss. ... Hello? I talked with my boss. He is now as angry with me as you are. He's sick and tired of my nagging questions. See, I'm supposed to tell all the customers that I'm the call center. But I also want to be nice in the process. I can't see any way out. Please hang up. I'm not authorized to end the telephone conversation because it earns us 12 cents a minute. I can't go on. You keep talking, at least it's earning us something."

In this way, Ms. Morose is using her intellect and her heart! She is concerned about the people and the whole! A Lean Brain person is not allowed to do that! That is why an intimidated Ms. Morose does not work well. She uses her brain and does not adhere to obligations. She is not moronized enough. She is worried and weighs alternatives that do not exist. Her boss then tells her this. He puts more and more pressure on her. He is the cursed amateur intelligence. Contradictions in the Lean Brain System are either sustained by the system or dissolved. It is not the task of simple employees to solve contradictions in the system. It stresses them out. It costs them time and mental energy that should be used for working, not ruminating. Lean Brain Quality is clear, fast, and can be done in one's sleep.

Classic insipid management thus does not lead to exceedingly safe negotiations but rather to overworking or overtraining, as they call it in sports.

Overtraining leads to fatigue, sleep disorders, burnout and damage to private relationships. Overtraining leaves behind the feeling of not having grown although so much was done (too much!). The entire package is called "Overtraining Syndrome." Athletes no longer excel, do not win, give up hope, and have aching muscles. Those who have hit rock bottom inform their coaches: "Infinitely empty." And the insipid manager will answer: "After exerting yourself so hard, fatigue is normal." – "But I feel so drained." – "Pull yourself together! Otherwise, I'll have to punish you! The press has to cheer! The next competition will be an even greater challenge for you!" – "I think I'm coming down with the flu." And the flu does come, indeed, because it has triumphed over the stupid manager.

Stereotypical, exceedingly safe behavior must be placed into the body, which works like a well-oiled machine. Lean Brain! No amateur intelligence that worries and weighs alternatives and is thus extremely expensive. People who need their head in extreme working speeds will collapse under the stress.

> The well-oiled body works faster than the brain can keep up. Lean Brain thus does not use it.

8. Effective, Practical and easily understood Advice for Managers

The most important management principle cannot be repeated often enough: Employees must perform the absolute little work they do extremely well. Employees must be utilized where they achieve a great deal. That sounds very simple. Sure, but just take a look around!

Things are organized in exactly the opposite manner. The work on hand is divided among the employees present! That is how amateur intelligent managers handle it!

These so-called executives do nothing to adapt work and employees so that they match. Lean Brain work for Lean Brain workers! Often, employees are overburdened or employed in the wrong area, and frequently "overqualified" individuals are used as assistants, who then become unhappy and lethargic. This is accompanied by the usual "bla, bla, bla" out of the management books and makes it considerably worse for those who have to listen to it. "Everyone has to chip in when there is work. Nobody shall shirk work. We have no patience for wussies. Nobody shall wriggle out of doing something. Even idiots should use their brains and at least seem beneficial ..." I'm sure you are familiar with this. This chatter is a sure sign that the work does not match the workers. It has thus not become second nature to them, and they contemplate their work dejectedly as they do it! That of course reduces their performance. ("Oh, when are they going to offer me partial retirement? What am I even doing here?")

Thus there are basically two main important points to remember:

> If you overburden employees, you burn them out.
> If you underburden employees, you make them apathetic.

These are trivial pieces of wisdom from scientific research on stress which has no doubt exploited the findings from Level 1 to 9 in Tetris.

Overstressing is similar to overtraining, discussed above, or overdoing, and leads to burnout. The brain identifies the state of the overexerted body as ill. The brain then makes sure that the body recovers again. It does not make any energy available that would maintain further stress. This makes the body tired. It needs to rest. Usually, the brain sends along a cold, headache, or a crick in the neck.

Understressing leads to agitation and fatigue. Feelings like the meaninglessness of existence flood body and soul. (Security guards keep watch in the dark night. Nothing ever happens. They are tired. Yet when they are no longer on watch, they can't sleep. – Polar bears in captivity pace back and forth in their cages, agitated in a senseless life. – So-called hyperactive children, who are burdened with under-stress in school, try to find something of interest: the birds outside, the person sitting next to them – they think about what pranks to play and they make noise.)

Unfortunately, managers do not give any thought to the work. After all, they do not need to work themselves and can only vaguely imag-ine it. Teachers consult the syllabus and start teaching. They do not know what learning is. The normal tactic in our society is constant overstressing. "Be the best! Otherwise you're nothing!" No one checks anymore to see if the people are even capable of the things they are expected to do. The completely overstressed burn out and are put in remedial schools or disposed into the realm of unem-ployment. All the while, the understressed are chewing on their nails and bothering everyone. If they bother the others too much (hyper-active), they are sent to even more remedial forms of work and school, where they are entirely underchallenged. "The drama of the gifted child."

Lean Brain organizes work such that it can be done by any person at all. It is just like the Tetris game. Anybody can complete Level 1, whereas not even I can get through Level 9. Lean Brain Managers allow their employees to play at the respectively highest level that the person can master in his sleep, without thinking. That is it. All of Lean Brain work is organized like a game of Tetris. Everyone plays at Level 9. Those who don't cut it receive an even more inane task because it is easier, one that they can complete at Level 9 in their sleep. Done.

- Reorganize all jobs such that any moron can master each smoothly and such that they can be performed as fast as desired once the morons have mastered them.
- Train your employees in the wisdom of overlearning so that they gradually become faster and can do more and more things in their sleep.
- With the exception of the higher training phases, let all employees always work at the highest level that requires no thinking of them.

In contrast, the systems today that are based on intelligence are bound to fail. If you leave school today with a high school diploma with honors, there is nothing you can do in your sleep – not spelling, not fractions, nor the rule of three. All you have done is had one good look at everything in an unnecessarily high degree of complexity, and then almost never practiced! And that is why you can't be on vacation in Mexico and know how to ask for a restroom in a hurry because your head needs to figure out what tense the verb takes. You can do nothing, nothing, I repeat nothing, in your sleep. Math, English, and foreign languages must become part of you! But instead, teachers all just drone on until our heads are stuffed. Lean Brain Managers will put a stop to that.

No drill – no skill!

Recently at IBM, we surveyed people as to what the difference was between training and education. Most IBM employees found the question odd and expressed the firm opinion that these terms are synonyms and thus mean the same. Isn't that terrifying? Only one IBM employee, who was Japanese, did not provide an answer, but rather sent us a counter question: "What is the difference between sexual education and sex training?"

Do you notice how you are capable of understanding this sentence with your body? Do you feel in your flesh and blood what I can only write here?

9. Take-Aways, Control Questions and Excercises

Think about where your company is top-heavy because the system is too inferior.

- Are the forms clearly understandable and can be filled out quickly without thinking?
- Do people keep racking their brains about how a job instruction was meant?
- Do you often faint because reality cannot be forced onto a form, such that you must painstakingly invent something fitting?
- Are there often special cases or cases of doubt?
- Do you often have to let the boss decide how something is to be done?
- Does your department argue with other departments about who is responsible?
- Do procedures lie untouched for long periods?
- Are suggestions for improvement implemented wisely?
- Does management value simplicity and clarity?
- Do you employ standards with which everyone is satisfied?
- Are you annoyed about quixotic rules from above?
- Are the core employees of the administration secret scientists because they can handle the business processes alone?
- Do you have several telephone conferences or meetings intended to agree on or determine how something is to be interpreted?
- Do you argue with others about the distribution of bonus payments and performance evaluations?

Search yourself. Imagine you are in an airplane, with your whole body.

"Boss, there's a yellow light on. What does that mean?" – "Oh, I've never had that before. Get out the manual. Where is it?" – "I have it at home. It got kind of mushy because I left it in my briefcase with a banana." – "The instructions should also be saved on the computer somewhere." – "We could call a meeting and the flight attendants could search the hard drive with me. We could apologize to the passengers and ask for their patience." – "Yes, let's do that." – "Ahem. Can you hear me? This is your captain speaking. There is a yellow light on in the cockpit, which has never been lit before. We still have to determine what it means. Since it has never come on before, it can't be too important. The aircraft we are in is fairly old and has really been through everything. We are going to call the ground crew. Hello? Houston, we have a problem."

Now imagine that you are at work.

"Boss, your star programmer had a broken computer." – "Get to the point." – "Right, Boss. The computer was repaired and checked for functionality, both for which we're being billed. But it didn't work, and we don't want to pay for it. That's the one thing. It was repaired again. They replaced the chips because the computer was really old, and now the operating system won't work anymore." – "Why don't we buy him a new one?" – "We have to save money, so we're not allowed to buy a new one, Boss. We have to repair the old computer to death. Anyway, everything has been repaired and they replaced the BIOS. Now the machine is dead for sure." – "So now you want a new one? I know the trick with the dead computer, but we have to save money so we're not buying any new computers." – "Boss, please let me finish. At the time, the computer was still just barely working. It was sent back in the mail but got lost. We made inquiries for three months and telephoned the transport insurance for another two months. Then we were very happy there for a moment. See, the insurance will pay for the computer. They told us to buy a new one and they'll reimburse us the following day." – "That sounds great!" – "Yes, Boss, it has been eight months now that the star programmer hasn't been able to work. Now everything's going to be fine. Unfortunately, we can't buy any computers because we have to save money. But we should buy one so that the insurance will re-imburse us the purchase price." – "True. We have to do that. We have to call together the entire company administration to find out how to do it while getting around having to order a new com-puter, which we're not allowed to do." – "I've already arranged that, Boss. The earliest date is already in eight weeks. We're call-ing a few top managers back from their vacation, that should be no problem." – Can't we just let the insurance company buy the computer, then send it in the mail?" – "Sorry, Boss, no can do. They've already had a big internal meeting about it. Besides, we don't know how to book the computer if we don't have an invoice and an order. We have to have another meeting to find out if we are even going to pay for the failed repairs, and we don't know how to charge off the old computer because it got lost in the mail. We've never had a case like this before." – "Write it off as having been stolen." – "Well, Boss, then that insurance wouldn't pay be-cause we have another policy for theft." – "Oh dear, I can see that this can't be solved with common sense. So we're going to need lots of meetings. That will cost the company a great deal of en-ergy. We'll have to economize even more. We have to put pres-sure on people to work harder!"

What percentage of your work time is spent with such amateur intel-ligence? Half? And what tasks do you execute practically automati-cally? What is second nature? How much of the work is so badly allo-cated that the entire system always has to give its approval if someone just wants to work?

Do you know what a bad manager would then do?

He would run to his assistant and have him or her prepare an as-sessment as to what the exact percentage is. After a year – he is on his second new assistant – the results are determined. "Fifty-three percent." – And the bad manager asks: "What does that result mean content-wise?" – "It's a good result, Boss. The average of the other departments is 56 percent." – "Oh, wonderful! Then you were better at fudging than the others, huh?" – "Um, don't forget your predecessor. What is he doing anyway? He suddenly disappeared." – "He had dizzy spells at the meetings. He's in the hospital. It fluctuates. They don't know if he's going to crack or not."

Take-away: Work must flow – and wisdom is required to know what the difference is between work and activity. "It is flowing." – Not: "I am working hard." – Not: "I am busy."

Lean Brain concentrates on inane, simple, clear work – without thinking.

VI. Suggestions for Concrete Transformations of the World

1. The Search for the Genuine that can be Faked

Now let's transform the world into a Lean Brain World to save lots of intelligence and emotion. Instead of genuine rum, we'll produce really cheap cut rum that can hardly be distinguished from the real thing. Oh, that reminds me, I was once very successful with the mathematical optimization of tobacco and coffee blends. The goal is to generate good taste without having to mix in too much of the more expensive varieties. Having to use expensive varieties is terrible! The blending process is a sort of faking. It must compose the flavors that are in great demand without having to use expensive types. That's the trick!

I was once in a chocolate factory on a similar mission and asked the manager if there were any considerations to observe, such as regulations similar to, say, the amount of genuine rum required by law to be in the blend. This was his answer – a one-hundred percent genuine quote: "If you can make chocolate from shit, that would be the best option and we'd have no problem with that." Well, I couldn't do that and considered that this proposed new raw material actually wouldn't be *that* cheap if it needed to be used in large amounts. I immediately reasoned that pork would then become cheap because profits in pig farming would focus more on what came out of the pigs. Or wouldn't they be slaughtered at all anymore? Then meat would become very expensive.

Another time, I was in a pet food factory in northern Germany, where we were discussing optimizing canned pet food. At the time, I had already heard the chocolate quote and wanted to make a good impression. So I was thinking out loud and rather naïvely said: "You could put practically anything in the cans, and the animals wouldn't notice. As long as the label assures customers that the contents are for selected, purely biological, organic animals." Of course, you know what I meant. They gaped at me and had to fight not to become impatient or even loud with me. They then went on for 15 minutes, speaking adoringly of pets and the lovingly created food blends with which their little darlings are nourished. After that, they didn't really want any more to do with me because they hated the Lean Brain philosophy with a passion and suspected it in me. Thus, I was very, very politely bidden farewell. And all the while, I just wanted to fake it for once, against my own better judgment, and was penalized for it! Perhaps mathematicians shouldn't attempt faking after all.

Both of those visits made a very strong emotional impression on me. The treasured and the cynical grow in entirely unexpected factories! Can we really still know where the genuine is and where there is only the cut version? I've heard of some surgeons who had submitted a small amount of no-name, brown soda pop containing caffeine to be passed off as a patient's urine specimen, which was then processed normally. This led them to conclude that the chemical consistencies were identical. Do you see? Sometimes the fake is "the real thing". However, I think that, in this case, the logic is fake, if not even the whole story.

Yet the Lean Brain vision of the future definitely only produces with a view to the result and does not undertake any emotional considerations such as I had done when I still lacked wisdom. Lean Brain Managers thus first put the entire system to the test and inspect exactly what genuine elements can be faked much more cheaply and where intelligence or effort can be replaced by, well – nothing, ideally.

We walk this world and ask: What in the church is genuinely from God? Can it be replaced by a fake? What is real in politics? How would it be with a fake? What is genuine in the façade of a woman? What would it be like with a silicon valley? How can we write a genuine scientific article that nobody can understand and thus that nobody will ever read, more inexpensively? Are there any Eastern European dumping scientists that can produce the incomprehensible in a cheaper fashion? If the effects of homeopathic medicines are only based on their placebo effect, do genuine, expensive herbs really have to be used for their production?

As you can see, we must now scrutinize the genuine from all sides and ponder whether we don't rather only need about five percent or less of it. So, let's look around: Where is it, the genuine?

Where in politics? It should be actively concerned with the good of the people and not with power fights and re-election. In professional sports? The best of the best should actually be competing for an athletic victory and not wage a hi-tech pharmaceutical war in the laboratory. In senior citizen care? It should enable people to spend their sunset years in dignity and not focus on efficient interim storage before the inheritance. Do you understand what I am trying to say? Take a deep breath and hold on:

> There is actually not much more that is genuine that needs to be faked. We simply recall the formerly genuine and – in a haze – maybe even believe in it. Because that which used to be genuine has completely degenerated. Lean Brain actually fakes the totally genuine – and not the kind that has degenerated into unrecognizability. By doing so, Lean Brain has the chance to make the fakes better than the meanwhile degenerated genuine. That is why Lean Brain cannot help but triumph.

Athletes still train, despite all the drugs! Why? They could concentrate on the new genuine, the show, just like in professional wrestling, where that tactic works well. In that field, the fake is the art. Politicians still stand up for issues and lose elections. What is that all about? Politics has degenerated into senseless debates on tax and contribution rates. Here, everyone tries to be an expert and is helpless in the process. So I ask you: What do we need to fake there? I mean, there is potential, but the greatest opportunities would lie in first returning to the real roots and faking what is worth trying. Perhaps we should begin by redefining the genuine and then producing it cheaply?

> Lean Brain fakes the truly genuine, not the current mishmash of degenerated, old genuine and new, helpless fake of the already corrupt.

2. Gigantic Savings Potential

Especially in places where people work with higher intelligence and where the salary level is relatively high, "nothing comes of it." I have repeatedly referred to this phenomenon in this book. In politics, the theoretical elite of our collective conscience battles for the well-being of our country, but so little comes of it that those that would be good politicians have turned their backs on politics. We as voters would like to see action, but we cannot find anyone who would take matters into his own hands. That person would be the one we would vote for. But the way things are now: Do we even go voting at all?

Science has made itself so independent from the goals of human collectivity ("theoretical basic research") that it has become irrelevant. With funding cuts and evaluations, governments are now painstakingly attempting to pull all of the hyper-intelligence out of the quagmire and at least use it for job training for young people.

The churches in Germany are dwindling down to nothing and still command the same church tax percentage rates as ever. God is no longer visible to the world because the only entities that count are those who appear on talk shows. One can only place all hope in popes and the like who are suitable for television; otherwise the church is through.

The politics of education is the source of horrifying evaluation results like the Pisa Studies comparing European schools. German students can recite the strangest things by heart but are helpless in real life. "Question: How much does a driver's license cost if you take ten hours of ..." – Oh, Daddy's paying for that!"

We all know that we are throwing money out the window with hands as large as goalie gloves. And get this: Go and accuse research, the schools or the army of failure! Scold them loudly for wasting so much money!

Then you will finally get a straight answer.

And that answer is: "We can't do anything good because we have no money!" The churches are groaning because they cannot pay for the places of worship and their pastors. Researchers complain about unacceptable working conditions and leave the country. Schools are sinking in agony. The army grumbles about sitting on outdated weapons arsenals, which, in an emergency, would amount to a death sentence. The Secret Service has communications equipment dating back to the Sixties and cannot utilize the Internet because it is not secure enough. It is clear: All of these intelligent systems are wasting endless piles of money, but when the cause is sought, they all point to a chronic lack of money.

("Annie, sweetheart, there's no more money in our bank account!" – "I had my hair dyed three times. I'm trying to change myself for the better!" – "But we have no money, Annie, sweetheart: I have to invest money because I work freelance!" – "That's a pity, Davie, honey." – "Sweetie, I need a computer in every room because I just invested in a wireless system.")

We could save money by using our cars and clothes longer, by living healthier or doing without air travel or our salaries. Yet that would be no fun and is not the point of this book. Lean Brain Management enters a realm of life where economizing does not hurt too much. Lean Brain examines the systems to see whether they are not overly intelligent and thus dissipate their own energies. Just the question as to whether they are necessary as a whole is very embarrassing for most systems – distressfully embarrassing. Do we need the church or the army or university courses in South African Studies? The Lean Brain movement will of course be the first to pose this initial, crucial question. Everything intelligent must be put to the test!

In any case, Lean Brain will cut costs to one-third; of that we can be sure!

3. Moronorgy as the Core of Lean Brain

Lean Brain thus begins with the fake of a true, as yet unadulterated genuine and seeks the best systematic procedure.

Now there is a problem: This function of constructing an intelligent system that can get by without the intelligence of morons is called moronorgy. Moronorgs form the very smallest level of human intelligence that constructs the system.

> Today, we have neither moronorgs nor a moronorgy, perhaps only moron orgies. We must establish an initial system of moronorgs who will lay the groundwork of the moronorgy and redesign the world.

The goal of a moronorgy is perhaps the clearest. Its purpose is to construct intelligent systems; for example:

- Nations that can be governed without intelligence.
- Churches that offer entertaining faith events.
- Profitable companies that are serviced by customers.
- Virtual instruction systems (currently called Education and Science).
- Satisfying media (pleasure, attention, distraction, ...).
- Etc. etc.

We will have to decide to entrust the most capable of the land with the construction of a moronorgy. Unfortunately, due to the current naïve and amateur intelligent politicians and managers, this is very uncertain. Politicians and managers see the exertion of power as the highest achievement. They view tasks such as those of moronorgs (generating foolproof recipes so that power is no longer necessary) as completely inferior. They generally entrust such tasks to forces and bureaus or sacked ex-politicians or managers that have long been laterally promoted. Everything that today already resembles a subsequent, noble moronorgy is currently seen as insipid work and distributed to so-called task forces as a charity. Perhaps you can see it according to this principle: The most capable among us currently wield power (ministers, line managers with profit/loss responsibility) or at least try to do so. However, if they are not successful, have no luck or flat-out fail, they then must work out the odds and ends. In other words, what they were not able to achieve in a practical situation, they are expected to theoretically design for all others to abide by. In the crepe example:

> Managers who can't take the heat in the kitchen should not be sentenced to generating recipes for the department.

Do we want eunuchs writing the Kama Sutra? That is precisely the typical criticism of the departments. The Lean Brain movement thus must never bow to such practices.

You see: The Lean Brain movement will cut out almost all intelligence in the country anyway and thus free it up for other tasks. At the beginning of Lean Brain, as long as there are still superfluous universities and schools, there will be a superordinate amount of stray intelligence in the world that will most likely need to be prevented from producing destructive nonsense.

For instance, as you know, aggression builds up in people if it is not let out to relieve tension. That is exactly how intelligence works. Intelligent people get all fidgety if they are confined to an inane environment. From time to time, they need a flash of genius to relax. They will hardly have a chance to experience this in the Lean Brain world because the Lean Brain movement fights the individual amateur intelligence situated in humans like an evil compulsion!

There will thus by a myriad of applicants for the few moronorg positions available. They can therefore be very carefully selected for their task of providing humankind with all Lean Brain instructions. After all, the moronorgs will recreate the world as a Lean Brain World. That is the greatest responsibility that humans have ever had in their history.

4. Walking the World with a Lean Brain Eye

Would you come with me now? I'll take you by the hand. True, it will be somewhat hair-raising as I pare the world down to its essentials, effectively reducing it to a third of its size, with completely audacious proposals. The fact is, we can save quite a bit if we could just overcome all of that intelligence and its related vanity.

I am going to get extremely radical, and a great deal of what I will now suggest will not be easy to implement. I am aware of that. Because the intelligence and above all the vanity of an anachronistic set of ethics will not surrender so readily. In addition, many Lean Brain cuts can only be implemented if the whole world participates. I know. You're wondering: Where do I get off intending to turn not only the world, but also your stomach, in ten short pages? I think: It won't work on an intellectual level, but it might on a Lean Brain level. At any rate, everything will subsequently have to be hammered out much more thoroughly by the moronorgs. I am only trying here to enchant you with the splendor of the Lean Brain concept.

To approach the various systems correctly using Lean Brain, we must ask the following questions:

- What is the purpose of the system desired by normal people?
- Is the purpose still current?
- Does the purpose require something that we cannot or will not contribute?
- What purpose does the system actually have today?
- Is the system in decline? Does it resort to survival tactics in stressful situations?
- How do we experience the system emotionally?
- What would a sufficient, conscious Lean Brain fake be like?
- How could an emotionally valuable Lean Brain System be built?

As I've already mentioned, we are roaming through the world of systems. We will take a look at the nation, religion, science and the media.

I am not going the route of a systematic saunter but rather a series of stations that can better be explained in this book.

5. Lean Brain Army

Let me begin with the German army. Let us simply refer to the above
set of questions – as intractably as a Lean Brain process or a food
recipe.

What is the purpose? – In the current peacetime, people do not exactly know what purpose the army serves. World police? Well, okay,
but not to guard American construction sites put up without consulting us first. Theoretically, the army should protect the country
from enemies and ensure its independence. If the country is in danger, it should be able to defend itself.

Is the purpose still current? – Heck no! Wars are economic suicide,
even for the so-called winners. A Western country cannot start a war
without a stock market crash and high indebtedness, no matter how
it ends. Western countries can hardly be attacked because the at-
tackers are laden with embargos. Several countries live on tourism. If
a European or an American is killed in such a country, the tourists
will stay away! Therefore, in Arab countries, the national army thus
protects their alleged enemies rather than waging war. In Germany,
the so-called threat has disappeared. In the Fifties, Germany decided
with a heavy heart to establish the Bundeswehr because it saw itself
as threatened. These grounds have evaporated. So what now? Do you
think the purpose is still current? A new purpose has been created:
Germany must contribute to the process of enforcing peace the
world over. What are the tanks for? Looking at the arsenal of our
army, you would think "the Russians are coming." And in fact the
Russians really are coming but now more to spend time in casinos
and luxury hotels than they did in Dostoevsky's day (if you read *The
Gambler*, you'll find it takes place in good old Germany).

Does the purpose require something too difficult of us? Heck yes!
Theoretically, we have to fight and put our lives on the line as soldiers! Nowadays, that is completely inconceivable; that is how cowardly we are. Most people lie or fake it when they talk about it. They
say they are Christians and do not wish to cause anyone harm. In
reality, war means being shot in the belly or having someone hold a
flamethrower in your face, which an English soldier once did to my
father. "The smell of roast," he would say often. "The smell of roast!"

And you could smell it whenever you imagined his face freshly burned. Since, meanwhile, more than 3,500 American soldiers have been killed in the Iraq War, the recruiting of soldiers has stagnated. Strutting around in a battle dress uniform? – Sure! Impressing the girls? – Great! But being flown home with half your body blown away? No way! Ever since war has become economic insanity, ever since there are no more winners and no triumph arches being built – ever since then, the demand to die for insanity is too difficult.

Is the system in decline? Does it resort to last-resort fakes? Troop sizes are sinking. A political administration that cannot balance the budget can hardly afford to spend money on new weapons systems because these systems are no longer necessary. Thus, everything is rotting away. In Germany, recruits only serve for nine months, and in that time, nobody learns how to fight anymore – even a spare tire around a rookie's waist will survive the nine months intact. Recruits barely have time to polish the museum weapons and do some sports. It is ludicrous to think of putting some black soot on their faces, sticking a few leaves on their helmets as camouflage and sending them off to die! They are not trained for it! That was already the case in 1970, when I was in the service. We handled equipment and shuddered at the thought that the others – over there – truly yearned to kill and die. We certainly didn't. And we knew that everyone who yearned to kill could send our whole army packing. Thus, our army is not capable of fulfilling its purpose. This is unacceptable, because it is costing far too much. That is why the army is now protecting Afghanistan. Of the more than 200,000 soldiers, almost 5,000 are keeping peace. Now the government is pretending that this is a good reason to engage 195,000 more soldiers. However, those 5,000 would not fight, just run around with weapons so that they are not shot dead themselves ... That is how the Bundeswehr justifies its existence with just a few people appearing to serve a purpose. Now 500 have been sent to the Congo. Man alive!

How do we experience the system emotionally? The army has been spurned for years and will soon be ignored, in a way. In Germany, we don't have the feeling that it is protecting us. We don't perceive ourselves as needing such protection. It is there because all countries have one, so that they can make their contribution. In wars, Germany generally pays other countries to fight and die for us. Germany thus does not even use its army when it must fight. We feel nothing anymore.

A possible Lean Brain fake? We could scrap the army, put the money used for it in the bank and, in times of war, pay mercenary soldiers to fight. They would be rented to fight! That would never amount to the 25 billion euros per year that the Bundeswehr costs! I remember that, during the Iraq War in 1991, Germany paid about 10 billion euros to the USA. Even if we had to pay as much every year as we did in that horrible year of war, we would still have 15 billion euros for 15 years left, and with interest, we would have amassed a good 200 billion euros. Companies act in a similar way, where that money is called the "war chest."

Thus we establish large mercenary armies on a global scale, consisting of unemployed individuals or low-wage countries and let them fight against each other. Those who pay more can afford more mercenaries. This system proved successful in the Thirty Years' War. Basically, the country that puts in the most money and can pay a charismatic leader wins the war. Logically speaking, this reduces the entire process of waging war to something like a poker game, which also revolves around skillful play and money.

The Lean Brain question is: Why don't we just forget war and play instead?

Why bother with all the bombarding and rebuilding? In the past, poisoning wells and chopping down olive trees were taboo because reforestation would have been unfairly much more of a hardship than breeding new young men. Today, blowing up nuclear power plants, spreading the bird flu or destroying Pizza Huts are frowned upon. Every age has its wise taboos, doesn't it? Lean Brain makes a taboo out of war altogether and transfers the conflict to the financial stage!

How could an emotionally valuable Lean Brain System be built? We let war take place in the form of a game that is emotionally stirring. The focus is on large sums of money (the only thing that can still stir some people today), such that the same results are achieved as when playing with mercenaries, only it is much more captivating. Basically it does not matter what rules are used to wage war, just as long as it is all about money and leaves behind a feeling of triumph for the victors.

Thus I suggest: We replace war with death matches in computer team contests. The best computer aces of a nation will fight it out. All virtual wars will air on television. Then, war will pretty much be waged non-stop, and the inhabitants of a country can hang on the edge of their seats, following it all daily on pay TV. The country that can assemble the best virtual death match players will always win the war. The fundamental principle that the money wins is thus preserved. In addition, war will then be fun, and everyone can get something out of it. Death will become grand again! (Just as it was in the Middle Ages with the much revered heroic death).

As the basis for computer game, I'd like to initially suggest the well-known, tried and true Unreal Tournament. It just has the perfect name for the war of the future. In that game, players fight virtual battles in various "maps," to keep it interesting. We can select alpine or desert maps, and dress our players in national jerseys with patriotic colors, which will also be the hues of the blood that is shed.

The stars will then earn incredible piles of money because they hold the fate of the well-being and suffering of the country in their hands. If a player is invincible, he can conquer the entire world. That adds extra pep to my Lean Brain recommendation. Then there will at least be some action again.

The best computer players are the heroes of the future, since they will be deciding the wars. Now, playing on the computer, once scorned, will finally receive a decisive purpose, giving the lives of a large class of the population meaning, which is also acknowledged by non-players. A left mouse click instead of the trigger finger on the Colt! I am completely convinced of this recommendation and will immediately begin practicing.

6. Lean Brain Science

What is the true purpose of the system? The sciences protect and expand the knowledge of the world. Science, be fruitful and multiply! The universities educate upcoming scientists – even those pursuing a career outside of research. They advise non-scientists in order to make fruitful use of science.

Is the genuine still present? Does it make hard, intense, unreachable demands? Several functions of science have become obsolete. In just a few years, all expertise will be freely available for every human on the Internet at Google. All books, publications, the content of the Library of Congress. (At the moment, copyright intelligences are whining about how to achieve this. The answer: Google will someday charge a ten-dollar flat rate per month – that'll do it.) Google will then be the keeper of knowledge. Especially in the humanities and economics, an incredible amount of time and energy will be spent finding and researching text sources. Scientists are working together with librarians and archivists in exceptionally painstaking efforts that Google will soon (and, to an extent, already does) execute for us almost automatically and for free. One example: My father's hobby was geneology. Our entire house was full of lists of ancestors and charts. I would always tell him: "Papa, you just have to go on the Internet and enter somebody's mother and father. Then the computer will fill in that person's family tree, and you're done. You can then print out the family tree any way you like." My father did not want a computer and, up to his death, continued rummaging around undisturbed in archives. And yet it's true: You really need only inform the computer of any person's father and mother! In this sense, geneology is nothing more than idiotic typing of data for morons. Someone phones up a call center: "Hello, a new person with a father and mother." On the Internet, the entire world is being displayed right now on Google Earth (I had specifically requested this in my book *Wild Duck* in the year 2000 and unfortunately was not able to convince IBM to take on the task). The history of the world, the constellations, everything is being put on the Internet in one huge structure. That's it. That doesn't leave much more for the universities to do.

True, there is still research going on. But the population is getting more and more agitated because scientific results consist almost exclusively of buffing up the old stuff. (That is what Thomas Kuhn called "puzzle-solving"). The population wants breakthroughs and Great and Important Things! Whoa … that really is too much to ask of scientists.

Just think for a moment. Who, I ask you, invented the loom, dynamite, the gasoline engine, the car, assembly line production, the lightbulb, the telephone, Morse code, the Internet, the computer, the airplane, ships, gold mining, cotton undershirts, instant noodles, Darwinism, wall plugs, SAP or the theory of relativity? Were the technological revolutions of our time primarily created at the universities by "scientists"? Huh? No way! It was the "entrepreneurs" and the geniuses.

What purpose does the system actually have today? Ask a scientific researcher at a university what he or she is busy doing these days. They record the smallest of results to publish so that they can be promoted or at least stay employed. If, for instance, there were no use for promotions or doctoral degrees (such as in a Lean Brain world), you wouldn't need such pseudo science! In addition to solving puzzles for the doctor/professor, researchers are additionally saddled by the state with the task of educating students as well as with executing the university's own administrative tasks. The college curriculum is anachronistically old and could easily have been uploaded onto Google by now and adorned with an attractive layout. ("At this great college, the curriculum is always up to date, at least for post-doctoral candidates.") Research is only allowed to be started in an endless bureaucratic process of self-justification. Money is not freed up for it until after eternal procedures designed to separate the unimportant from the thoroughly unimportant. Typical research proposals sound something like this: "In the first three months of the project, I will attempt to finally understand the problem for whose research and solution I have hereby submitted this detailed application. After another 57 days of introductory work, I plan to have a great idea between Day 58 and Day 60, followed by the implementation phase on Day 61. I have taken out a complete cancellation insurance policy for Days 58 to 60." Soberly speaking, universities today are nothing more than inferior vocational schools. As they themselves claim, they cover a diffuse academic demand, but no one knows what that demand is. "Study whatever interests you, Son. In the light of all of this uncertainty, there is nothing more you can do. There is hardly a course of study left that offers the prospect of employment." (Universities are already feeling the Lean Brain revolution.)

Is the system in decline? Does it resort to last-resort fakes? Many scientists today already work in such special niches that they suggest five years of study before one even gets to a respective miniature specialty field of research! The specialized literature is hardly even read. Most are only cited once or twice, if ever. And yet, considering the time spent at university, they cost perhaps 100,000 euros each. Is this miniature expertise really worth it? Four years of work and wages for one desk drawer dissertation? The whole field of research will soon bend under this destructively simple criticism. That is why they have invented third-party financing. For this, universities campaign for money from the outside, such as from industry. If industry spends money on university research, then the research must be of use to the industry, otherwise industry would not be so stupid as to spend its money. So the universities fib in this manner: If they receive money for something, that something must be useful and thus valuable. (It makes absolutely no difference what that something is! If there is money for it, it's valuable, they say. Of course this is not true, and neither is the opposite! That is the problem!) In reality, many university employees hire themselves out as cheap labor or programming drones in industry and work their tails off. Industry pays the university fairly well for it, thus confirming the usefulness of the work as research service. The university, in turn, gives the researcher a modest assistant's salary and, at some point, an academic degree. In this way, the researchers can stay at the university and conduct real research a bit in the evenings or on weekends. When seen as a whole, traditional puzzle research protects itself with the fake of self-earned money, allegedly given out for the research. The written work is read and cited even more rarely.

How do we experience the system emotionally? Well, as basically useless, smart-alecky, and hair-splittingly specialized. "The absentminded professor," overqualified for life in general. A good half of all students in Germany give up their studies during the first year, change their majors a couple of times, and take an average of seven to eight years instead of the necessary four-and-a-half to five. They are tremendously disappointed by their dry activity, find no satisfactory approach or interest, and try to earn a degree simply because it seems necessary to get a job. Industry is finding it increasingly less necessary and is banking on students who rapidly complete their studies at technical or vocational colleges.

What would a sufficient, conscious Lean Brain fake be like? Google for the benefit of science. While on the Internet at Wikipedia not everything is accurate, it is nevertheless well explained. At a university library, everything is difficult to find and just as hard to understand! The library has become obsolete. (My wife is a certified librarian at the Max Planck Institute for Astronomy in Heidelberg; we discuss the matter in detail.) I myself have a fairly large number of reference books and a few fat textbooks, most of which are located on my laptop hard drive, which is sufficient. New science is primarily seen as a development or advancement of already existing ideas – right up to product development. ("This project will generate operable computer code for which we see a market.") Whatever that is, science or not, it should not be one of the responsibilities of the state.

The state should close the universities down altogether, organize vocational training differently and separately and instead establish large institutions completely dedicated to the moronorgy, the training of moronorgs and system construction.

How do I surgically remove an appendix in a foolproof way? How do I manage an Internet company? How do I write a movie script? How do I win court cases in a foolproof manner? Which 10 successful steps can I force neurotics to take? How do I learn everything they teach in school in just 30 days? How can I use simple exercises to make my work as a moron bearable?

For every realm of life, moronorgy universities work out the basic recipes, which the system moronorgs can adapt somewhat on site. ("Can we afford to always make the crepes with orange blossom water?")

Lean Brain universities should be made useful for the moronization of the population. They will then enable people to get by without having their own intelligence. This would give today's universities a new mission that is worthy of them.

How could an emotionally valuable Lean Brain System be constructed? Google with emotion! The Internet today is much too businesslike. It should organize and electrify events. Emotional science is like Einstein's tongue: We should show off geniuses in public, discuss their private lives and celebrate them without end. "Mirror neurons prove that nice people are allowed to exist!" – "Black holes can swallow us whole without chewing!" Geniuses have nothing to do because they first need to have an ingenious idea for people to know that they are geniuses. Yet they almost always have only that one idea! This means that, precisely from that point on in which we can recognize their genius, they are no longer ingenious. They can thus be immediately channeled to a media system that spurs on the adoration of morons for knowledge and strengthens their trust in the system. They hold petulant lectures, appear on quiz shows and engage in discussions on talk shows. "How I suddenly understood the nature of gases while bathing. First it was just a vague bubbling, but I immediately smelled an idea. Then came the Big Bang of my life!"

7. Lean Brain Education

What is the purpose of the system desired by normal people? Normal people expect life competency skills from school. The old, true purpose of the education system is education. This purpose has now become foreign to us. "The educated person knows about the most precious elements of a cultural group and has brought them into a personally accessible form." That sounds noble, doesn't it? True education goes hand in hand with a talent for fine differentiation to be able to tell the precious from the trivial. It forms personality. The educated individual enjoys the precious and ethical and basically only these. (What, may I ask, do you watch on television?)

Is the purpose still current? School hardly serves education anymore and doesn't really care about a young person's life competency.

"Learners know the life cycle of the mayfly, but they cannot do math or write. They know a great deal more than twenty years ago, but they are filled with unimportant garbage." That is approximately what a prominent appointee recently said on the matter. He literally said: "Their hard drives are full of garbage." I didn't want to write that myself in that formulation because then you would have resented me, the mathematician. But a tradesman would be allowed to say it. That sounds convincing, doesn't it?

Does the purpose require something that we cannot or will not contribute? The poor schoolchildren creep along. They most likely theoretically know that, in school, they should be forming their personalities and learning life competency – but this purpose does not seem too worthwhile to them either. Imagine a student saying: "I want to be educated." Or "I want to form my personality." People would make fun of him and think he were strange. The older pupils read that there are no jobs and that math, writing, English and personality are important. "Johannes, this is not about learning vocabulary. In real life, you have to speak normal English and be able to express yourself well. You especially need to have something to say." – "Dad, tomorrow I'm going to have a quiz on exactly these one hundred vocabulary words. That's all. That is what matters. When I graduate, nobody is going to know whether or not I can speak English really well. I only have to always know what is being required on the morning that it is required." Through such discussions heard at my home, you can see that the normal purpose of education is no longer considered or not even known. Students want to get to the next level and earn points, nothing more. They are already orienting themselves toward the new Lean Brain World.

> "In every moment of your life, you always have to know the next instruction of the system – and nothing more."

In this sense, there is no purpose for the individual. The purpose comes later in the Lean Brain System – just as the purpose is in the anthill and not the ant itself, who is just acting according to simple rules.

What purpose does the system actually have today? The current education system is cluttered with garbage. It relies on old teaching methods that communicate certain subject matter for which kids cram. This subject matter is written in the sacred curriculum and for purposes of better stuffing the student, is divided into modules that can be infiltrated using a modular system. Students change schools or states, they move to a different residence within the EU or change elective, gut courses on a whim. That is why education cannot be allowed to build on itself. If that were the case, that it would progress from the simple to the difficult, then there could be no movement back and forth! That is why knowledge is funneled into students' heads in brick-sized portions, whereby difficulty is to be avoided whenever possible. Statewide, uniform tests are designed to verify whether all of the modules are in students' brains and correctly stored. The lobbyists at the universities fight with the school superintendants to regulate the knowledge portion sizes. "Everyone has to do three additional brain units in Economics!" – "No, in First Aid! That's more important!" – "No, in Personality Theory!" – The schools scream back: "What are we supposed to cut back for that?" Then all are at their wit's end and ultimately caught up in endless discussions about the "purpose of education." In reality, much of the subject matter is tailored such that, right after secondary school graduation, one can start studying physics right away – have you noticed? In college-preparatory school math, kids don't learn the theory of probability, statistics, the evaluation of numbers, tables and elementary business relationships but rather differential and integral calculus! You only need those to study physics but then never again in your life. The purpose of education – as if! It is a forgotten lobby.

Is the system in decline? Does it resort to survival strategies in stressful situations? The educational system in Germany is now continually bombarded by Pisa Study crises. Germany is relieved to be at least average. The politicians say: "In Germany, wages are much higher than anywhere else in the world because we are simply more productive and better. Education in Germany is unrivaled." Perhaps it once was! We claim to be the best and are happy to be average in the Pisa Studies while at the same time earning high wages! (That's ingenious, isn't it?) Of course, that is pride, or even blindness before the very deep fall. Nevertheless, actionism rules. The examinations of the brick system must be more difficult, and more – yes *more* – students must pass them! Naturally the supervisory school authorities are happy that the system is so bad because they can then requiest more money for teachers. That's the way such authorities work. But at home, it's more like this: "Son, I am appalled at your report card!" – "But Dad, there is not much I can do with the little allowance I get. Increase it and I'll see what I can do and what I can't. Please don't be too miserly. You have to be generous. Because I'm really bad." More teachers! Smaller classes! More stress for the students! Harder tests! Oh, right, with all the stress, you forget that, in the end, pupils need only know writing and arithmetic, speaking and taking action. The high school diploma, known as the "Matura." A certificate of "maturity." Personality. Life competency. All of that is forgotten in the stress. They cry: "When there is enough money, everything will work itself out."

How do we experience the system emotionally? There are as many positions as there are people. Pupils searching for education will do extra reading to attain it and tolerate school as a necessity. Others execute instruction for instruction and leave the school "cluttered" with garbage and apathetic enough for the life of a moron. The energetic ones that wished school were interesting either curse or flee. "Johannes, don't you want to become a teacher?" – "Oh Dad, school is so boring, but if I were a teacher … do you know, the job itself is not so bad, but socially speaking, you're completely disregarded. I don't like that. I think I could be an elementary school teacher. They are loved." That reminds me, I think we need centralized testing in order to be accepted into a college-preparatory high school so that it, too, will end up being a gloomy place. Many studies confirm the normal impression in life that children happily skip off to their first day of school. Yet after three years, this spirit ebbs from them – more and more.

What would a sufficient, conscious Lean Brain fake be like? The Lean Brain school not only fakes the essentials, but rather, right from the first day, it only teaches children to be future morons. Lean Brain does not need education, only the skills of a moron: following recipes quickly and without thinking.

The Lean Brain school practices operating computers, cell phones, DVD recorders and digital cameras. Within minutes, students learn to find just enough information at Google for any topic in the world to be able to talk about it for ten minutes and sound like experts in the process. Today, that is the most extreme amount of intelligence that would be virtually expected of morons. Nowadays, for instance, sales clerks google a bit before conducting a sales consultation, or when a customer asks a normal question. Managers google before meetings, unless they are executives, in which case they have everyone in the outer office do the googling and are then subsequently briefed. After the sales consultation or meeting, the googlers forget everything again, so that their brains can prepare for the next meeting.

The brain is always old! The young brain is filled up once and then lives with those modules of knowledge. However, when googling, the information is always current. That is why it must immediately be forgotten again after use. The statement that "you always have to learn anew" is not accurate. It's not about continually updating the hard drive in your head. It's that we should not even be using it at all! Lean Brain is the virtuosic handling of short-term memory or, to use a computer metaphor, your RAM.

School and university education as a whole fill up the hard drive of the brain with knowledge, as if Google and the Internet didn't even exist. Knowledge is on the Net or in the system! It is not needed in the brain. That is why I say it is cluttered with garbage. We no longer do math in our heads; we use a calculator. Similarly, we know everything from the Internet and no longer from our heads. In math, we are to learn how to get results from a calculator. In language, we learn how to extract knowledge from the Net and babble on proficiently like an ueber-expert.

The highest aspired intelligence level of school could be roughly equivalent to the requirements needed to be interviewed by Catie Curric or Oprah.

On the whole, state-funded school as well as the universities should be eliminated in their form with their outdated missions. Today, the state has already begun conducting nationwide testing as it has been done for ages to acquire a driver's license. A German driver's license can only be had via these national testing organizations in combination with private driving schools. Please keep in mind that the school system is outdated, not properly developed, and deeply discourages young people. On the other hand, driving schools must hammer tediously uninteresting and useless knowledge into the heads of these young people. ("How long must a giraffe be dead before it can stick out of the trunk of a motor vehicle? How is the rigor mortis test performed? How far may the giraffe extend out of the trunk? How large must the exterior rear view mirror be? Why are the warning flags for dead giraffes in transport not allowed to be yellow?") And yet the private auto schools still manage to have even the least intelligent of its students pass the written test, whether they can read or not. These results are crushing in comparison to the performance of the schools. It shows that the individual learns everything immediately if he or she can understand the sense of the material relatively well and can pay for it all.

Now let's imagine that everyone would suddenly recognize the sense of a college-preparatory high school diploma so completely that they would pay for private lessons. It is impossible to imagine what a flood of intelligence there would be in Germany!

What do the morons of the future need to learn? As a rough guideline, I would say: They have to be able to do the things that a normal computer requests of them step by step. These are the occupations of the future. The system takes care of almost everything itself. Most of these occupations will disappear altogether if people can be made to feel emotional satisfaction from automatic apologies generated by computers.

Lean Brain is the opposite of the education system – I'm sure you realized that from the start. Here is where the large-scale savings can be had. Morons in a Lean Brain System save a few years of schooling, a year of military service and a few years of college study. They do not cost much, no more than today's trainees. If, for example, we would provide excellent medical care to morons in accordance with today's standards, then the medical treatments alone would cost more than one moron is worth. Today, medical insurance costs about 15 % of the average income. In the case of morons, this could quickly become 60 % or even more than 100 %. We can see that we can only implement Lean Brain in society as a whole, and not isolated in a single area, such as in education. Everything must be faked cheaply – not only the humans themselves but also their entire periphery.

Allow me to summarize what expert knowledge people must acquire:

- Googling, googling, and more googling.
- Downloading.
- Obtaining PowerPoint transparencies on all topics from the Internet and talking about the subject fervently for ten minutes.
- Sitting at computers and executing the instructions provided.
- Being capable of serving companies as a customer, that is, filling out questionnaires even if they are incomprehensible, which is the general rule.
- Understanding and complaining about invoices.

In addition, it is advantageous if the moron demonstrates a personality:

- Morons must convey competence and charisma via all media (email, text messaging, calls, video telephones, face to face, stage). Otherwise they can only be employed as back-office morons.
- Morons must be able to authentically fake any request. (An observer must be able to greatly appreciate that you are professionally faking, whereby it is always clear that you are indeed faking. I see role models today in the cast members at Disney World who play the great white shark every five minutes for a new boatload of spectators.)
- Work process steps are to be executed without any fluctuations in disposition, without questioning the meaning or wishing to understand it. Morons are to be even-tempered and empty inside. Under no circumstances may the mind disturb the work. At no time is the customer to be bothered by the employee's brain.

8. Lean Brain Spirit Service – Bless for Less!

The savings in religion are not only related to intelligence but also and primarily to faith. If faith is cut out, religion becomes superfluous. Many people have already undertaken this step. Nevertheless, there are still churches; that we cannot deny. It can't be due to the faithful, who are most likely a very small minority. The cause is a hearty, solid pillar of citizens who do not actually believe in God anymore but still pay taxes to the church because it is standard practice.

This section has been written for exactly those taxpayers who do not believe. They probably would like to see their taxes as being utilized in order to make things Lean Brain efficient.

What is the purpose of the system desired by normal, non-believing people? Oh boy, that is hard to say and not even possible to answer in a politically correct manner. But here goes:

The normal fake-faithful Christian wants a service from the church: Christmas worship services, weddings and funerals, in addition to communions and confirmations. Thus, the point is to provide people with an emotionally valid framework for the important events in their lives. Especially in the case of funerals, the deceased desire personal treatment. They want to hear something nice about them; a fake among the emotional tears is allowed.

> When giving eulogies, a fake of any quality is usually better than the real thing.
> This is also true for government policy statements.

Normal non-believing churchgoers primarily enjoy the introspective, quiet, fulfilling community experience that is pleasant for everyone. They really like it when the church is full and when they can get together, when they open their hearts after church in the grateful October sun. Some people (including non-believers) secretly wish they could experience, live or witness true faith in church. True faith, however, has most likely retreated to the monasteries for good.

Is the purpose still current? The churches in Germany are empty. Faith is, to a greater extent, situated in the few believers, not in the empty churches, which are mainly only viewed and serve as lively, noisy tourist attractions. A few scattered believers do not comprise a festival of faith. The church only "functions" at Christmas nowadays, and even so, on the last Christmas Eve, it was half empty. The pastor couldn't even speak German. There is a lack of pastors in Germany. He read a canned sermon from a fat book and harshly accused us of having come today of all days (and not on any other). There was no vibrancy wafting down from the pulpit. The holy element was absent. We were hardly in the mood to leave a donation. We left the church like we were turning our backs on a lost homeland. I was sad. Where can I find anything genuine?

Does the purpose require something that we cannot or will not contribute? Christ wants us to accompany him into heaven and prepare ourselves for this journey. We are not doing that. Much to my alarm, most of the people who claim they believe are not doing it either. I assume the consensus is: We should at least want to be good people and try to do so every day. We aren't even doing that consciously anymore. Life is all about being successful. Whoever is successful is good! "He's *really* good!" – "She's *really* good!" Plain old "good" is no longer even the object of attention.

What purpose does the system actually have today? It is shrinking in agony. You can tell by the current retirement discussion that there will soon be many old Christians. When they are gone – in just a couple of decades – the church will shrink dramatically right along with them. So, what indeed is the purpose of the system today? Is the system redefining it? Unfortunately, it is attached to the old, official purpose that hardly has anything to do with the humans of today. We now admit with much pageantry that Galileo was right. We ultimately accept Darwin, we discuss celibacy, although it evidently doesn't really exist anymore or perhaps never did and will certainly be officially abolished in about 200 years. These are discussions about retreat – hundreds of years after the alteration of actual reality. Positions are only being changed after being ignored or generally condemned for centuries (abortion, birth control, women of the cloth).

Is the system in decline? Does it resort to survival strategies in stressful situations? I believe that, in the whirl of income development in the '70s and '80s, churches estimated that church taxes would explode because if everyone earned more and more money, the income tax percentage rate would increase dramatically. However, the church tax in Germany is a fixed percentage of income tax revenue. Thus, the church tax increases more steeply than income itself because it rises according to the income tax revenue percentage. What happens if incomes increase by six percent every year? Then churches will get rich. That is why they became bogged down – just like the state that just had to construct spa clinics and swimming facilities everywhere. The churches invested in kindergartens, hospitals and universities. Now, however, incomes are no longer rising, they are falling. Now ten percent of the population has become unemployed. And what is much, much worse: Income tax progression and the top income tax rate have been reduced continually for a while now. The foundation of their financing has broken down on several fronts at the same time. Long-term obligations, though, have remained. What now? Cheap pastors? Lay preachers? "A funeral is not a sacrament and thus does not need to be conducted by a pastor." Precisely what we, when dead, want, is cut. The last word is no longer spoken over us by the sacred. Instead, communities are collected into districts, and central church services are held. Rotating pastors come by from time to time. The Sunday congregation is dying out for good. "Hey, people, why aren't there any french fries and Mars ice cream bars at the church meeting?" I asked, and shouted passionately: "We should rejuvenate the church!" The answer: "People here only want liverwurst sandwiches and pickles – after that, Teewurst and blood sausage. That's the way it has been for centuries."

How do we experience the system emotionally? Unfortunately, we feel almost nothing anymore and are dejected because we don't feel anything. Thus, it is like experiencing the silent mourning of the godforsaken, which stays within limits because no one is exactly sure anymore whether God is among us or not. In contrast, we revel in delight when, for instance, the Pope comes to Germany. The BILD newspaper put it very cleverly in its headline: "We are Pope!" Hundreds of thousands of people are deeply moved by the death of the Pope and are joyous when the new Pope brings them together once as a community. Once! The next day, the newspapers wrote: "Will the youth that cheered the Pope come back to church?" The newspapers don't get it. God can only be perceived by the non-believers or almost non-believers in a community of people and they no longer congregate in churches. Unless of course if it is holding a special event.

What would a sufficient, conscious Lean Brain fake be like? The churches can economize on services for individuals, in fact they have to, because they have no money. However, at Christmas, they could really try to attract a full house and offer the event-hungry community something special. The churches could specifically train Christmas clergy who would exclusively professionally stage the Christmas Eve event. To do this, you wouldn't have to study theology. Anybody can read from Isaiah. Then, of course, *Silent Night* is sung and *O Come all ye Fakeful*. That's about it. The only other thing we'd need are people who can authentically fake some faith; or of course we could relocate the entire event to a different media, such as digital television. There, the Christmas celebration can be viewed at varying, staggered times, just as the various German television stations traditionally show *Dinner for One* at diverse times on New Year's Eve. Then the mass can be timed to coincide with the automatic oven finishing up the Christmas roast.

A Lean Brain church would serve the church taxpayer, off of whom it lives, to a greater degree. We should allocate a single, national human voice for the Pope – just like the voice actors who always dub the voices of the same film stars. Perhaps it would be better to have several Popes that can serve a variety of target groups (using the Spice Girls as a model). Maybe a special Pope just for heathens wouldn't be bad either, as it would open new markets for church taxes.

The church can save a great deal if it broadcasts the sermons of the various Popes globally and completely abolishes local church services. It has to change, completely transforming its functions so that they take on an event-like character. People have to be able to sway and sing together in the dark while holding up lighters. This creates goosebumps of emotion that is felt by almost everyone as a fake of God among us. The motto of an economizing Lean Brain Church must be:

> Bless for less!

As in all Lean Brain systems, the church must largely step away from its own, expensive activities and let the customers, in this case the believers, do the work. Priests should limit themselves to their core business, transferring most of the work to laypersons, volunteers, and all believers and people willing to help, just as Lean Brain companies have their customers do the work. Similarly, the church must let its assistants serve it. (Not only at funerals! It would almost be better if there were funeral bishops. That job requires good Hereafter management). One might consider holding church services in people's living rooms, alternating from one to another, at least in winter, when heating the church costs a great deal of money.

These helpers would be honored by the church through gold and platinum badges, or they would receive a thousand Lufthansa frequent flyer miles for every sermon. The state must be forced to offer tax breaks on private rooms used primarily for sermons, just as is the rule in other occupations. And so on and so forth.

I have only addressed the Lean Brain organization of a currently completely ineffective church. Yet we would also actually have to rethink its significance.

The significance of the church is to safely accompany believers on their way to God.

Let me repeat: This is a big problem in a time where people do not really believe in God so much any more. In the past, our parents would tell of the bogeyman who attacks naughty children in the dark or puts leaches on them when they don't do their homework. When such children subsequently find out that there is supposedly a God, they are relieved, and clearly feel protected in their religion. Then praying is like a piece of cake! Today, God is farther away than ever. Can the church even build bridges that big? Aedificatio pontis ultima? Should it even try? I'm afraid it can't anymore. Real faith today is much too intense for the watered-down contemporary Christians.

Real faith requires dedication to God and the careful preparation for eternal life. That is far beyond the potential of a normal Lean Brain person. Normal church services today don't even broach the subject of faith anymore, instead preaching only the positive useful possibilities of faith. "It has been statistically proven that on average 50 % more faith corresponds to a 10 % rise in income. Whoever doesn't want to accept that can go to the Devil! How is he going to top that?" This simple appeal to the genuine completely replaces the genuine. The state of being moved performed by mystical believers in movies is probably the most intense form that can be tolerated. (The sacred, reduced to normal-strength faith). Lean Brain tries to insert this bearable holiness, that does not demand too much of the church taxpayers, as a fake into the needs structure of consumers of religion in a cheap and optimal manner.

Try reading a book about shamanism. In the past, the souls of shamans could leave their bodies in long-practiced ecstacy techiques and etablish contact with spirits or capture the escaped souls of ill individuals and bring them back to be healed. In this way, shamans served as sacred doctors. Today, they often only simulate epileptic attacks for money and subsequently offer well thought-out advice – and after their hard work, they cry a bit about the general decay of shamanism. I only mention this because the loss of the real and its fake in this case are much more obvious than in the Christian church.

Lean Brain Spirit Service does not grumble about decay and does not attempt to save any anachronistic elements over time. Lean Brain Spirit Service contemplates systems that, through the simple execution of instructions, can keep morons in a positive spiritual state which will enable them to bear their inane work and give them the feeling that their life as a whole is worthwhile. Basically, the Lean Brain movement feels it is free; so free that it would possibly like to act autonomously to establish new Lean Brain religions.

This is not so easy! We need religions that are precisely tailored to the needs of morons. I could imagine commissioning the construction of virtual private gods. We could base them on the principle of the Tamagotchi, whose name itself sounds divine, but in Japanese, "tama" means "egg" and "gotchi" is based on the Japanese word for watch. The original Tamagotchi device looked like an egg-shaped pocket watch. Let's give our device a different name; how about Kamagotti? Kama in Hindi is the desire for good. Every evening, a Kamagotti asks what good deeds were done and remembers them. He prays with the child or later with the people and reads to him or her from the Bible or tells stories of saints and good deeds, of white knights and the black evil. The Kamagotti exchanges information with other Kamagottis via the Internet, communicating arguments between various children and about their Kamagottis. Through people's good deeds, the Kamagotti develops further, as is also traditional with the Pokémons. People thus advance the Kamagotti, who in turn expands their desire for the good and allows it to grow. Every child acquires a Kamagotti as well as he or she can.

The Lean Brain church moronorgs design the official Kamagottis for the Christian church and demand a monthly flat rate for unlimited use of the virtual god. The Lean Brain Church can follow the development of the Kamagotti via radio communication and the Internet, and thus possesses much better information about the believers than was ever possible in the confessional. Using simulation programs, mainframe computers determine what type of god for the current moron age is the most optimal at any given time. It can support this advancement of God officially on television or through various Popes. The moronorgs can use the Internet to program the Kamagottis with the wish to visit various church events and to donate money to the church at these events. Kamagottis could be happy when their people pay a fee to light a candle in a friendly church with which a profit-sharing agreement has been stipulated.

Just think about the laborious procedure in Catholic churches in which you first must deposit the money and then light a candle. Then you have to pray for someone. It would be better to set up electronic input devices where the amount of the donation, the name of the donor, the saint being prayed to and the relative who is the subject of the prayer are all entered. Then a banner would appear on a screen in the church in the manner of a Donor TV, where a crawl text like the following would appear: "Mueller has donated a virtual candle for Myer. 10 euros. This message will remain on display for a total of 20 minutes. Thank you." Then the churches wouldn't be so smoky – they could dispense with all that frankincense. This electronic message could then be transferred to the Kamagotti, who would be really thrilled and pass on the story to the Kamagottis of the person's parents and friends as well as the tax revenue office. The other Kamagottis would also be happy and communally praise God. The mother Kamagotti bursts with pride because the child Kamagotti was good, and she gets more frequent flyer miles for her saintly status. When their children do good deeds, mother Kamagottis develop further; similarly teacher Kamagottis advance when their students' performance is good. In this way, the total network of Kamagottis connect and reconnect humankind, and humans and God become closer than ever.

The Lean Brain Kamagottis thus generally lead to a Lean Brain convergence of God and humans who then truly become one. Bless Kamagotti.

I have used the Catholic church as an example here, but I mean pars pro toto for all other churches. The other churches are much more difficult to moronize because they are organized much more loosely, that is, they do not even need a system that needs reforming. I myself am Protestant, where the pastor simply preaches what he wants; it is still a long way to a central TV message or a Master Fake Group that puts the crowd in a good mood at events.

Just one more thing: When I suggest Kamagottis, we are already on the brink of a completely new world that is returning to a spiritual element once thought to have been lost. With these Kamagottis, I have suggested something totally wonderful that can make the world happy. Can! If a prophet like myself preaches something good, they will come crawling out of their holes, those evilest of the evil. They will invent Yammergottis for the Germans or Famagottis with lots of dirt from the tabloids. The Satanists will put their own version on the market, and hackers will infiltrate other gods and thus grind down and disgrace the new sanctuary. Up with Kamagottis! Unfortunately, all that glitters will ultimately not only be gold.

9. Lean Brain Sex

Now we've reached the roller coaster segment of our journey! What better topic to follow religion than sex? Sex, the deadly enemy of religion! It's all due to the Lean Brain solution, which would also work with Tamagotchis here, too. Yes, you've guessed it: We're talking about cybersex. Sex in its current trivial form does not generate business, it shatters relationships and indirectly costs society loads of money: 35 % divorces, the troubled souls of children, school years repeated and useless spiraling semesters at the university, a decline in the desire to have children, conflicts at the workplace. Sex must be possible without stress and emotion.

What is the purpose of sex desired by normal people? This is a difficult question. Naïvely speaking, it is procreation. From a somewhat more sensitive standpoint, it is that shot of endorphins related to being in love that can last a good 18 months: It is the most magical chemical state of the body that we know. After approximately 18 months, the partners take a fresh look around and are surprised to realize that they have married each other. That is the problem.

Is the purpose still current? Another difficult question! You need two partners for sex who must have time at the same moment and be in an appropriate emotional state. These two prerequisites are becoming increasingly more difficult to fulfill in these modern times. Both partners work incessantly, perhaps also take care of children, and have a myriad of obligations hanging over their heads: jogging with a friend, the gym, the pottery course at the community college, bringing kids to and picking them up from somewhere. You notice this when you try to schedule an evening with somebody. You can't do it. "Well, let's just try again in the next quarter year!" That is also what your boss tells you when you really need something important from him or her. Scheduling an appointment has, in the meantime, become next to impossible! In the past, marital cohabitation was often planned for a Sunday afternoon, when the children were asked to be absolutely quiet. That is hardly possible anymore, either, what with the car races on TV every other Sunday, and the like. And let us not forget the second condition: For a few decades now, it has been necessary that *both* partners must be in the mood. That wasn't always the case. Previously, only the man would need to be desirous of sex, which of course he always was. Now everything has become tricky ... and you want me to answer that tricky question? Hmm. Statistically speaking, everyone is dissatisfied with sex. It's too fast, never practiced enough, no time. The young generation of party hoppers sees sex something like smoking: A few still want it – but they have to go outside to do it. Sex is on the decline. Many avoid sex because they compare their performance to that of Sharon Stone in *Basic Instinct*. When a man is faced with such demands, he can easily turn into an ice pick. The woman could be tempted to try to look like Ms. Stone ... The actual feasibility and the theoretical expectations diverge immensely. In addition, from other realms of life, we are used to everything but everything being available immediately. And here?

I have already cited the damaging effects of sex above. Being in love is threatened by cell phones ringing, tears, separations, family ties, a lack of professional mobility and career disadvantages, divorces with considerable asset impairment and the baseness of the opponents of sex. The risk of suffering damage exceeds the joy of sex significantly.

Does the purpose require something that we cannot or will not contribute? In principle, real love would be just fine. Dedication and understanding. Loving attentiveness. Most people mistakenly think that sex must have something to do with love. That makes the issue even more complex. Ever more and ever new conditions! Is that what we really want? The effort required for the pleasant experience continues to escalate.

What would a sufficient, conscious Lean Brain fake be like? Cybersex.

Are you familiar with cybersex? In chat rooms, couples describe sexual scenarios over the Internet. "Now I'm touching your knee. You're still a virgin." – "No, I had a fig leaf slip cup on." – "I didn't see any!" – "I wear the cup as mock pubic hair." – Oh, so that's why it tickles. I'm allergic to cats." – "Hey, I have to stop for a moment, my husband is coming." – "You're a woman?? Oh, this is my climax!"

Or: "Okay, I'm taking my cell phone now. I'm putting a condom on it. Can you feel that over the computer? I'm putting it on vibrate, haha! Guess, oops, where it is now? Now call me with Skype. I want to feel you waiting for me to answer! Say something, you can talk to my insides now." – "You're going to have to answer it sometime, otherwise it really will vibrate! I want to say something!" – "My cell phone is brand new. It doesn't stop ringing when I answer it." – "That's stupid. It'll drive you crazy." – "Not always. Hahahaha, oh man. I can set it so that it asks me what background music it should continue playing when I answer it. When my husband calls, it makes office noises." – "So everyone will think you're working." – "No, for work I of course set it to moaning. I don't want to have to do everything by myself." – "So you fake it during cybersex? How horrible! Hello? Say, am I talking with a vibrator right now? Is this conversation costing me money? Hey, what a character you are. Hello? Hello?" – "Please hang up. Please." – "You are a different voice. I can hear it." – "Please hang up." – "Who are you?" – "I'm her Kamagotti. I am so embarrassed. She sets me to vibrate whenever she does something bad so that she can become a good person. I am her conscience, you know." – "Well, good God, where are you now?"

For true cybersex, we still lack those luxurious end devices that industry is still working on. A type of diving suit would be conceivable, one that always vibrates in places corresponding to where the chat partner types on his remote keyboard. Then the virtual universe will provide quite a kick. "Honey, I'm holding the Russian Roulette revolver to my temple. Press any number from one to six on your keyboard." – "Okay. Four. ... Hello? How was it?"

Cybersex is always available and requires no preparations such as heartsickness or getting close, not to mention those many frustrating failed attempts. Every sex fanatic goes on the Internet and searches the servers for partners. There always are some out there! There are absolutely no coordination problems. If you want to indulge your lust between tasks at work, you can have it immediately. The endorphins don't disappear 18 months after they burst on the scene, like they do when you are in love. They can always be renewed! The sex partners are virtually as attractive as in the movies. We never again need to feel ashamed! We never again have to be nauseated by a sweaty partner with bad breath and bleeding gums. Everything is always perfect, and if not, we immediately switch cyberpartners.

Real love is too intense. Cybersex is a good fake! A Lean Brain person can now virtually live out all his or her fantasies suggested by the tabloids. (A true Lean Brain person no longer has fantasies. After he's watched all the afternoon shows, there is no more room for it). Thus, people approach a certain ideal sex drive. Thanks to cyber media, they never again satisfy their drives in an authentic manner, but rather only as a fake. But there are absolutely no more limits set on the faked drive satisfaction! No more conventions! No permission from partners! No unwanted humiliation!

The Lean Brain faking of desires takes a lot of the tension out of human relationships. True love and true sex pale in the face of Wagnerized cybersex, which can be inflated to any desired size. (Nothing against Wagner. I love Wagner. I have all his operas. Wagner is genuine. Wagnerizing is faking Wagner – the intoxicating effect of a fake such that it has the same effect as Wagner. Do you remember when Wagner was still alive? He divided his listeners. Wagner was too intense for many people.)

Sex has never had anything to do with the brain. Sex has always been a zero-brain activity, at least good sex. That is why the jump to Lean Brain sex isn't so big. Lean Brain sex maintains all of the necessary cybersystems and end devices. Now, completely brainless indulgence is possible, without any considerations, without foreplay and questions, without the block caused by subsequent, teary phone calls, without depression, and without Clambergotcha.

10. Lean Brain Relationships and Communication

You can see how simple relationships become if we hold people at a bit of a distance and if they can be replaced practically at will. The best human companions after dogs and horses are, once again, the Tamagotchis, right?

All joking aside – relationships in modern times waste incredible amounts of emotion and necessarily end in awful arguments. Lean Brain relationships are light, loose and easy. This is possible because the people in our lives come and go.

What do normal people expect from relationships? Depth. Trust. Resonance. The same wavelength. We wish for true friendships and intimate relationships. Above all is the love of a partner and the mother of her child (son?).

Is the purpose still current? Through the Internet and globalization, distances between people have fallen away. We are constantly available via mobile phones. The charges for the calls are no longer very high. With Skype, you can telephone all over the world on the Internet for free. Anne sits here at home and talks late into the night for hours with Matthias, who is away from her for a year, studying in Boston. The Internet offers us a plethora of new relationships. Families will soon only see each other on a video telephone. I myself have only ever seen half of the people I work with. I look at their photos in the IBM intranet. The Internet removes all boundaries, to such an extent that we don't visit each other any more. Long-distance relationships will become the norm.

What do relationships really look like today? Two words: Life stage partners and life stage children. Everything changes. We work at a life stage company in a life stage city. School classes are disbanding, several people are calling for afternoon school, such that the time spent with the family is sinking to a minimum. We live with several alternating people. Now more than ever, it is important to make contact with strangers quickly and understand them. Employers demand social competence, empathy, and human resilience. ("She's crying because she got fired. That's not professional behavior. It's a good thing we're rid of her.")

What could good Lean Brain fake relationships look like? "Hello!" I've mentioned the greeting at the cash register a tedious number of times. Morons will serve customers in call centers. "Hello!" Teachers do not really know their pupils anymore, not to mention professors and their students. The telephone is becoming the primary communication medium. We have seconds to conceive of what to say, formulate it in a determined manner and very politely get our way.

"Hello, good morning. This is your friendly bank! Am I speaking with Mr. Drip?" – "Yes, why?" – "Our computer knows your cell phone number, Mr. Drip. What can I do for you, Mr. Drip?" – "I'd like a large loan in the amount of a half a million dollars. And at zero percent interest." – "I'm not sure if we offer a service with zero percent interest, Mr. Drip. I doubt it. Let me check quickly. Yes. We have loans, but only at seven percent, Mr. Drip." – "I see. Would you be able to secure a loan for me today at zero percent?" – "I'm afraid we only have loans at seven percent, Mr. Drip. Please understand, I'd very much like to gain you as a client for our friendly bank. You would make me personally very happy because then I'd get a commission." – "I want zero. Otherwise I'll go to the competition." – "Mr. Drip, I work in the call center and have no idea about banking. However, as a layperson, I have the feeling that no one offers zero." – "Ha! Toyota and Nissan offer zero percent financing for cars purchased at the list price. So you as a bank should be able to do that without the car, otherwise I'll go there." – "I'm also personally very sorry, but we only have seven!" – "That's highway robbery in comparison to the zero percent at the car dealers! Can I talk to your boss?" – "Just a moment, sir, of course you can speak to my boss. Strictly speaking, he isn't exactly my boss, this boss, only a slimy customer stealer. From this point on, when I put you through, the call will cost 49 cents per minute because, um, it's the boss, just like you wanted." – "Thank you! You had zero sympathy. In my experience, a boss is generally more accommodating. I can get more out of bosses." – "Yeah, sure, see if you can get him to give you a discount, if you even want to accept our money." – "Thanks for the tip!" – "I'll put you through ..." Hangs up. Her colleague at the next desk: "Hey, Jenny, that guy was a real drip, huh?" – "Nina, he's just a nice customer for our friendly bank. All people are nice. I treat them all with the same amount of friendliness." – "Especially that guy who was in such a hurry to end the conversation." – "He makes a lot of money, Nina. Kindness always pays."

Once I bumped into an American woman who was a friend of mine downtown. She seemed very sad. She was walking directly toward me. Then she saw me, and her face suddenly lit up like it was touched by heaven! "Hello!" I was very touched, and my heart swelled. She quickly walked past me. With a friendly expression, I looked over my shoulder at her. To my horror, I saw her face droop, become bitter again and revert back to the sad expression I'd first seen her with. How she managed to beam like she did, I don't know. But to this day, I still carry that reversion to bitterness as a lasting impression on my heart. Fake.

There is the one side of me – the private me. Then there is the communicative surface me that reacts professionally. Relationships are becoming more and more professional. The part inside is not really locked tight – it's not that what is inside is nobody's business – but that relationships are often so deep as to make what is inside important. Generally, feelings are economized. In a way, we are ending the intensity of our relationships. We only meet in telephone calls, emails, text messages, events, parties, in discos, fitness studios or on short getaways. There, we treat each other in a professional manner. Either things go well or we "hang up."

> Lean Brain Communication is aimed at enabling everyone to be able to tolerate anyone else at any time. We now love all people. "Hello!" We smile the Lean Brain Smile.

The real trick is to really believe in the surface fake.

> "I like whoever says 'Hello' to me." If you cannot believe that, you either will go crazy or you already are.

We only have real relationships with Tamagotchi or Kamagotti – and perhaps also to our reflection, if we can pay for the surgery.

11. Lean Brain Health Care

What is the purpose of the system desired by normal people? The health care system keeps the entire population in good physical and emotional health. It is uncomplicated and humane. It does not cost too much. It generates well-being.

Is the purpose still current? Definitely not! We keep reforming it in our heads. We only see grievances of the greatest magnitude. The health care system is thrilled about this and cries for more money! More money for expensive pills and fashionable doctors! A few see health care as the business of the future. There are theories stating that, following electricity, the invention of the airplane and the Internet, people are now increasingly paying more attention to their health and paying a lot of money for it. In fact, health insurance in Germany currently costs about 14 % of our income. In addition, we spend money on ginseng and aloe vera and premium-priced compounds to fight Jaffa skin. And let's not forget the thousands of diets and special athletic attire for thumb wrestling or for active power breathing. Then there are expenses for homeopathic doctors and psychotherapists not covered by insurance. We have out-of-pocket payments for eyeglasses and teeth, new legs, wigs, braces and vitamin-enriched nail polish. How much does health care cost again? Thirty percent of your income? And it *will soon be* big business? Right. We'll be having surgery soon. Body-Modding. Silicon at age 13, permanent Viagra for the high life. "You want me to marry you? Show me your inspection pass first so I can see if you're outdated!"

So? Are we healthy? Statistics show dramatic increases in stress neuroses and depression, allergies, back problems and addictions of all kinds. Currently, we are getting really sick! And morbid! And fat!

Does the purpose require something that we cannot or will not contribute? Definitely! We are supposed to stay healthy. That is about as difficult as being a good person or living a life agreeable to God.

What purpose does the system actually have today? The repair of serious damage. In the past, we took as attentive care of ourselves as we did of our cars. Cars were always taken to be inspected, and we would wax and polish them. Their insides were neat and tidy. They were fed super super fuel and Hyper Formula One Oil. We took off our shoes when we got in. If we had an accident, we became depressed, and could only be consoled after the car was repaired and looked nicer than before. Our cars! But today we pay no attention to scrapes, dents and inspections. The car is a utility object and has to hold up to driving the garden cuttings to the recycling center, which causes scratches in the paint and the ceiling.

That is also how we treat ourselves now. We only go to the doctor when we are no longer capable of driving – er, I mean working. This procedure is much cheaper for cars! We've known that ever since we started abusing them. The death of a car costs about 100 euros. Either junkyard to trade-in. Your death, dear reader, will be very expensive, depending on how many inspections you have skipped. Now death has become extremely costly because we don't want to let ourselves die like a broken car. That is why doctors and pharmaceutical companies can command 90 % of our income if they want – we still can't be cured. We run around like rust buckets with makeup.

Is the system in decline? Does it resort to survival strategies in stressful situations? The entire system, according to all sources, is ailing. Now everyone is battling each other for a piece of the shrinking "pie," the money of the insured. The pharmaceutical industry regularly "improves" medications in order to keep prices high, physicians use cost optimization programs to calculate the most expensive therapy possible that a private insurance company would still be willing to pay. Hospitals juggle with bed occupancy quotas and lengths of stay. The whole system is on the lookout for expensive loopholes. An army of medical equipment is let loose on the patients. "Before the doctor himself examines you, we're going to check everything out and get a better idea of your situation." Politics is all but powerless against the whole lobby. The bargaining chip of the health care system is the health of the people. "If we receive less money, people will die from the inferior quality." That makes a deep impression on us, so we pay until we drop.

What would a sufficient Lean Brain fake be like? A friend of ours was in Shanghai, and there was a flood. The poor person was wearing a dark suit and had to cross the street to get to his meeting. He ran off, and then stepped in a puddle concealing an open drain hole. He fell, twisted his foot and suffered a complicated splintered fracture. They treated him in the hospital. He went through each station, from admission, to the x-ray procedure, to anesthesia, and so on, was examined and finally treated. He had to pay at every single station, a sum amounting to a dollar or two. By the time he was discharged, he had paid just under 50 dollars. He flew back home and had the splint and leg construction assessed in an elite hospital in Heidelberg. The doctors were surprised by what the Chinese had done; they found it highly irregular but original and good.

In Germany, one day in a hospital costs about 500 euros, and in China next to nothing. If we add a cheap flight for 70 euros with Ryan Air, China is a real bargain. A hip operation with a 14-day hospital stay plus six weeks of rehab would thus cost well over 10,000 euros in Germany, and in China hardly anything. Without using our brains, we immediately notice that we should reorganize our health care system. A good cheap surgery airline would offer the operation plus a day on the Chinese Wall for a third of the cost. Already, our x-ray images are being examined in China. A German patient unknowingly approaches a German x-ray machine that is connected via the Internet to China. The Chinese doctor studied medicine in the USA and can roughly imagine what the German body is like. He prepares a diagnosis and sends it and the very small bill back to Germany. The patient's general practitioner announces the results with an important expression on his face. I heard somewhere from a reliable source that recently, nobody was able to see what was wrong with a freshly-operated lung – nobody: not in Germany, not in China or anywhere else. Then a non-medical person came by and discovered a German rag left behind from the operation. Yes, these things happen. In China, the washrags used are of a different type. But this special case is more of an amusing anecdote and wouldn't soak up a fraction of the criticism that other medical economizing must face.

The second way to save in health care from a Lean Brain standpoint is to have patients themselves take care of all of the work they can. In addition, doctors will be so specialized that they no longer need to study but rather can be trained in half a day.

The Lean Brain health care system would thus take on a hierarchical call center structure. The patient must call when he is ill.

A computer asks: "What are you suffering from?" – "Either the German measles or scarlet fever." – "Please pick one." – "I have no idea." – "Don't you have a 10-month Lean Brain high school diploma?" – "Well, yes." – "Then please google German measles and scarlet fever and call back." *One hour later*: "What are you suffering from?" – "Scarlet fever." – "What type?" – "Normal with a strawberry tongue." – "Why did you first think it might be German measles?" – "What, is every computer a know-it-all now?" – "Please be as brief as possible. You are paying for this call. Do you also have rheumatic heart disease or kidney glomerulonephritis?" – "I'm not sure." – "Okay, then it looks like you don't, otherwise you would be whining more. I'm going to ask you something. Please answer clearly and articulately, as the answer will be recorded for legal purposes. Question: Do you agree to being treated for normal scarlet fever without septic complications?" – "Yes, well, I'm not sure." – "That answer is not permissible. If you are not sure, you must speak with a much more expensive computer that has specialized knowledge. So, once again: Do you agree to being treated for normal scarlet fever without septic complications?" – "Yes." – "You will receive some penicillin in the mail today. We will send you the dosage instructions via email with a receipt confirmation request. You will receive via email the code of behavior you are to follow. The post bundle will contain test materials for blood in the urine. Test yourself for blood over a period of 14 days. If blood is present, call back and tell me that you have a renal corpuscle infection. Have you understood everything? Please answer clearly. Your answer is being recorded for your further legal tracking purposes." – "Yes." – "Good, then I will initiate the healing process and invoicing procedures. Beep. My liquidation has already been executed online. Beep. Goodbye. Good luck."

Outpatient treatment will thus be automated. Hospitals will be organized in a similar manner. A clinic will be constructed for each operation, such as the removal of an appendix or parts of a stomach, in which only that operation is performed. Surgeons would then only need to know how to perform a single operation. They would thus have a maximum training period of one month. That is a great deal of time for Lean Brain; however, all hospitals in Europe will be shut down and moved to China. Only the most extreme emergencies involving self-paying patients would perhaps be treated locally.

Lean Brain outpatient services only offers standard therapies for self-diagnosis. Lean Brain medicine completely refrains from making precise diagnoses whenever possible. This cuts out all the current medical gobbledygook that costs so much money nowadays. All experts today agree that more than 80 % of illnesses are based on emotional causes. For instance, shamans consider physical illness as an ailment of the soul and approach the problem accordingly. German conventional medicine almost never addresses the emotional side of illness. It potters around on the body of the patient. If nothing is found, the patient is referred to a psychiatrist, who then regards the illness as a gene defect and treats it by swiftly obliterating it (and usually the ailing soul as well) with psychotropic drugs. Yet if 80 % of all illnesses are of an emotional nature but the soul is never treated, then practically all diagnoses of modern medicine are erroneous, and the therapies, in turn, as well, unless they address the soul. From a completely brainless standpoint, then, it is much more successful to treat the patient for something he himself believes he suffers from.

On the whole, it is not perfect, but the practice of allowing patients to make their own diagnoses is better than the current state of affairs. Doctors cannot possibly know everything, but patients can be expected to understand that one single illness that affects them.

Only specialized doctors skilled in one single illness can become Lean Brain doctors. What is more, they can be trained in approximately one week. Whenever a patient thinks he or she is suffering from Illness No. 13,556, he goes to the specialist for 13,556. The patient has only that disease, and the doctor is only familiar with that one. That is pure, unadulterated Lean Brain.

Perhaps you will shriek in objection and desire doctors with a wider spectrum of education, but that is just exceedingly expensive security thinking. It also has no basis in reality because doctors are much more Lean Brain than you think. Professors or chiefs of staff at hospitals only ever research their own favorite disease, about which they write scientific articles their whole lives! That is why they do not really know more than one disease anyway. Yet our health care system demands that they treat all patients that come to them, which for privately-insured patients indeed makes sense. But these doctors really only want to treat guinea pigs that have their special illness that they are researching!

It would be like heaven on Earth to all of those research doctors to be able to do the same thing over and over in a specialized clinic – exclusively treating patients with their special disease. Then nobody would read their articles anymore because they are the only doctors who even care about that special illness! They'll love it, I tell you! They won't admit it, mind you, and it was only writer Henry Fielding who first spoke the truth: "You should never go to a doctor without knowing what his favorite diagnosis is." Marcel Proust came to the same conclusion: "Almost every doctor has a favorite diagnosis. It costs him quite an effort not to make it." And Nietzsche said: "Every doctor and every politician has his favorite diagnosis."

Thus, medicine has always felt sympathetic to the Lean Brain approach.

In the above section, I have naturally only explained how our health care system can be made more efficient. Of course, the bodies of people are still being treated where – as I've said – the fault as a rule cannot be found. Do we have a chance with Lean Brain Psychology?

12. Lean Soul and Psychotherapy

What good is a healthy soul? It lends vitality and radiates warmth from the heart into the environment. People with a healthy soul experience their normal lives as meaningful and rich. (I'll just let that stand as is instead of expanding this section into its own book.)

Do we care about having a healthy soul? No! Today, we chase success and affirm global competition and social Darwinism as the number one recipe for success. The incomes of all surviving humans will pile up to the heavens! But not our souls – we sacrifice them. Neoliberal economies currently have the upper hand. They apparently prove that radical attitudes toward the individual responsibility of people and a renunciation of social Darwinism accelerate progress. That may even be true. But our souls are all kept on a high level of stress in the process. Our bodies function in a biochemical state that does not benefit the soul. There has already been extensive philosophizing on the subject. For instance: "For what doth it profit a man, if he gain the whole world and suffer the loss of his own soul?" Christ says this in the Gospel of Matthew. Unfortunately he could not argue biochemical processes – so I'm sure that's why you'll believe me instead, right? Seen as a whole, theoretical wealth increases because technological developments come hard and fast due to the rush, but emotional illness also increases, doing immense damage to people and their savings accounts or health insurance policies. We complain of an appalling increase in cases of depression, hyperagression, antisocial behavior, crime, schizophrenia, addictions of all kinds (alcohol, drugs, etc. – of which you are aware – but also the most difficult addiction, that of incessant work so as to avoid the fear of failure). I know that some of you will not take well to my Bible quotes, but perhaps you should consider the Jesus quote for a moment. We are gaining the world outside and suffering damage to the world inside.

Does the health care system care about our souls? No way! The conventional health care system unswervingly repairs broken bodies like mechanics fixing defective cars. Since documents exist depicting the original construction of the cars, it is considered repaired when it looks like new again. With some limitations, medicine also treats people similarly. Psychologists heal the soul, just as physicians heal the body. Unfortunately, no one knows how the soul was in the first place, before it shows up damaged at the psychiatrist or psychotherapist. Thus these experts are forced to view the soul as healed when it is "normal," that is, when it no longer negatively deviates to any great extent from normal souls. (Mathematicians shudder to hear this – they can also imagine the positive deviations! Psychologists and physicians cannot because they only ever see sick people and never especially healthy ones. A deviation, from their standpoint, is always negative. That is why, for instance, they always treat gifted and extremely intelligent people as if they were ill.) Psychology thus eliminates deviations of the individual soul from the statistical average.

> The goal of psychological treatment is not a repairing of the soul but rather a transfer of it into a statistically normal status.

I just thought of something awful: What if we were all depressed? Then people would be depressed on average. That would render depression normal! That is why depressed persons would be healthy because they would be normal. And if somebody were not depressed but rather optimistic, he would be abnormal and would need to be artificially depressed. I am getting the feeling that we have indeed already come that far. I've heard of an employee who was denied a well-earned raise with the following reasoning: "You're not suffering! You're completely satisfied with your work! Your other colleagues are suffering. I'm going to give them the money to raise their spirits." This is the way happy people are normalized and depressed. The health care system, in its normal state of insanity, can always fulfill its mission by constantly generating new tables stating what is normal. "In the year 2025, the average German will weigh 330 pounds, so any weight above 385 pounds must be considered overweight."

Lean Brain Cynicism! I have just suggested a Lean Brain solution. The statistical average is declared normal, and the only thing that is treated are deviations from that average. If values in general are in decline, which happens to be the case at the moment, you don't have to take any action at all! What is more, good people who are not involved in the decline become extremely abnormal with time and must be resisted. In this way, *good* people become the greatest enemy to the degenerated average. Several intellectuals have already written about this problem but haven't explained it quite as lucidly as I have. They hate statistics, but I coincidentally was required to learn them.

How can we care for the health of the soul in a Lean Brain fashion? Let me just briefly repeat the classic Lean Brain approach of inexpensively faking the entire psychological realm. Subsequently, I will discuss the radical Lean Brain approach of electronically optimizing the soul, which will be possible in a few years with implanted radio chips ("RFID").

Global Lean Brain psychology, just as medicine, will be placed in the hands of morons. Every psychologist is assigned one single behavioral abnormality and treats only it exclusively. Physicians – as I have explained – actually like being moronized, because they then only have to treat their favorite illness. This is not the case at all for psychologists. Psychologists are not fixated on illnesses but rather a specific form of therapy that can be applied to all illnesses. While physicians act as if every patient has his or her favorite disease, psychologists or psychiatrists always select the same therapy, no matter what emotional problem the patient suffers from. Psychological experts are thus NLP experts, group therapists, psychoanalysts, motivational trainers, re-enactment coaches, client centered therapists or homeopathic pastors. They always use the same technique, which they swear by. (Imagine such narrow-mindedness in auto mechanics! Every master mechanic would only work with one tool!) Lean Brain psychology will probably be met with heavy resistance because it prescribes one single, global therapy that the computer in the call center uses. Psychologists are very familiar with resistance, let me tell you. There are long-term scientific experiments that confirm the revolutionary discovery by Sigmund Freud that psychologists offer strong inner resistance when patients disturb the way the psychologists wish to treat them. Psychologists exhibit a compulsion for a certain method regardless of the diagnosis. That is why they are very difficult to moronize ...

A patient calls: "I'm depressed." The computer answers: "Is your suffering more emotional or physical?" – "Both." – "Please decide." – "Okay, emotional." – "Why didn't you say that in the first place? I can only process clear answers." – "I answered physical last time, but that didn't get me anywhere. You prescribed massages for me and forced a height-adjustable desk on me for the office so that my back wouldn't hurt anymore." – "So emotional, right?" – "Right." – "We are going to send you a form that you can fill out on the Internet. I can also ask you the questions myself, but there is an additional charge for that because it is assessed as active listening." – "Please ask me the questions, I'm afraid I can't write." – "Fine. Are you overweight?" – "Yes." – "Are you planning to commit suicide?" – "Yes." – "Then I'll have to insist on online payments from this point on, okay?" – "Yes." – "Do you suffer from examination anxiety?" – "Yes." – "Do you hate yourself?" – "Yes." – "I must stop the questioning now because the costs for the treatment of the problems already cited by you are too high. We require a ten-percent downpayment before treatment begins. The treatment procedures will last approximately ten years and already cost ten times more than you have in your bank account. That is why I cannot consider any further symptoms until you have saved up more money." – "But I'll be paying for ten years!" – "You said you were planning to commit suicide. In that case, you have to pay in advance." – "Okay, then forget it. I'm not planning to commit suicide." – "That's great! That is the most expensive ailment, and it is very difficult to cure. At some point, everyone who plans it dies. I'll just cross that out. Oh, see, now you have much more credit. If you also take back the statement that you hate yourself, I could listen to you for hours." – "I love myself." – "Fabulous. Now we only have examination anxiety. That is very expensive. You must understand, examination anxiety is deliberately forced into people. They want people to be afraid of exams, so that they'll do all that work for nothing. Examination anxiety is normal for studying and in daily life. The only time it is not normal is if you have it when you are taking an exam. It should never pop up in an exam situation. It is hard to part with when someone has such a severe case as you do. Is it really such a disaster?" – "No, not really." – "Fabulous. Now we just have the overweight situation. That's no problem, but only being overweight is physical. You would need to display an emotional disorder." – "Yes, I feel so light. I've taken drugs. I'm floating, otherwise I can't bear the sight of the flowing blood. It's really warm, like milk fresh from a cow's udder!" – "Do you suffer

> from a communication disorder with call center computers?" –
> "I'm floating. Everything is dripping off of me …"

Radical Lean Soul! I want to dream of better times – the technology isn't ready yet. Besides, those dopey scientists are always thinking about inserting brain supplements into the heads of people so that they will all be incredibly intelligent. Scientists dream of brain expansion like gurus dreaming of expanding consciousness. A strange idea, screwing an additional, external hard drive onto somebody! It's like Google in your head. What for? You can have Google on your cell phone! No, not good enough. I would like everyone to have a chip implanted (like in my vampire novel, *Ankhaba*). This little computer continually measures the concentration of emotionally significant substances in the body: adrenaline, endorphins, dopamine and so on. In this way, the chip knows the emotional state of the person. Via the RFID part of the chip (Radio Frequency Identification), this information on the emotional state of the individual can be transmitted via radio waves, as is currently done for heart patients. When the heart frequency becomes irregular, the chip radios a paramedic, or a doctor calls the patient and gives him instructions ("Sit down!").

- The chip can inform the patient.
- The chip can display the emotional state of the patient outside on the patient so others can read it ("The boss is hopping mad right now!").
- The chip can inform the host computer so that it always knows if everything is normal and so that it can generate new statistics.
- A computerized chip can order adrenaline, endorphins or dopamine to be released into the body to normalize the soul. The individual substances are surgically inserted along with the chip, much like multi-chamber color ink cartridges in your printers at home.
- People that lose their tempers too often and must repeatedly be normalized should be made culpable in the eyes of the law. The chip can also immediately debit the fine from the person's bank account. This will also soon be the procedure in the case of cars, when the car chip communicates with the traffic sign chip. Then the car can immediately pay autonomously for traffic violations.

An additional gauge is situated next to the speedometer; let's call it the feedometer. It displays the fines.

- In rare cases, people losing their temper can be treated remotely (remote diagnosis and maintenance or shutdown).
- Roughly put, the Lean Soul model is based on the possibilities already utilized in car repair: Cars send data to a remote diagnosis station and send an alarm if they have been improperly handled or stolen.

Let me explain it once again from a radically mathematical standpoint. People are unfortunately multi-condition machines. They can change their emotional state. By this I mean: In the presence of anger, sorrow, joy, triumph, and hurt, their biochemical consistency is so altered that the entire brain programming is changed. They thus react in a condition-dependent manner, which varies from instance to instance. So the whole problem with the souls is that they can change their state. Almost all relationship trouble between people results from this feature. Lean Soul attempts to avoid all other emotional states through a radio monitoring of the soul. All morons are to be held in one and the same emotional state. This one humane and good state is that of the uniformly pleasantly greeting moron during initial customer contact. That is what we must aspire to. Morons must always remain in a healthy, uniformly cheerful condition, which indeed does occur. This state is closely related to that toward which the large founders of religions strive; I'll get back to that point in the discussion of the metaphysics behind Lean Brain. All great thinkers demand equanimity from people, that is, remaining in a healthy basic state never to be abandoned. Stoics! Lean Brain uses RFID technology to establish this ideal emotional state for the long term. All great thinkers claim the world would be much richer if equanimity could be used to cut out all other emotional states. Lean Soul economizes and makes you rich.

13. Lean Brain Law – Bills instead of Rights

What is the purpose of the system desired by normal people? The legal system is intended to provide justice, order and legal certainty. Justice should be in harmony with normal thought, seem uncomplicated, and be legally enforceable. Ideally, the people would have such high ethical standards that the law would only need to appear on paper – just in case. "It is prohibited to burn paper money." Do we need a law like that? Surely not. "It is prohibited to kick babies in the stomach, hammer their heads against a wall and/or rape them." Surprisingly, this is a law we need. "It is prohibited to slaughter people upon their own request, eviscerate them and eat them while performing sexual acts on them." In Germany, we could have used a law like this a few years ago! The judges in that case did not want to admit that the defendant may need to be acquitted because there was no law on the books to match the crime. The media generally regularly sprinkle us with such abstruse individual cases so that we can slaughter, eviscerate and inhale the stories in front of the camera. Yet we only want to live together in peace.

Is the purpose still current? Yes and no. The law is good and secure, but it is dreadfully complicated and thus also very sluggish. We hope for wise judges that will hand down simple decisions – and not 200 days of trial with all manners of defense, diversions and finesses, all of which cost nerves, money and our faith in justice and thus in the legal system. Court cases are absurdly expensive. Every additional law that tries to make things better increases the complexity problem and leads to additional costs and bureaucracy, both of which we are inundated. The notion of trusting wise judgments based on laws that are not wholly unambiguous seems to be too heavily based only on good people, with whom attorneys and judges are not really familiar. Legal practitioners are like service technicians who – like physicians and psychologists – are focused on repair. Doctors are given ill bodies or souls, and attorneys diseased facts of a case that need repairing. There is no such thing as "healed" in the eyes of lawyers. They fight against limits being exceeded, just as the psychologists fight against "deviant behavior."

Physicians are out of luck; they are faced with visibly and profusely bleeding wounds that need to be healed. Psychotherapists deal with a deviation of the soul from a statistical norm, and they must force normalcy on the soul. In contrast, legal practitioners are faced with an overstepping of limits that they themselves arbitrarily set.

Then they complain because "laws are not enforceable" because these laws are completely ignored. Yet the laws must be in harmony with the people's normal sense of justice, otherwise they are bound to be ignored! We have the feeling that we, as people, are ignored by the legal system and so we ignore them back, as much as we can. We want laws with which we can live, not barbed-wire fences running through our lives. The things we consider righteous should be the law. Then we wouldn't need any judges because we could judge for ourselves.

What purpose does the system actually have today? The legal system, just like the economic system, is slowly being dissected into partial processes that are controlled by the procedures and the bureaucracy. The document traffic and legal procedures outweigh "justice." The procedures must be in order, not society as a whole. That is a correct approach that is not unfamiliar to the Lean Brain movement. However, the attempt to construct an intelligent legal system is smothered by complexity, just as management systems of large corporations and states are smothered by convoluted matrix structures. Today, the system only stolidly executes the procedures. It hardly ever questions the meaning because it is already too late. "Sense" has now become synonymous with "simplicity," which has slipped out of our reach.

How do we experience the system emotionally? As sluggish, unpredictable, and threatening. We appreciate that justice prevails in our country, but we tremble with fear at the thought of getting caught in the gears of justice because we are not confident that the result will be healthy.

What would a sufficient, conscious Lean Brain fake be like? I suggest replacing laws with charts and accompanying deals.

Laws require a hard, black or white decision. Guilty or not guilty, yes or no. However, because in life the dividing line is hard to draw, and because it must be drawn in court, it is difficult for us to reach an agreement.

If I go speeding through a small town, the police are ready and waiting, and pull out their chart. I pay a fine based on the severity of the excess speed. I cry a bit and suggest that the radar equipment must be faulty, then they say they'll be willing to take the next cheapest fine on the chart. I am happy at having been able to get out of paying the top fine, and really like the police. They like me, too. I pay and continue driving in the same manner. I complain a bit about the highway robbers that the state pays to disturb the traffic flow in sensitive areas. And then I'm satisfied again. I've paid the coincidental portion of the car tax – that's what I call the speeding ticket. Even better, though, would be an RFID chip in the car itself – but I've already gone there. You know what I mean:

> Bills instead of rights! Invoice, not inconvenience!

A Lean Brain legal system would enact foolproof laws like cooking recipes. Intelligence would not be necessary to distort the laws but to design them.

A Lean Brain legal system will no longer determine laws but rather generate foolproof charts for everything according to which penalties are calculated. Lean Brain law no longer needs to painstakingly determine whether a defendant is truly guilty or not. Lean Brain law works with tabular intermediate stages. The penalty is now negotiated as a deal, and that's that. The legal systems have been exhibiting this Lean Brain tendency for quite some time now. "The charges were dropped in lieu of payment of XYZ." That was a deal! "The defendant confessed and as a result, only received 10 years." That was a deal resulting in abbreviated court proceedings and a reduction in incarceration costs. "After the politician resigned from office, the state did not want to add insult to injury by commencing legal proceedings which would bring truths to light that would hurt all good people." According to statistics I once saw in the newspaper, more and more legal cases are being decided in advance through deals. In the process, the focus is less and less on justice and more on procedural efficiency. The law only serves as the weapon or the threat of the district attorney with which he or she can force a deal.

If we make the yes/no, guilty/not guilty morale of the law obsolete through deals, we should be consistent and formulate laws as charts in the first place. Then, if we do not respect a law, we can decide, like a driver, how much we can afford to cross the legal limit and how large the risk would be of being caught. Such economical decisions are already being learned today by schoolchildren on subway trains.

In addition to the charts, Lean Brain will equip the entire world with cheap RFID chips and monitoring sensors. The chips could then immediately send a text message to my cell phone presenting the bill. Polite sensors could explain to my cell phone that I should not go any further, otherwise it would cost me X amount of money. Each sensor always contacts my implanted chip. Thus, it knows that it is me and which cell phone is mine. It knows my daily rate for one day in prison ... all of the information is there to help the law achieve relative retribution. The state will always set the fines exactly low enough that lots of people will gladly pay. (That is already the procedure with regard to taxes on alcohol or tobacco.) If the state does a good job, it may even be able to abolish income tax because the fines would cover it.

> Total electronic monitoring transforms evil into the foundation of good.
> The good lives off of the bad. The bad is good!

Bills instead of rights! In addition to public law, a Lean Brain legal system could also include private law. The defendants would then either be private or public defendants. Those who pay a great deal would have a certain amount of crimes free. For a couple hundred million dollars, one might even be able to buy a penalty exemption flat rate. Isn't that a great idea? Hmmmm. Perhaps ... well, okay, it is possible that this procedure has already been unofficially implemented, only ... where is all the money?

Those who have no money to pay fines will simply have to obey the law – that's a given. Or, to put it the other way around: Those who obey the law save a great deal of money or can consider themselves rewarded.

If we undertake such expansions of the legal system, virtually no intelligence at all will be necessary any more – at most only for skilled negotiation and the ability to fake in front of the judge. The legal system thus becomes a part of the economy and follows economic rules. The economy – with the exception of the media, of course – has already developed much further in the direction of Lean Brain. If the legal system joins in, the result will be a savings of incredible quantities and especially qualities of intelligence and, as we have seen, lots and lots of money.

14. Lean Brain Democracy and Politics

What is the purpose of the system desired by normal people? The state should prosper, and we want to live in it with pride. The ruling powers are to make sure this can happen. There are various ideas as to how this is to be organized and take place. In general, it is thought that a kind dictator would be best. Since there is no such thing, we have lapsed into democracy, which distributes the powers of the leaders so wisely that everything works well on average. Democracies are more likely to be insisting or unmoving in comparison to dictatorships. If a nation is healthy, a democracy is ideal; but if things are not going well, democracy tends to fixate on the problems. Then the cries for a strong hand or a multi-party coalition grow ever louder – something has got to happen. This presumes that the democracy has difficulty allowing things to happen.

Is the purpose still current? Nations today are largely not prospering. There are several suppressive problems: impoverishment, obsolescence, environmental pollution, climactic changes, a slowing of innovative power, a decline of culture which is largely and morbidly dependent on sponsors. Those in power are overwhelmed by the superiority of the problems and also suffer under global economic currents. In a global world, individual administrations hardly have the power to be a source of influence. Who can influence the Internet? Who can influence corporations, raw materials, or the environment? We citizens understand the problem, but we are nevertheless peevish because politics achieves so perplexingly little that we practically consider them superfluous or even dangerous (when politics presents itself as an expensive arena for power struggles). We all can see that the administration lacks efficacy and efficiency, is practically lacking in good will but at least is lacking in energy.

Does the purpose require something that we cannot or will not contribute? Yes, a farewell to the prosperity of the '70s and '80s, when we were enveloped by the feeling of an eternal upswing. Basically, the assumption of an eternal boom indicates serious general brain damage, but we had a theory of unhampered growth through technology, in which we believed. This theory may be correct on average over a period of centuries but not for the ups and downs of decades. The invention of the computer, for instance, must be paid for with a complete reorganization of the world. That is one valley of tears through which we must wander! In fact we are in it now – and will be until Lean Brain rules everywhere.

What purpose does the system actually have today? I actually think no one knows. In the newspapers, you can read a great deal about democracy being a power struggle. Politicians practice "content free communication." Voters' hearts' beat faster when a presidential candidate declares his love to his wife on live TV, and immediately elect him! Politics, if it really did exist, cannot take place because partial elections are always being held in individual parts of countries. Content splits the constituents and must take a backseat before elections. After the election is before the election! Content must be avoided. It is torturously forced by the circumstances. "Germany is lagging behind! We have the lowest sales tax rate!" – "Raise it!" – "We have no children!" – "Increase child benefits!" – "We have no innovation!" – "Increase research money!" – "We have no money!" – "Postpone the procedures!" Only after something is going incredibly bad, such as the general mood, is something raised, for example the general mood.

Is the system in decline? Does it resort to survival strategies in stressful situations? Yes.

How do we experience the system emotionally? We are sick and tired. Tired of the state. Tired of politics.

What would a sufficient Lean Brain fake be like? Lean Brain transfers the intelligence to the system and does without the intelligence of politicians. The current administration is still banking on the intelligence of its politicians. But it never really makes way for it. That is a mistake Lean Brain will not make. That is why Lean Brain has so much freedom for action. A good government administration system primarily relies on its system of laws and regulations, which we addressed in the previous section. This system will be transformed by Lean Brain into a chart economy. The state will then appear as a large system with thousands of adjusting screws that are optimized and set by good moronorgs. In this way, the moronorgs lead the state to prosperity. They open up the country to many new options, such as the realization of various classes of humans, as is the case in banks. There, people are categorized into different risk levels from A to D, and in classes like Platinum and the like. As we have seen, we lend out various levels of citizenship for the corresponding amount of money. In the long term, nations will give up the territorial aspect of their existence and virtualize themselves. The state will then be the sum of its citizens, just like the bank is the sum of its customers. Just think of how the state would try to court us then! "Become a Golden Greek!" – "Become Lapis Lazuli Senegalese with a free house if you sign a ten-year contract! Offer expires April 1!" – "Be a Secret Swiss! Nobody will know you except us!"

Moronorgs are thus responsible for the prosperity of a nation. But we also wish to live in that nation with national pride and bask in its glow. "Hey, look! Hot! A real Chilean!" Maybe we could even name nations after enterprises! For instance, perhaps Germany could be "Adidas Arena?" Or, if they came up with enough cash, Germans could be known not as Germans but instead as "Gummy Bears"? Americans could be called "Jiffies"? Or perhaps "McMericans"? Generally, we need a mutual, glittery presentation of ourselves, something like the Emperor of China above us; something that will give us the feeling of a Lean Identity.

Politicians must give us a Lean Identity!

Just as I have wished for several popes for various target groups, I bet the election of entire girl and boy groups would also be exciting.

Lean Brain Managers will use public casting shows with a lot of TV pomp to find various actors who only ever rattle on about the opinion planned by their party platform, without actually personally representing it or doing so all too officially. (After all, stars make commercials without really using the cheap stuff they sell). This is not about achieving the represented standpoints but rather about making the respective part of the populace happy.

"Law and order must rule here!" calls one of the Chancellors and several pensioners sigh at the coffee klatch and whisper in admiration: "She must be reading my mind!" This and primarily this is expected of the politicians: They are to speak from their hearts. Since there are different hearts (and souls), Lean Brain Systems require several chancellors or presidents.

The Spice Girls solved the problem well. Their names are Posh Spice, Baby Spice, Sporty Spice, Scary Spice and Ginger Spice, to represent their traits. One would have to name the candidates after their respective areas of expertise and present them in public. They could have names like Oily George, Tricky Dick (no wait, we already had one of those), Woody Al, Baby Barack or, to go with a trend, Billary. Their bellies, hairdos or exciting girlfriends would be marketed. Nowadays, this only happens sporadically and coincidentally.

Lean Brain builds up politicians for a party that are completely fake or boy/girl group in nature, such that a party can be elected by everyone. The administrative work is completely separated from the politicians. This enables them to pursue permanent election campaigns or visit banquets. All they need to do is showcase the party, get people to talk loudly about them and win everyone over for the party. Behind them is the administrative apparatus, conceived by moronorgs as a Lean Brain System. The administration can be dissolved, just as churches, schools or universities, through privatization. The registry office, identity card and finance office will be taken over by the banks. The people who issue bank customer cards will also be able to print out driver's licenses as well.

And the army would be gone because we will buy Lean Brain mercenaries. The police will also be replaced by mercenaries. Schools will be long gone, replaced by people's initiatives. Basically, there is hardly any more administration needed for the moronorgs to construct.

Fake politics provides us with the illusion of order. It unswervingly exudes faked confidence, so that Lean Brain citizens will feel good. "Social security is stable and the economy is growing fervently. Unfortunately, the numbers do not yet reflect this. But who needs numbers? We are a wonderful people! Several enterprises would cancel our debts with them if we named ourselves after them!" Fake politics rationalizes all problems away. When the people are unsettled, fake politics whips up an enemy from outside, globalization or Googlization.

Elections give the Lean Brain populace the feeling of having their own identity. Thus, elections must be styled into an event. Recently – I read this with half an eye – I saw that 60,000 tickets for an open air festival were being given away in a drawing. Anyone who called in could participate for "99 cents a minute." One-hundred million calls were placed; in other words, 99 million euros for 60,000 tickets. A good deal. Just as many people call in for American Idol and Big Brother. How crazy! That is why the Lean Brain election will be conducted fully automatically via cell phone for "99 cents a minute." Everyone can vote as often as he or she likes. The parties are financed via a portion of the caller fees. The intermediate results are displayed on TV 24 hours long. The beautiful hosts that look like they are straight from a chewing gum commercial motivate the people to grab their cell phones. "Call me, call me!" they demand, like goddesses. That is going to be some great atmosphere. Again and again, the fake troops of the individual parties come on stage and campaign for their party. Stars from sports and culture support them! It will look like the Super Bowl, only there is not so much riding on the election as on the ball game. Politics is now a fake that makes people happy.

15. Lean Brain Management

That's the name of this book. So I don't actually have to write anything more here. Let me break out of the structure for a moment and turn to a small remaining point. If politicians can act like the Spice Girls, why can't the faked executive boards do so as well?

I need not say much more about managers. They have served often enough as examples for Lean Brain in this book.

The tendency to force all business procedures into insipid business processes is increasing everywhere. Most procedures in businesses don't really work, lead to chaos and false decisions, and have thrived far beyond legal procedures. The management of the world has a great moronorgic advantage, namely the SAP system. There, the world is already relatively consistently preformed.

At the University of Göttingen, I once learned the composition rules of composer Palestrina. The professor said: "When you write music that conforms to all of Palestrina's rules, it already sounds like pretty good music – that's how good the rules are."

The following applies in business:

> Once a company has implemented SAP, it can never really be bad again.

SAP software is an ideal workbench for moronorgs who wish to define the procedures of a foolproof recipe.

Of course, this takes skill, but SAP at least serves as a possible template for the whole world. You just have to adapt the reality of an enterprise or state to SAP for it to work live …

The primary problem of most companies is this: They do not explicitly allocate the position of the moronorg. Companies have managers for human resources, production, marketing and sales (all of which are Lean Brain areas), but they do not arrange for any explicit system intelligence. They have no CMO (Corporate Moronization Officer). That post – and only that post – should be occupied by an intelligence. The CMO must make the enterprise foolproof. Everything must function properly on its own!

Most companies today are not prepared to come up with the money for intelligence. They attempt to solve everything via trial and error or by employing edgy or double-edged decision-making personalities. When these makers and breakers run aground, they'll be put out to pasture via lateral promotions into staff functions where they can apply their experience and experience frustration. These lateral existences are entrusted with one task: contemplating the procedures of the firm. They make up the staff function. These former managers, of course, can't possibly have a clue as to how business procedures are actually designed. In their active time, after all, they only accelerated or goaded such processes, and perhaps also satisfied them – but there is no way they understand their construction. For them, the company is like a car: They want to drive it fast, but they could never build one themselves. They also do not know how it works, even though they repair it continually.

> Someone who beats cows so they will produce more milk doesn't need to know how cows work.

The former managers usually accept this and make the best of it; that is, they leave the company with a large sum of money. This leaves the actual job of the moronorg with the other class of staff employees, the controllers. They only know how much must come out of the cow when it does big business.

The problem is, they have never even seen a cow before! Controllers are people who count the vehicles in the company fleet! They know exactly how much the cars cost. But they cannot drive and do not know how cars work. To expand upon this, they only know the quantity, not the quality. Therefore, controllers are completely unsuitable to be moronorgs.

> Companies must institute the position of CMO, Corporate Moronization Officer.

The previous chief executive officer of a company now only takes on the ceremonial and representative part of management. Every small measure of the CMO and moronorgs is sold as a triumph of the company's technology. "We supply you with software for every complicated situation!" if the software is too complicated. "We wish to congratulate you, dear Customer, for doing business with us. That shows your good taste!" when a good business deal has been made. The executive board will become the Spice Girls of the company. They herald joy as when "men rejoice when they divide the spoil." They announce successes and praise reorganizations. They eat with customers and provide a dignified context for all conference openings with their salutations read from cards.

16. Lean Brain Media

Already weary from all the fakes? I suspect you are. It really is quite enough, but I do need to say something about the media, don't I? I'm sure you can imagine what I am about to say, so I'll keep it short and then end this chapter of examples.

What is the purpose of the media desired by normal people? Fun, entertainment, information and officially also education. Media give people a certain common focus. "Did you see that offsides goal yesterday? We of the Bayern München soccer team are cheated out of a goal at every game. If we still end up being the champions, that will really mean something – not like with all of the other teams." – "Who did you phone in for on Big Brother?"

Is the purpose still current? Not really. There are still a few educational offerings, but the information is becoming ever thinner. Humankind itself could collapse and it would hardly be shown on the news. It seems as if there are reporters everywhere, out to film explosions and visit the scene of highway pile-ups.

> There is no accident too small to become a fake ad!

Every crashed bus, every tear of a supermodel appears to be worth money. Fears or overwhelming emotions must be stirred. News about new laws or interest rates are so dry in comparison that we no longer take them in anymore, even when they are broadcast. Everything is squeezed dry to produce emotion. All factual content is emotionalized and personified. Even the once rather sober animal documentaries have now become happenings with animal dialogue. The media has gone overboard on the fun and entertainment side. The standards are becoming more and more trivial and bawdy (e.g. soaps). Education is slowly fading from the media altogether.

Does the purpose require something that we cannot or will not contribute? Concentration and interest for what is broadcast. We cannot achieve that. We come home from work as tired morons. We don't have to learn anything and only want to be drizzled on under the shower and in front of prime time television.

What purpose does the system actually have today? "Bread and games for morons." We have the need to enjoy life in a flat state. Our jobs are so content, experience, and emotion-free that we come home in the evening and fill up on emotion in the parallel media world. We comfortably experience fear, are shocked at disasters and donate money, we suffer and tremble, we rejoice and celebrate. We are fans in the grandstands of substitute emotions, and feel like stars.

In real life, we are forced to consistently cling to the same, politically correct position. The media allow us to let our hair down in a parallel world. This includes horror films, first-person shooter games and cybersex. We wallow in emotion and feel momentarily free from the systems and constraints of other people.

What are Lean Brain media? The media are even further along the Lean Brain path than management. The media serve our viscera. They flaunt unvarnished, trivial life. People like us love and hate each other in reality shows. They are mercilessly vulgar and trivial. That is just what Lean Brain wants! The media used to show us role models. The message was always: Be like Muhammad Ali, Vince Lombardi, Albert Schweitzer, Albert Einstein! You can do it! These kinds of messages are only sensible in a Lean Brain society for elites and moronorgs. People have to watch their peers. "She's got such a tiny bust, but she still manages to have a cushy life!" – "He used to stutter, now he raps."

Thus, the media mainly address common instincts. You don't even need your mind at work so it is not unnecessarily resuscitated after work because it cannot provide joy or satisfaction anyway.

Hollywood films repeatedly modulate the same old themes such as murder, mummies, dinosaurs, knights, or love, and Wagnerize them with the latest technology, which is becoming ever more perfect at injecting these themes with intense emotion. The films fake a feeling of luxury in us. We feel faked honor, love, and humiliation in a tolerable amount that can be considered as pleasure. We leave the theater, the live concert of a superstar, or the sports arena as if anesthetized. Our bodies feel satisfied. It can now resume performing Lean Brain tasks for a few weeks without protesting.

17. Effective, Practical and easily understood Advice for Managers

If you, as a manager, now wish to convert your entire system to Lean Brain, start with the hiring of a CMO, a Chief Moronization Officer. He or she is responsible for the construction of an intelligent Lean Brain system according to the latest facets of moronorgy.

The CMO will hire several moronorgs that will gradually embed foolproof processes in the system and make it serviceable by morons. I have referred many times in this book to the fact that an obvious but unfortunate option is to entrust former controllers, staff managers or laterally-promoted ex-talents with such construction work.

Don't ever do it that way! That is the first and biggest mistake you could and would be expected to make. Take the responsibilities of the CMO and moronorg seriously! Give the CMO the true power in your enterprise. Rejoice in Lean Brain. This is true here and universally.

> Lean Brain succeeds in its own anticipation.

Eliminate any cultural problems among the board of directors. This can often be achieved simply by swapping out high management. Think about the concept of the Spice Girls. They have to take on a variety of roles and represent them to the media:

- Power Spice: Gives everyone in the company the feeling they are working in an important system: "We are somebody!"
- Number Spice: Declares any random numbers from stock analysts as successful. "Everything is right!"
- Pushy Spice: Demands higher performance and motivates people to work harder.
- Team Spice: Stands for a team spirit of togetherness: "We are one."
- Vision Spice: Can describe the future of the firm in a stirring manner.

Power Spice talks of world dominance and the purchase of all competitors, succinctly shows the way to success and exuberant power. Morons can fill up on confidence and pride with Power Spice – despite the tough love they get from Power Spice at work.

Number Spice conveys the current reality as the highest in the world. Shareholders cheer him or her on and stimulate other buyers to drive stock prices up. "Without the one-time burden for social plans and one factory closing, we would have faired two percent better in comparison to the quarter before the company launch under consideration of adversary tax rates. These burdens are non-recurring! In the next quarter, we are going to write off all of the worthless junk that we cannot sell. This one-time burden appears negative on the balance sheet, but we will then enter the next quarter unburdened, whose unique problems I prefer not to know, to the advantage of stock prices, otherwise I would not appear before you with such confidence of victory. There is a great deal to do. We are economizing severely, hardly anyone can work decently, otherwise we'd come back and economize some more. We always take on more than we can handle. We are proud of that. We are right in the midst of reality."

Pushy Spice whips people into action. "I feel proud when I see our future before us. I'm proud of the great numbers that Number Spice has just cited. Great! I am totally excited about what you guys are capable of achieving. But I want to see better numbers, not like the crappy ones in the last quarter. I'm going to crack down, ladies and gentlemen, let me tell you. I won't tolerate another bad quarter like the one we just had. I'm going to inundate you with measures, and you know I will! Now let's go full speed ahead! Go! Keep going! Sell! Sell! Sell!" (There is a Muppet film about this.)

Team Spice: "I'm here today to tell you how wonderful it is to have such a team. I would like to honor a few of you that I especially like with some worthless little prizes and appoint you Player of the Week. Please accept this as a small, humble thanks. Please. I cannot tell you how moved I am. People are so important to me. Employees are our greatest assets. I am now going to name the people that I have especially come to love. My secretary has prepared the list for me; I of course don't know you personally. I am standing here on stage looking forward to seeing how you look in person. I love you. Please come up onto the stage to me! To me! Take this certificate, have your picture taken with me as a team and say thank-you into the microphone. Don't forget to say that this prize isn't really for you, but for the team. Mention how great the company is to you. That is all that matters; I don't care one way or another about you."

Vision Spice: "I have a grand vision. I am so grateful to the company that I am allowed to have one. Today, I'd like to share this passion of mine with all of you. We want to build the new XXL, incredibly wonderful at the price of an S. I already have nods from the entire management crew. They are all excited about going down this path that will shower us in profits. I only need a bit of money for the initial investment and a couple of permits, but, right after these five years of delays on the part of the bureaucracy, we will be churning out the profits!"

You can also fill other and/or more roles, but there should be at least one Spice Team member that can hold the prescribed Lean Brain speeches described above in a convincing manner. The Spice Team is only responsible for representation, not for the function of the system. The CMO must keep the executives out of it. If the top team confuses presentation with true management, it will only end in catastrophe.

The Spice Team has nothing to do with the operative side of the company. It motivates, mobilizes and communicates. The Spice Team must be cast expertly, not to mention the CMO. For the future, I could also envision a virtual Spice Team. Moronorgs write the speeches and large media firms animate them with virtual characters. Today it is standard practice anyway for the Spice Team of a large corporation not to come down for personal appearances, but rather impart a video message on a film screen. Virtual Spices would be ideal for this purpose. They are the perfect Lean Brain fake: prettier, more eloquent, with a quicker wit … simply completely satisfying.

18. Take-Aways, Control Questions and Exercises

Look in the mirror:
- Do you look good?
- Do you have nice teeth and a charming smile?
- Are you introverted? (Take the test at www.keirsey.com in all languages)
- Are you extroverted?
- Are you moronorg material? (Can you design recipes?)
- Can you fake well? Are you capable of investing 10% effort to make look like it's the maximum?
- Do you like saying the same things over and over with unshakable enthusiasm?
- Can you quickly assume new roles upon the request of a system?
- Has your personality learned how to let go? To let go of itself?

Time will tell if you will become a Spice, moronorg or moron.
    Everyone has a role in Lean Brain.
    If you aren't good at anything, switch over to the customer side. There, you will be allowed to continue existing in strict limits as a

human being, with all of your faults and/or your brain, but you have to bring lots of money with you.

There really isn't a third option.

VII. The Metaphysics of Lean Brain Thought

1. Is the Renunciation of Intelligence Humane?

Before the grand finale, I would like to add a couple of thoughts on Lean Brain itself. (Can you stand another three to five pages?) After reading the above, you are sure to be shocked that the world can function with so little intelligence. You probably asked yourself repeatedly: What will become of us? I would like to address that now. But first I would like to tell you that the question "of us" has to do with our heads. Our bodies will remain as intelligence-free as ever.

So, if you are asking yourself that question, you probably went through long periods of your life where you did not listen or you understood little about the important things in life. Jesus doesn't say anything about intelligence. Nothing at all! I have the entire Lutheran Bible on my computer. The word "intelligence" does not surface once, but then again, it is not Martin Luther's style anyway. Thus, I also looked for "smart," which is also nowhere to be found. I searched for "success," but, once again, nothing! What does that tell us? It tells us that, in the eyes of God, all of those things are not important. God is not impressed by our intelligence and has no desire for it. In his mission to us, there is no mention of success. We are to go forth, be fruitful and multiply ourselves, not our intelligence.

I hardly even know anyone who claims that intelligence makes you happy. Okay, some have written to tell me that they only know cerebral pleasures and reject sex. I answered that, in a world without sugar, oatmeal can taste like sugar. Everyone talks himself or herself into being happy in some way. Those who do not achieve this constantly complain about being unhappy, which in itself is also a kind of pleasure. "We are fine!" Try saying that four or five times a day at work – you'll make everyone mad and there you'll have your happiness.

I think that, in our society, intelligence is simply one of the important sports in which one can garner fame if one is good at it. It is not much more. If the Lean Brain movement places intelligence on the negative list, along with "costs" and the like, then of course all of the brains will protest at having lost their benefice. I can understand that – I myself don't know what I'm going to do with my intelligence in the new world. Perhaps I'll become a metamoronorg and, as the founder of the theory, train other moronorgs! I can thus evaporate into the teach-o-sphere. (Teaching is simpler than doing, which is why that occupation is so popular. People often overlook that fact – as they do the advantages of being a eunuch instead of a man). So you can see – my future is set. If you, too, are intelligent – oh dear – then you'll have to see how to get rid of it yourself.

If you are not intelligent, you are already much farther along. Ask yourself the following: Have you got dignity even though you are not intelligent? Have you nevertheless earned love and honor? Can you pray without blushing? "Yes, yes, yes!" you will say. And I, as a Lean Brainer, will beg you: Enlighten the intelligents! Diminish their fears! Take them with you into the new Lean Brain age. Lean Brainers are the heralds of the new age! Let that intelligent arrogance with which intelligents greet you just drip right off. They can't help it! They are complete prisoners of their intelligence! They cannot break free! Oatmeal, I say! The existence of the moron is a relatively happy one. Morons press levers like laboratory rats in cages and earn plenty of rewards and cheese.

2. Lean Brain envisions People like Lab Rats!

In the realm of psychology, Watson came out with his thoughts on behaviorism in 1913. People perceive something from outside (a "stimulus") and react to it ("response"). Watson declared psychology to be a pure science that examines how people respond to various stimuli. Observations of the inner goings on and feelings of the subject were never meant to be part of his research because science is impartial and feelings are non-scientific. (Today, people hope to be able to define feelings by observing brainwaves. So now they could also be existing impartially. This example shows how science shuts its eyes to the things it cannot immediately understand – until they are understood! So scientists mainly boast about things that are comprehensible, and fear those things most that are vague and unclear.)

Since Watson's famous explanation (*Psychology as the Behaviorist views it*), almost a century has passed. His vision of people as a scientific object peaked in the behaviorism of Skinner. Today, we are familiar with the *Skinner box*, in which the responses of laboratory rats to various stimuli are recorded.

The Skinner box is a glass or grated container in which various devices are designed to confront the rat with stimuli. Most Skinner boxes contain bells (acoustic stimulus) and light sources (optical stimulus). They have a lever that the mouse can press in response to the stimuli, and a food hatch which releases food or "reward cheese" into a trough. The floor of the cage consists of a grid upon which the rat can be punished or stimulated with electric shocks.

So, psychologists went about using a reward system to get the rats to demonstrate all responses that were imaginable for rats. It looked as if only the correct ratio of cheese and electric current were all that were needed to "program" the rat. And indeed – the rats learned the programs!

I am describing this only to carve out one important thought:
Stimulus systems teach a living thing to enter into a symbiosis with a system – in the above case, a Skinner box with its stimulus system. The ever more insipid stimulus/response way of life machinates the creature and teaches it to be part of the system. It is programmed.

> Rats in a Skinner box become any predetermined machine. They represent an animal fake.

This is a very important and wonderful thought! You have got to remember this! Skinner was wrong! He cannot teach a rat to be like *any* other rat. He can only reprogram them into any other *rat whose response recipes have been precisely defined*. Through electric shocks, behaviorists can implant any and all desired habits into a rat. Thus, the rat can be planned in advance to exhibit perfect responses through recipe-like descriptions. In the box, it learns to carry out all instructions step by step. The rat presses the lever and gets cheese. After being trained for an extended period, the rat reorients its life to the system in power and from then on only reacts to the business processes of that system.

Therefore, the rat can be forced into almost any system. In that sense, it is an animal fake. However, it is no longer 100 % animal but rather only a bit animal, namely that amount which is allowed and commanded by the system.

Thus, the retraining of rats is precisely the Lean Brain process described in this book. It's not about economizing on intelligence but rather carrying out instructions. For rats, pressing on the lever may even mean an increase in intelligent performance. From that standpoint, the mechanization of rats has less to do with Lean Brain than will be the case for the mechanization of people. Yet we can very clearly recognize:

> Rats are moronized in the Skinner box.

Made very optimistic through his very positive experiences with rats, Skinner supposedly claimed (with an impish cockiness?) to be able to retrain any person to behave in a certain way using the corresponding stimulus system. I don't know what gave him that idea. I mean, just imagine …

> People in a Skinner box could be exposed to a whole lot more stimuli. Lights of all kinds and colors, tones – shrilly painful or

harmonically soothing (pop or classic), ideally a computer screen that displays commands. Small tasks can be entered into the computer. "Call and ask if the party is interested in a home building loan." Or: "Execute a foreign money transfer." Or: "Make an appointment." When these tasks have been completed successfully, the person in the box can be rewarded with small amounts of money. In the case of failure, he or she could be threatened with a financial deduction; however, good old electric shocks have proven much more effective.

Skinner's claim that people in one of his boxes can be made to do anything was evidently taken completely seriously. Ever since, we have plenty of stimulus systems for people that involuntarily place us before a relationship between electric shocks and money-cheese. We press the keys for pleasure and pain. Observations of the employee's inner life, that is, the actual motivation of the subject, are not taken into consideration. As Watson would say, they cannot be examined on a scientific level. They require too much profound contemplation beyond the obvious, as I would say. This mechanizing and simplifying view or procedure has, in the meanwhile, entered our lives under the moniker of *scientific management*. Managers imagine sitting at the controls of a cockpit, surrounded by buttons and throttles, skillfully suspending incentives or rewards in the hopes that we will exhibit the desired work response.

There are raving opposing theories from many of the more "humane" psychologists. Freud almost *exclusively* focused on the inner life of people! He was chasing their drives! Maslow and Fromm preached fervently about *humanistic management* which places the inner motivations of people in the spotlight.

Well, those are the fronts. I have discussed them seriously in other sources, such as in *Duecks Trilogie* ("Dueck's Trilogy").

Let us think back to people in a Skinner box. I would like to emphasize the same important notion for people that I have already presented for rats.

So: We place electroconductive wires on people as well as sensors all over them and put them in front of computer screens to have them process certain normal tasks as test cases. The test cases consist of series of instructions. If they are completed successfully, a few cents are put on a blocked account; otherwise pain is applied to the groin, temples or testicles.

And, just as in the case of rats, I ask you: Can every person be retrained to be any other person? The problem is easier to discuss here than it was for the rats. The stimulus/response pattern can only be applied if the response to a stimulus can be observed. Thus, there cannot be a task like: "Imagine a naked female minister."

For such a task, there is just no way of measuring its execution and subsequently rewarding it with a brief electric shock. All tasks that affect a person's inner life, that is, his fantasy, trust, and love, cannot be executed in the Skinner box. In other words: I can only teach a person things via programming for which program commands have been generated. They do not exist for everything today. A person's emotional existence remains closed to measuring devices (at least for now).

Thus the following summary:

> We can retrain people to any other form for which instructions and a reward/punishment scheme can be described.

This means: Whatever a moronorg can design as a *program* can theoretically be constructed as a *person*. Again: the view that any person can be made into any other person is incorrect. The truth is that every person can be remodeled into any moron. It depends on the quality of the instructions and the stimulus system. When rats are moronized, it increases their intelligence. When people are moronized, their normal intelligence is no longer needed. It is superfluous because the instructions alone can serve all purposes.

> Lean Brain makes every person into a precisely prescribed human fake.

This solves all ethical questions. If a person reacts as instructed, he cannot commit any sins! After all, sin is inside his body. Yet this body has become part of the Lean Brain System through its computer workstations and the accompanying headphones. From there, the body is moronized and maintained.

The moronization of rats or people leads to mechanization. It is true that ethical questions are solved, but we still have the economic problems. The largest and most important question is: How much cheese and electricity do you have to give a rat so that it will exhibit all of the prescribed responses or completed all of the instructed tasks? Electricity costs money! The same is true for people. How must the ideal incentive system be constructed so that people can get by with few rewards and punishments? That is one task for the new moronorgy science.

> One of Lean Brain's goals is to fake humans *as cheaply as possible.*

The faking itself must also be executed according to Lean Brain principles! Today, when people are to be reeducated, this usually involves armies, inquisitors, social institutions, psychotropic drugs, examinations, revisions or police, who must mercilessly obey the rules, much like railroad conductors. These black-knight institutions cost society enormous amounts! Lean Brain must be in charge of cheap reeducation. The new moronorgy must research how people can be made subservient through little kisses, hair stroking or encouraging looks. Often, even presenting them a bouquet of flowers for 50 years of hard work can work wonders. One might also consider giving them aluminium badges upon which the work performed is symbolized. A merit badge for merit!

> Lean Brain replaces wages with gimmicks.

Unfortunately, rats are not able to be dumbed down to the point that they would work for a gimmick. They want cheese. People, on the other hand, will fall for gimmicks. So you see, humans are vastly different than animals!

3. Ameba Nirvana

In the Lean Brain era, morons only serve systems whose will they carry out step by step. After work, which stretches for long hours each day over a long life, morons fall into a kind of lethargy or sink into the couch to watch TV. They also indulge in cybersex, instant lottery cards and peanuts on the side, to recover from the disaster reports in the media. "A child locked into a condemned office building lived for months on the skeletons in the closet. He has just received a telegram from People-Person Spice."

Lean Brain people are good people. They are so used to instructions that they do not need to seek nirvana. They no longer need to lie on a bed of nails, like a fakir, to numb the sinful energy of their bodies. They love themselves. They have no desires, no will and no responsibility. They are truly free.

> Lean Brain people are not humans, not animals – they have become amebas. As such, that is, as fakes, they are ideal.

Buddha would have been pleased because an ameba can live its life without any desires. Jesus is happy because an ameba is docile and good-natured. Lao Tse is satisfied because the ameba is going the way. Confucius is tickled because morons live in devotion to their rituals. Nietzsche's Uebermensch is the Lean Brain System. Goethe would write:

> Ameba's Night Song
>
> In full brains
> Is calm,
> In your harlot
> You feel
> No breath of love;
> Your bird fallen silent in the wood.
> Just wait, soon
> You'll also be at rest.

The ameba knows that it knows nothing. It is not like Wilhelm Raabe's character Stopfkuchen, whose motto was to "get out of the box." The ameba stays in the box. It lives in the box. It has enough to eat and drink, and gets enough electricity.

4. Lean Ethics

Lean Brain is very constructive! People are perfected! The damaging aspects of intelligence are driven out of their bodies! Without intelligence, a body is a good person, just like in the animal kingdom!

There are no philosophical problems for machines. They function and run. Any questions as to meaning or ethics only pertain to the machine's builder but not the machine itself.

Does the machine serve a beneficial purpose?
Does it work satisfactorily?
Is it treated and maintained well?
Does it receive enough oil and rust inhibitor?

If we observe human fakes instead of machines, an ethical moronorg should be able to answer "yes" to all four questions with good conscience. Yet we must also take cultural differences into account. Germans, for example, love to fill out questionnaires, but – to put it delicately – they are not the best at harvesting asparagus. Germans like to serve machines but hate to serve people! At work, they need to have the feeling that they are masters and that they are respected. I am reminded of those dry Germans that are employed as tour or museum guides. They are the masters of the area or era through which the tour leads – they never see themselves as service providers to the patrons. Oh, no: They are exhibiting their art of mastery!

> "Here you see this modern painting. It is only blue, all blue. It asks the question as to what about it is art. It is my task to explain it to you. If it were not art, it would not have been so expensive,

but we bought it at an auction for 100,000 euros. The reason why it was so cheap is because that price was the minimum bid. The artist actually didn't want it to be sold at all. He wanted it to be donated to a good cause, but no suitable location could be found. Thus, someone had the idea to put it in a museum. The blue color – it was thought – is so supernaturally blue that it never occurs naturally on Earth. However, in the context of a dissertation during a four-year search, exactly that blue was found on one single day in the Caribbean Sea. Thus, we must assume that the artist wanted to immortalize that spot. We precisely reconstructed the artist's life and found out that he was helpful, for a large fee, in supporting a research team to determine the one day in his life in which he was the closest to that very spot in the Caribbean. We know today that the artist was at least 1,266 miles away from his own painting at any given time in his life. That is amazing. The artist is using the payment as an inducement to continue his blue period. However, I am not going to rest until I find out what the significance of the number 1,266 is. I'm going to write a dissertation on the subject so that I can soon appear before you ignoramuses with a doctoral degree."

Thus, when the new Lean Brain systems are being established, they should, despite all of the economizing on intelligence, be adapted a bit to the culture of the future morons. For Germany, then, the systems should be designed in German, Italian for Italy, and Bavarian blue for Bavaria. Why don't we use this thought in an exercise?

How might a Lean Brain Germany look like? Would you like to contemplate the question with me? A Lean Brain book cannot close with thoughts. No, we need a huge exercise to serve as an example. It will function as a reference for the lean efforts you will surely soon be attempting in your own environment.

VIII. Musoleum Germany

A reference example! Germany! At first, I'd wanted to attempt one for my family or for buying perfume. "Come in and find out!" as a popular German perfumery exclaims. But while I was writing the last chapter, I decided to make the example larger, much larger, which would be more in step with the significance of this book. Well, that's not entirely true. Actually I am worried about Germany. "I think of Germany in my bed, and crashing noises fill my head!" Or: "I think of Germany in power, and bet we should all start to cower!" Did you know (oh, there's that word: *know*) that Germany is the land of poets and thinkers? That higher intelligence is at home here, even if it, as a prophet, hardly matters in its own country? Will not there be a weeping and gnashing of teeth if Lean Brain befalls us like a wolf in a herd of sheep?

That is why I did not want you to close this book without a comforting hope. That is why I have already done preliminary work on the design of a best-possible Lean Brain Germany. Whew! Now I know how hard moronizing will probably be! At any rate, the best of all Germanies cost me a good week of thinking: poor me.

The results will astound you – I certainly was flabbergasted! The solution is simple. It will give us Germans all a wonderful life, and we can continue doing what we love to do best: be German. Of course we won't really be German, we're just going to fake it. That goes without saying. Germans are still Germans, even in the lowest possible concentrations.

1. What would the Lean Brain Form of Poets and Thinkers be like?

Up to now, I have treated the economizing of intelligence in an abstract manner. Now, let us focus directly on Germany, since it has the largest potential for economizing on intelligence – the largest in the world!

> Lean Brain is the great epoch-making chance for Germany.
> Where much is wasted, much can be saved.

Germany is the famous land of poets and thinkers. Naturally, there are also other countries that can be proud of a rich and valuable culture, but Italy, for instance, is only clearly leading in art and a lightness of being (not in intelligence). The truly difficult core intelligence is attached to the acutely gloomy Germans. I'm sure Immanuel Kant is partly to blame! He wrote intricately complicated books that are evidently meant to be taken completely seriously. While there are several books in the realms of modern science, psychology, sociology and even in pure mathematics that are quite a bit more difficult to understand, it seems to be purely deliberate, serving sadism or a veiling of a vapidity of content. Many unclear thinkers have the courage to write books before the fog in their heads has lifted. They then bandy about heaps of foreign words, so that the fog, which everyone can see, is at least obviously from the authors themselves.

The German is weighty or difficult. It is deliberate or sadist. It is arduous – authentically arduous. It just isn't easy, you know? The culture of Germany has only produced one single real comedy of literary status, I once heard an important person say. He must have been referring to *Minna von Barnhelm* – I can't think of any other. To be German is to be serious to the point of being morose. Morose? It comes from the Latin morositas, or morosity. What a coincidence, it sounds a lot like moron, doesn't it? Morose – oh, right, that was that very German woman in one of those call centers ... where was that again? So now the Germans not only have to be morose but also morons too?

As I have already mentioned – Germany can save more intelligence than the rest of the world because the Germans know so much and are so educated. (The Pisa study does not measure knowledge, but rather practical applicability which is something like transferring what is in your head to your hands). Unfortunately, the German penchant for morosity has the disadvantage that the Germans will surely not be able to or want to see that they have the most Lean Brain potential. I bet they'll all say:

> Germany has the most to lose through Lean Brain. That makes it morose.

That is why hard times are moving in. The writing is already on the wall in the job market. Cleaning women, asparagus harvesters and waiters are being sought in droves. However, the Germans do not wish to practice such occupations. If they feel they are in an emergency situation, they are more apt to buy themselves a Mercedes and add to the overcapacity of taxis in front of the train stations, where they sit and wait.

The Germans are not satisfied with their jobs if the jobs are not "dignified." A job is only dignified if it matches the maximum intelligence level that they can prove they achieved in school or university. "I have a diploma and was a manager! And now you want me to tend graves? I'd have too few people under me. Forget it!" When working in civil service, you are primarily paid according to the proven state of your head when starting the job at age 25: either in the lower, middle, upper or higher grade of civil service. Only in top positions, such as a governmental minister, does intelligence not matter because the state of your head is not the important element. "Experience," they say.

So, people faced with working in a job that is beneath them would rather do a headstand! They refuse to get their hands dirty when their own heads have worked fine in the past. Let other people use their hands! Germans are poets and thinkers.

However, if we ignore Lean Brain, we will fall.

"Mene, mene tekel upharsin," it says in the Bible.

2. FAKe

Today, industrial enterprises are increasingly and shamelessly raving about foreign workers from low-wage countries. They are willing Lean Brain employees!

They could work in the call centers! We Germans don't do such insipid work! Foreign workers from low-wage countries would otherwise have no work at all! So they are told to quickly learn German, then they could work right in their home country in the Far East providing call-center consulting to German customers for a couple of euros per hour or per day. Those workers would then enthusiastically learn the German language in a few months and be completely happy with a Lean Brain job. And their ticket in was a command of the German language, which Germans have been speaking well since they were four. That is all we need to work! Nothing but language! Soon, maybe even typing on a keyboard will be enough.

Since the Germans do not want to take advantage of their incredible chance, they are systematically being transformed into low-wage workers. Firms are beginning to have everything taken care of by "externs." These external workers have no wage agreement, no rights, and no high wages. They must bank on the hope that they will be needed frequently. In a large, genuinely German corporation, external workers are called "Fremdarbeitskraft", whose literal translation is "foreign workers." They use the abbreviation "FAK" or "FAKe" in German for such workers, in the singular and plural respectively. These FAKes take on all cheap legwork, not only that directly related to cleaning the rooms or delivering the mail. FAKes can also be academics that, for instance, generate presentation transparencies and new strategy proposals for internal managers. Thus, the FAKes generate fakes that the managers in turn present to the corporation as their own ideas. Managers in that company can, for instance, also outsource their own intelligence via FAKes.

FAKes are a beginning. Once FAKEs have taken over a large percentage of German legwork, these tasks can gradually be relocated with the aid of data transfer to low-wage countries. If we do not allow ourselves to be moronized, FAKes, and at some point, Martians, will be found to do the job.

(Yes! Or newts! That's it, newts! Are you familiar with the book *War with the Newts* by Karel Capek? It is a forerunner of the Lean Brain philosophy. It was written in the 1930s, before there were computers or good systems, only morons and newts. Capek is considered to be the originator of the word *Robot* and is a must-read in addition to Huxley and Orwell.)

We are sitting in a Skinner box, people, and we are refusing to press the lever. We hope that it will nevertheless still rain cheese. We deserve it! Manna will rain down! German intelligence deserves it, just like ... um, when a beautiful woman automatically becomes a manaqueen. She doesn't have to do any thing else ...

3. Lean Brain Rescue for Germany!

It is of no use to hide your intelligent head in the sand.

Let's ponder this, just one more time.

> What can a German without intelligence do to still earn lots of money?

Everything that can be executed via telephone, Internet or computer can pretty much be performed abroad. That is why all of this work is given to people that have learned German or can operate a computer. Production of the software will also be relocated abroad. Many people believe that a great deal of intelligence is contained in these realms and is now being transferred out of Germany; lately, though, software industrialization has been seriously promoted.

The programmers will then construct more and more programs using code components, thus resembling masons building a wall, only without the bad weather allowance.

Production is organized such that there are almost no people. The few people who are still needed in the factory could also be Germans, if necessary. The factory is very expensive in contrast to a couple of overpaid guys, so that is no problem. However, it would definitely be better to build the factory in a low-wage country. Then, when the factory is no longer needed, we can just let it rot – a practice that is prohibited in Germany.

Agriculture has long since stopped being necessary. It has been in the throes of death ever since I've been alive. (I grew up on a farm and thus grew up with death. We used to bring our carrots to the canning factory, pickled pigs in stone coffins and buried vegetables over the winter in sand so that we would have something to eat ...)

That is how our entire working world is dying.

The naïve question in the box above is not so easy to answer!

What in heaven's name can an East Indian not do as well here on Earth as we can?

What?

What?

The Indians can't stage the Bayreuth Wagner Festival, although all of India is situated south of the Bavarian veal sausage equator.

Anything else?

It' simple: Indians are not Germans!

People in other countries may well practice loan dumping, they may trump us and drive us into an economic corner, but there is one prized asset that cannot be bought or sold with money: We are original German.

Being German is the only thing in which we are clearly superior to the rest of the world.

We have to uninhibitedly market this solitary and incredibly valuable unique position characteristic, and then we only need to be German, do not require intelligence and can earn as much as ever.

What is truly German and can secure us a unique position in the world except for excessive intelligence? Sweeping the streets on Saturdays and then bathing and eating herring with fried potatoes? I imagine that Germans can complain the best when something is not in order. So they should be in charge of checking for errors in bank balance sheets or dog family trees, or for trichina inspections around the world. Something like that? Perhaps each German will get a large permanent rubber stamp, inspect everything like a true German carping critic and mark it all with the stamp? I have already published this suggestion as a serious proposal in another publication. The response was disappointing. When we stamp things, we mark them. Thus, we are just substituting things here: Instead of the stamp "Made in Germany," we'll now stamp "Marked in Germany" on things because everyone was envious of our German mark. We'll get back to that later.

Well, as I have said, I could not drum up enough enthusiasm for reform. What else can Germans do uniquely besides stamping things?

Hmm. Recite Schiller's poem about the bell by heart, sing like the folk music star Heino because there is only one Heino, a ubiquitous German folk singer whose light blonde hair and sunglasses make him a favorite target of impersonators. Wait! Yes ... that's it! There are masses of Heino fakes! You basically only need a blonde wig and a pair of dark sunglasses, and the singing will happen all by itself. In an emergency, we still have all the CDs by the one and only Heino. Yes! Heino would be a good place to start faking German cultural assets.

We'll put on powdered wigs and play Schiller or Goethe. They, or their fakes, will both be on the evening political talk shows, sitting on the west-eastern divan and showering us with distiches!

> Heino fakes are the paradigm of a new Germany.

Yes! We'll all play poets and thinkers! Whoever isn't serious enough for that can happily play pop singer Nena or folk singer Marianne Rosenberg. We could get plastic surgery. We'll all become famous! I'll have surgery to become Hildegard Knef, you can be Klaus Kinski!

Nobody will get out of this with his or her skin unscathed! And then we'll start faking away, without inhibitions!

Hmmm ... now all we need is someone who will pay my way when I sing the jingle for a famous bra ad: "It's quite a help, like little elves, No need to haul your bust yourselves ..."

I've got it! We'll put it all on for the Indians! For the Chinese! For the Russian millionaires! We'll play intelligence! You see – my hands are trembling while I type, my keyboard is slipping – we Germans are the only people that can play intelligence genuinely because we take it so seriously! And people living in low-wage countries will come from far away to Germany just to see the faking of intelligence in its pure form for once in their lives! There must be an enormous global demand for viewing the old, complicated human once again, just like seeing the prehistoric man of Mauer, here near Heidelberg.

I've got it!

I propose that all of Germany be turned into a huge amusement park under the motto "Poets and Thinkers." Yes, that is it!

4. World Heritage Site of Germany as a gigantic Intelligence Fake

In America, the Native Americans earn a great deal of money simply by being present in intricate, feathered dress. The old-fashioned Christian Amish people let themselves be viewed for a price near Philadelphia. They are examples of superior cultures that can impress the nouveau riche of the lower and already degenerated cultures for a brief admission time, and receive good pay for this service.

When we were on vacation in Amish country, where the people live as if "in primeval times," and reject industrialization, average Americans flip out, with their ooohs and aaahs. For them, it was inconceivable to live by candlelight.

I, however, sat there, self-absorbed, thinking back to my childhood in the '50s in the town of Gross Himstedt. We roasted coffee substitute in rotating pans, hand-churned butter, cooked treacle and heated the bathwater on Saturdays on stoves with iron rings. We only had an oven in the living room: In the evenings, we'd go upstairs to bed in the freezing cold in winter or in the summer in scorching heat, fighting off mosquitoes. We washed ourselves at the porcelain washbasin and had a large outhouse with four parallel seats. I spent the weekends cutting the local newspaper into squares, or searching the garden for eggs because the stupid chickens refused to lay them in the coop.

I had the feeling that the Amish in America lived with more industry than I myself growing up. I bet our old farmhouse would make a sensational museum today! If we still lived there, we could show you our washbasins and our porcelain pitchers! You could all stay at our house for a day when Auntie Stoppel comes by and makes all of our clothes. You could take care of all of my chores and wax the stone floor with the extremely heavy floor-polishing brush until everything shines. You could eat pig potatoes with me straight out of the steamer – those are the very little potatoes that no one wanted – the same kind that are known today as princess potatoes and cost twice as much. We used to cook them in vats for the animals. "Gunter, we're having delicious rutabaga soup and you've spoiled your dinner by filling up on pig food!"

Can you feel it? That is German! That is original German. And we will now transform the entire country into a primeval German idyll. Then, all of the low-wage country millionaires will come to Germany for their vacation. Once the world has converted to Lean Brain, all people will be moronized. But some will keep all the money; that is why people are moronized. These people will come to Germany and spend their money again. Since there are not so many Germans, we can split the spoils and live well again. During the day, we'll work as Germans and then recuperate in the evenings.

Due to the climate changes, considerable global warming will soon take place. The Southern European countries are going to dry out and suffer from shortages in drinking water. The summer climate, with its excess of 100°F, will be uncomfortable. Germany, on the other hand, will profit. It will be a paradise. Green forests and a bright sun. The millionaires will flood in just as the Russian nobility used to when they fled Russian winters by gambling their money,

which they had earned by blackmailing moronized farmers of Po-
temkin villages, in Bad Homburg or Baden-Baden. Read The Gambler by Dostoevsky, who met his ruin in Wiesbaden in his day.

Yes, that is how Germany can become good! We have so, so much
more to offer than Indian feathers, Ephesus or three pyramids and a
valley of kings!

In Germany, we are rebuilding the Germans as one gigantic fake. We
are integrally raising ourselves to become a world heritage site. We'll
construct Germany as the ultimate Lean Brain System just as thoroughly as we Germans do everything else.

The attractions in the Disney parks serve as a Lean Brain paradigm.
There, one rides through an "attraction" in a boat (you may get
splashed on a bit; it's so cute!) or a train (boy is that a bumpy ride!)
or in a rocket (must keep my lunch from taking the seat next to me).
A sort of student or boy or girl explains with the skill of a Hollywood
actor what we should be feeling. "Great, America." The entire ride
lasts anywhere from three to eight minutes, at which time we are
drunk with glee and can endure waiting in line for an hour to take
the next ride or eat Goofy-shaped popcorn.

The scout or cast member of a particular attraction, insofar as it is
not a Lean Brain speaker's voice from somewhere in Kamchatka
coming out of loudspeakers, must only perform this one part for
four minutes, for an entire lifetime! If cast members need to learn a
new part (that is our destiny: a life of learning!), he is taught another
four-minute part. If that does not happen too much, it will go well
and perhaps be a welcome change. So we can see:

> The occupation of presenter is Lean Brain.

In an amusement park, there are only routine occupations! No intelligence, only amusement! All the employees have to do is master
their four minutes and be an integral part of a large-scale greeting
offensive as is practiced by the supermarkets mentioned earlier.
Some sell two kinds of ice cream, another coffee, and another one

still French fries. Each person is an underpaid cog in the machine. In all, however, the park is a gigantic fake for pleasure.

> An amusement park is a highly intelligent system composed of Lean Brain parts.

Germany should become the global modal.

> Germany will become a Las Vegas of thought and culture.
> Here, intelligence will forever remain a cheap fake.

5. Musoleum Germany

We will remodel all cities into theme cities.

Consider Weimar: An entire city has been built around one and a half poets. Nevertheless, there have been other historical great minds from there, but only Goethe and a bit of Schiller can animate an entire town.

We could consistently goetherize all of Weimar: We could have Lean Brain students standing around everywhere who would recite the *Erlkönig* or perform the *Sorcerer's Apprentice*. Highly-paid Lean Brain workers, accompanied by the encouraging applause of bystanders, could even manage *The Bell* or *Faust II*. Basically, each inhabitant must only be able to recite one of the platinum hit poems to present it among the amusement park attractions. Weimar can also market genuine Thuringian Sausage, thus placing that extra special something next to the normal Goethe. My favorite way to drink coffee is out of a black mug that has the word SALVE on it, which I got at the Elephant Hotel in Weimar. A Guatemalan blend with Goethe!

Weimar has Goethe and Salzburg Mozart (and the Mozart chocolate truffle balls instead of the sausage). We have to make a long list in order to reconstruct all of Germany. I suggest that we search German history for attractions and consistently expand everything into an amusement. The paradigm of historical amusement is the currently modern custom of medieval meals. I now have to suffer through one of those after my talks. People dressed up like medieval sages, sing and play music and amuse us with ribald sayings. All the while, we must consume a frugal meal with our hands and be blithe in the process. That is pure Lean Brain. It can also be very nice but not every two months. What I am trying to say is that not every city can construct the same attractions: For instance, they cannot have the same hamburger restaurant or an identical pizza station.

No – Germany will be converted into a Lean Brain Musoleum that fakes the German culture of all centuries. Do you know the nine muses?

There is Clio for history, Calliope for epic poetry and elegy, Melpomene for tragedy, Thalia for comedy, Urania for astronomy, Erato for love songs and dance, Euterpe for music and lyric song, Terpsichore for choral lyric song and dance, and Polyhymnia for dance, pantomime and solemn song.

Obviously, dance is weighted too heavily here, but you understand that the muses can really kiss when we think of Germany.

Here is a spontaneous list of things that can be offered as amusement:

- A whole lot of stuff about wine (harvesting, tasting, eating, dance)
- Sauerkraut
- Jousting tournaments in stadiums like the bullfights in Ronda
- Cloisters of all kinds
- Hiking rallies
- Poets and Cities, hikes through Mark Brandenburg (according to Fontane)
- Book printing in Mainz (like the historic Gutenberg)
- Witch trials with burnings; you can bring your own defendants
- Walpurgis Night in the Harz region
- Public tortures and execution (as fakes, of course)
- Following German National Parliament meetings
- Autobahn races
- Public mixed bathing in tubs followed by a party

- Dwelling like the old Germanic tribes on the Limes Romanus
- Scrubbing clean real antlers of dead dear and taking them with you
- Bread-baking and the science of sourdough
- Touring beer breweries
- The relics trade
- Collecting beech-nuts
- Fairy-tale parks everywhere
- Heino faking
- Looking for Nibelungen treasures and dragons with a cloak of invisibility and a Nothung sword
- Battue hunting for Lean Brain bunnies
- Outlets for clothing from various centuries
- Theater castles and opera centers
- Participating in coalmining
- Palace tours
- Championships in thumb wrestling, shrimp peeling or eating kale
- Presentation of German school instruction in cram schools, with beatings
- Duels with sables or pistols
- Student fraternity drinking competitions
- Fake historical lectures by Hegel or Schopenhauer
- Performances of Ruebezahl or Stoertebeker (this already exists – more!)
- Riding on sailing ships, mudflat hikes, …
- Wellness clinic water drinking contest for tourists with medal of courage
- Health spa lady/man-friend moron service
- Life in a German fake family with a Christmas party based on the writings of Böll
- Life in a sect (Anabaptists, etc.), selling of indulgences
- Bumper cars, coated burnt almonds and gingerbread hearts
- Yodeling diploma
- Inquisition
- Reinstitution of the Deutschmark as a semi-euro fake
- Traditional costume group festivals
- Butcher's Festivals and distribution of broth throughout the village

- Skat and Doppelkopf for card-crazy fools
- William Tell Shooting Extravaganza (well, maybe not ... there would be problems with the Swiss)

Every German town will look for a dominant Lean Brain theme or fakeulty and become pure Lean Brain amusement. Every city will have its equivalent of the Oktoberfest or another megatheme, whether it be one that centers on Beethoven or a daily half marathon past the miles of files of the Stasi. As long as it's German and as long as it's fun – that is a bit of a stretch, but that is how Germany will become the Lean Brain cultural core of the universe.

In that way, Germany will end its own development, while the other nations will still change in the direction of an uncertain future. The musoleum that Germany will become will be set up like a snapshot, a summa germaniae of all historical ages. Germany is faking its intelligence today, at a time when world history is experiencing the largest known squandering of intelligence.

Now we are entering the age of Lean Brain.

Germany will remain – in a faked, Lean Brain form – the way it was when it was the best of all time.

The world will go on.
Germany will stop where it is best.

German women, German wine, German loyalty, German song! The whole world will envy us for the way we have preserved ourselves. The brilliance of Germany will surround us for all time. Because our fake of ourselves will be wonderful.

Everything that is in the past will become big Lean Brain business, and the Germans will become specialists, each individually, for his or her song, poem, or palace tour descriptions as an actor or tour guide.

6. "I speak perfect German! I have a right to exist!"

When a Lean Brain System such as the Musoleum Germany is perfect, its management will feel obligated to maintain it and allow it to operate over millions of years.

Lean Brain Managers do not try to set off for new shores.

The final idea of Musoleum Germany must be implemented, unchanged, forever!

It is my idea! And I want it that way! Dammit! I'm not going to let it perish! Otherwise we will be in serious danger!

You see, I know for a fact what will happen if my idea gets into the cerebellums of diluters! Of course, all other people will be totally jealous when the Musoleum harvests the money of the global millionaires and when the financial currents of the world flow together here like a giant ocean.

Several non-Germans will apply to be able to work in Germany, in order to fake being German. Many will offer to do German cheaper and play it better. They will practice and become Cheap Germans and Loyal Germans. "I can play the perfect German."

Yes, and everyone will contemplate how they can fake Germany even better. They will establish Germany in other locations true to its fake, or try faking Italy or France as a competing event! They will try to fake all countries!

They will want to export Germanness. There will be German franchise countries. We will rent out universal German hospitality as a licensed product in a pay-per-use model, and …

He that hath ears to hear, let him hear:

Stop when it is best.
Then the game is over.
Do not ask what is to come next.
At the climax, everything will stand still forever.

There are highest truths that we are not allowed to know. I will divulge them to you because it is better that way than if you were to figure them out yourselves because that would mean discussing your thoughts with others, thus inviting big trouble. However, the trick is to be able to recognize the highest thoughts immediately at their inception and instantly repress them. You must lock your highest thoughts deep in your heart. There they will sleep like the most dangerous vampires in their coffins. You, however, are the keeper of these horrible truths that must never get to your brain. A true human is one who has irrevocably locked the truth away and carefully guards the dungeon. That is exactly what Socrates wanted to say about himself. "All I know is that I know nothing." You must know that you know nothing. Only then will nothing more come out of you.

This is the truth:

> The Lean Brain World needs a Musoleum Germany but no Germans.

And psychology needs Skinner boxes, but no rats. The Lean Brain World makes everything cheaper and cheaper. Maybe gene-altered animals could also be used for the fakes? Do we even need humans? Who will be spending all the money when it slowly and inexorably flows into the Musoleum Germany? Whom will it benefit? Behind this question is another of the deepest truths.

> Money learns to grow without human involvement.

It doesn't need us anymore.

Money has taught us to worship it and serve it. Now, however, it has taken possession of the systems through which money is fruitful and multiplies. Money is doing away with us. We are left sitting here – with what little residual reason we have. We ask: "Money, how can we survive in this situation, if you no longer stand over us and protect us?" Then money says unto the people:

> Your little brain is sure to suffice for this little bit of life.

IX. Brain Rest

Let this book sink in.

Digester's Night Song

In my brain
Is calm,
Beneath my forehead
I feel
Nothing but my belly;
The bowels filter the old.
Just wait, soon
There will be sound and smoke.

Even I am still finding this book rather hard to digest. I wanted to construct the world as intelligentless as possible so that it would finally be able to get by without brains or humans, when individual bodies can no longer be used for hard labor.

Don't think it will be so easy! Repeatedly, my residual intelligence, which technically needs to write this book, drove me. Again and again, annoying flashes of wit came over me! Luckily, Bärbel Nietzold, my editor, has diligently stuck to the Lean Brain concept and repeatedly admonished me. She pulled my head out of the clouds and got me back to reality. "Gunter, not so complicated!" She relentlessly pushed me to provide you with consistently high-quality and simple thought patterns and patent recipes and not fall into journalistic complaisance. The Word file would often have blazing red comments (from her): "Gunter, that is not new at all. It is not a new Lean Brain train of thought. You are describing normal reality here. That has no place in this book." And I would sigh. See, she was always right. She is the first editor who dared to coolly reject a chapter, so dear to me, four or five times, until every last trace of reality had vanished from it. That really hurt – and I am so thankful to her for it.

The first test readers of this book found my conclusions to be distressfully close to reality. No, no! We are still far away from a Lean Brain world! The path is still before us! It is a truly notorious dirty trick against revolutionary thought to disarm said revolutionary thought by claiming that a good portion of the road is behind us. No, no, it is not intelligentless enough! You probably cannot imagine how little intelligence we still need.

Most people that discover reality in this book are once again confusing stupidity with a lack of intelligence. Yet it is not about laughing at stupidity but rather rejoicing at a lack of intelligence …

Are you already capable of that? Has your brain already come to rest? Now, very, very honestly – your hand on your heart: Did you laugh while you were reading, or were you rejoicing?

I am not in a laughing mood. That's how far I've come. But I'm not really rejoicing either.